THE

ANCIENT HISTORY

OF

UNIVERSALISM,

FROM

THE TIME OF THE APOSTLES TO ITS CONDEMNATION IN THE
FIFTH GENERAL COUNCIL, A. D. 553.

WITH AN

APPENDIX,

TRACING THE DOCTRINE DOWN TO THE

ERA OF THE REFORMATION.

BY HOSEA BALLOU, 2D.
PASTOR OF THE UNIVERSALIST CHURCH IN MEDFORD.

SECOND EDITION, REVISED.

PROVIDENCE:
PUBLISHED BY Z. BAKER,
GOSPEL MESSENGER OFFICE.
1842.

PROVIDENCE: BENJAMIN F. MOORE, PRINTER.

PREFACE

THE reader will perceive, in the commencement of the following work, that I have not introduced a statement of the Scripture doctrine upon the subject of my History. For the omission, which some may consider a defect, I submit these reasons : it seemed to me that a brief statement would prove useless, since every one would form his own opinion from other authority ; and it was thought that a satisfactory discussion of the important question, belonged rather to the Polemic than to the Historian. Accordingly, for the commencement of my undertaking, I fixed on a date posterior to the publication of most of the New Testament ; and yet, as it was desirable to take into view every other Christian production extant of the first ages, it was necessary to begin as early as A. D. 90, before some of St. John's writings were composed.

The attentive reader will also discover, as he proceeds, that the Ancient History of Universalism is naturally distinguished, by certain peculiarities, into three successive Periods : — the FIRST, extending to the year 190, and embraced in the first two chapters, affords but few indisputable traces either of that doctrine, or of its opposite ; the SECOND, running through the third, fourth, fifth and sixth chapters, to the year 390, or 394, is distinguished by the prevalence both of Universalism and of the doctrine of endless misery, without producing the least disturbance or uneasiness in the church ; the THIRD, reaching to the Fifth General Council, in A. D. 553, is marked with continual censures, frequent commotions, and some disgraceful quarrels, on that subject.

And, as I have endeavored to vary my general plan, so as to suit the peculiar character and circumstances of each of these periods, I would here bespeak the reader's attention to the method I have pursued. In the first Period, then, I have been careful to state, in his own words, the opinion of every Christian author, who has left us any remarks concerning future punishment, or the eventual salvation of the world ; and down to the year 150, I have, with still more particularity, inserted every passage which I thought belonged to either of those subjects. Accordingly, it may be expected that, to many, the first two chapters will prove more tedious than the rest of the work. In the second Period, while it has been my principal object to give a full account of all those fathers, who, during that time, advocated or favored Universalism, I have also aimed to present a correct view of the opinions entertained, the meanwhile, by the Christian world at large, on that point. In the third Period, I have pursued nearly the same course ; leaving, however, the common sentiment of the church, concerning the doctrine in question, to be gathered from the controversies and quarrels which then occurred, and which I have minutely described. Thus far, I may venture to pronounce the History complete, in one respect : it contains an account of every individual of note, whom we have now the means of knowing to have been a Universalist.

In the Appendix the plan is very different, since a regular and connected history of Universalism, from the Fifth General Council to the Reformation, is, with me, utterly impracticable. Here, therefore, nothing but a sketch is attempted, pointing out those traces of the doctrine, which I have happened to discover in the course of reading.

1 would also take this opportunity, once for all, to apprize my readers of the sense in which they will find certain terms and phrases used in the following work. The title, *bishop*, is supposed to have signified, at first, only the chief minister of a city, or territory ; though it afterwards became confined in its application to a distinct and superior order of clergy. By the popular epithets *orthodox* and *heretic*, I mean, not the true and the false, but the predominant, or catholic, and the dissenting, or anathematized. To conclude, I have frequently spoken of the *Western or Latin Churches*, in distinction from the *Eastern or Greek ;* though they were not finally separated from each other's communion, till the ninth century.

Roxbury, Oct. 22d, 1828.

1*

ADVERTISEMENT

TO THE SECOND EDITION.

NUMEROUS changes are made in this Edition ; but the most of them are merely verbal. Some sentences and paragraphs are omitted, as unnecessary or irrelevant ; others are transferred from the text to the margin, as belonging more properly among the notes. A few accounts are inserted of those whom the author has, since the publication of the work, found to have been Universalists.

No occasion has been discovered for correcting any material statement, except perhaps in what relates to the fact last mentioned in the history, — the condemnation of Universalism and its advocates by the Fifth General Council. Though the ancient Greek historians agree that such was the fact, and though the acts of that condemnation are found among the other acts of this body, yet there is some reason to suspect after all, that they are the acts of the council held under Mennas, at Constantinople, in the year 540 ; and to doubt whether the General Council ever meddled with the matter. As the point, however, is not fully settled, the statement in the first Edition is suffered to remain with only a hint or two of uncertainty.

No one can be more sensible, than the author, that this history needs to be written anew, and on a more philosophical plan, especially in the former part. This, he has long desired to see done ; and should his life be continued, and an opportunity of sufficient leisure occur, he hopes to undertake the labor, at some future season.

Medford, January 1, 1842.

CONTENTS.

⊤

CHAPTER I.

Opinions entertained by the Christians, from A. D. 90, to A. D. 150, concerning future punishment, and the eventual salvation of the world, exhibited by means of all the relative passages in the Orthodox writings extant of this period, and by a summary statement of the doctrine of the early Gnostic sects.

A. D.		SECT.
90	Number, condition, and common faith of the the Christians.	1
	THE ORTHODOX. Titles and character of their writings yet extant. - - - -	2
90—95	Epistle of Clemens Romanus. Date of St.	
94—100	John's later writings, and time of his death.	3
107 or 116	Epistles of Ignatius. Relation of his Martyrdom. - - - - - -	4
108 or 117	Epistle of Polycarp. - - -	5
	Corruptions growing in the church.	
116 to 126	Papias. Aristides. The Greek Philosophy.	6
131	Epistle of Barnabas. - - - -	7
About 150	Shepherd of Hermas. - - -	8
90 to 150	THE GNOSTIC CHRISTIANS. Their general doctrine and character. - - - -	9
About 120	The Basilidians, Universalists. - -	10
do	The Carpocratians, do. - - -	11
About 130	The Valentinians, do. - -	12
	What notions of the Gnostics were peculiarly odious to the Orthodox. - - -	13

CHAPTER II.

Opinions of the Christians from A. D. 150, to A. D. 190, concerning future punishment, and the eventual salvation of the world, illustrated by extracts from all the authors extant of this period, who have introduced the subject.

A. D.		SECT.
150	Increase of Heretics. Ebionites. Character of the Orthodox. - - - -	1
	Change in the character of the Christian writings. Titles of those extant of this period. -	2
—150—	The Sibylline Oracles, containing the earliest explicit assertion of a restoration of the damned.	3
150 to 162	The works of Justin Martyr. -	4

A. D.		SECT.
160—170	Relation of the Martyrdom of Polycarp.	5
170	Oration of Tatian.	6
173	Ecclesiastical History of Hegesippus.	7
177	Epistle of the Churches of Lyons and Vienne.	8
178 to 180	Works of Athenagoras.	9
181	Treatise of Theophilus.	10
180—190	Works of Irenæus.	11
	Summary of the first two Chapters. Remarks.	12
	Necessary change in the plan of this History.	13

CHAPTER III.

Clemens Alexandrinus, and his Cotemporaries; or, the Opinions of the Christians from A. D. 190, to A. D. 230, concerning the future state.

A. D.		SECT.
190 to 196	Clemens Alexandrinus, a Universalist. His own testimony. His views of the future state.	1
	His general system of doctrine. His standing in the Orthodox church.	2
	His life.	3
	His character.	4
200 to 204	Tertullian, a believer in endless misery.	5
210	Minucius Felix.	6
	Opinions of the Orthodox concerning the state of the dead, and the near approach of the last judgment	7
	State of Universalism among both the Orthodox and the Gnostics.	8

CHAPTER IV.

Origen, and his Doctrine..

A. D.		SECT.
230	Origen's renown. His books Of Principles.	1
	His testimony in favor of Universalism and Pre-existence.	2
	His Life from A. D. 185 to A. D. 203.	3
	" " 203 " 216.	4
	" " 216 " 230.	5
230	His first publications. His general system of doctrine.	6
	His method of interpreting the Scriptures.	7
	His life from A. D. 230 to A. D. 245.	8
	" " 245 " 253.	9
	His character.	10
230 to 253	Universalism a favorite topic with him. Additional testimonies.	11
	The manner in which he taught it.	12

CHAPTER V.

Origen's Scholars and Cotemporaries; or, Opinions of the Christians from A. D. 230 to A. D. 270, concerning Universalism.

	Difficulty in ascertaining the extent to which Universalism prevailed. Origen's influence.	1

A. D.   SECT.

206 to 270   EASTERN CHURCHES. Alexander, bishop of
             Jerusalem ; and Theoctistus, bishop of Cesarea
             in Palestine. -   -   -   -   -   2
             Heraclas, bishop of Alexandria. -   -   3
             Ambrosius, Origen's patron. -   -   -   4
             Firmilian, bishop of Cesarea in Cappadocia.   5
             Gregory Thaumaturgus, and Athenodorus, bish-
             ops of Pontus. -   -   -   -   6
             Heretics of all kinds. -   -   -   7
249 to 258   WESTERN CHURCHES. Cyprian bishop of Car-
             thage. -   -   -   -   -   8
250 to 270   Character, condition, and general doctrine of
             the Orthodox. -   -   -   -   9
      APPENDIX TO CHAPTER V. *The Manicheans.*
             Extensive and lasting consequences of their
             heresy. Life of its author, Mani. -   -   1
      265   His general system of doctrine. -   -   2
             Its reception among the Persians and Greeks,
             and its appearance within the limits of the Roman
             Empire. -   -   -   -   -   3

CHAPTER VI.

History of Origen's doctrine from A. D. 254 to A. D. 390 ; and of the opinions entertained by the Christians, in the mean time, concerning the future state.

             Design and plan of this Chapter. Nepos re-
             vives in Egypt the doctrine of the Millennium,
257 to 263   against Origen ; but is refuted. -   -   1
             Origen's popularity. His doctrine attacked by
280—290   Methodius, bishop of Tyre. He is imitated by
290—300   Victorinus. -   -   -   -   -   2
About 300   Peter, bishop of Alexandria, reproaches his
             memory. -   -   -   -   -   3
305, 306   Arnobius and Lactantius, concerning the future
             state. -   -   -   -   -   -   4
             Complaints in the East against Origen's doc-
307 to 310   trine. Pamphilus and Eusebius's Apology for
             him. -   -   -   -   -   -   5
             Evidence that Universalism was not unpopular,
             and that Pamphilus and Eusebius were favorably
             disposed towards it. -   -   -   -   6
             Account of Pamphilus and Eusebius. -   7
             Arian controversy. Origen's name and doc-
320 to 360   trine somewhat involved. Marcellus, a Univer-
             salist. -   -   -   -   -   -   8
             Origen's notions attacked by Eustathius of An-
             tioch, and by Apollinarius of Laodicea. -   9
347 to 370   EASTERN FATHERS. Athanasius, Cyrill of Jeru-
             salem, Ephraim the Syrian, (and Hilary of Poi-
             ters, a Western bishop,) concerning future pun-
             ishment. -   -   -   -   -   10

A. D.		SECT.
350 to 370	Fabius Marius Victorinus, (a Western writer,) a Universalist. - - -	11
360 to 370	Titus, bishop of Bostra, a Universalist. -	12
370	Basil the Great, bishop of Cappadocia. -	13
370 to 376	Rise and establishment of the monastic institution. The Origenists. Their chief retreat at Nitria. - - - - -	14
376	They are attacked by Epiphanius, bishop of Cyprus. - - - - -	15
370 to 383	Many of the Orthodox fathers in the East, are Universalists. Gregory Nazianzen's indecision.	16
	His life, eloquence and character. - -	17
	Gregory Nyssen's testimony in favor of Universalism. - - - - -	18
	His general system of doctrine, works, life, &c.	19
	Didymus of Alexandria a Universalist. His life, character, and works. - - -	20
380 to 390	Jerome a Universalist. His early life. His friendship with Rufinus. - - -	21
390	Evagrius Ponticus a Universalist. -	22
	Most of the leading Origenists, perhaps, Universalists. Palladius of Galatia. Isidorus of Alexandria. John, bishop of Jerusalem. -	23
378 to 394	Diodorus of Tarsus, a Universalist. - -	24
384 to 390	WESTERN FATHERS. Ambrose, bishop of Milan. Ambrosiaster, or Hilary deacon of Rome; their opinions of the future state. - -	25
	HERETICS. The Arians of this century. Sabellians. Novatians, and other schismatics. The Manicheans; their opinions concerning Universalism. - - - -	26

CHAPTER VII.

The Contest with the Origenists, from A. D. 391 to A. D. 404; in which Universalism is for the first time censured, and in part condemned.

391	Principal bishops, writers, &c. in Christendom. Banishment of the Arians. Quiet of the Church.	1
393	Epiphanius's attack upon John of Jerusalem. His ordination of Paulinianus, Jerome's brother. Complaints of John. - - -	2
394	Epiphanius's Letter to John concerning Origen's errors; in which Universalism is for the first time censured. - - - - -	3
395	Disturbance in Palestine. Jerome sides with Epiphanius against John and Rufinus. -	4
	Letter of Isidorus. Attempt of Archelaus at reconciliation. Mission of Isidorus from Theophilus, archbishop of Alexandria. - -	5
396	He assists John in composing an answer to Epiphanius, or Apology to Theophilus. -	6

A D.   SECT.

396   The Christians at Rome variously affected by these publications ; some of them request information from Jerome. He writes them an An-
397   swer to John's Apology. Receives a letter from Theophilus, and replies. His application to Augustine. - - - - - -   7

        Reconciliation between Jerome and Rufinus. Rufinus goes to Rome with Melania, translates and publishes the first book of the Apology for Origen, and Origen's books Of Principles, and covertly attacks Jerome. Spread of Origenism
397, 398   at Rome. - - - - - -   8

        Jerome receives those works, writes to Rufinus,
398 or 399 and composes a Defence of himself, in which he denies a restoration from hell, and states Origen's chief errors. - - - - -   9

        Theophilus quarrels with Isidorus and the Nitrian monks, and takes up against the Origenists. Assembles a council at Alexandria ; in which
399   Origen's doctrine and books are, for the first time, formally condemned. Nitria. Theophilus drives away the Origenists ; who flee to Palestine. Conduct of John of Jerusalem. Exultation of Theophilus, Epiphanius and Jerome. Council at Cyprus, and decree of the Roman
400   Pontiff against Origen's works. - -   10

        Points of his doctrine condemned in these proceedings. How his condemnation was received
        by the orthodox in general. - - -   11

400   Theophilus sends a deputation against the Origenists, to Chrysostom, bishop of Constantinople. The Origenists proceed thither, and are favorably
to   received. Persecution and exile of Chrysostom. Death of Epiphanius, Isidorus, and the leaders of the Origenists. Reconciliation of Theophilus
403   with the rest. - - - -   12

        Paschal Epistles of Theophilus to the Egyptian
401 to 404 churches, against Origen's doctrine. -   13

        Italy. The Roman Pontiff cites Rufinus, on
400 to 404 charge of heresy ; rejects the Apology which Rufinus sends ; and condemns him. Rufinus's Invective against Jerome. Extracts of it privately sent to Jerome. - - -   14

        Jerome, in answer, writes his Apology against Rufinus ; in which he denies Universalism, and gives a catalogue of Origen's principal errors. Rufinus is exasperated, and threatens. Jerome adds the conclusion to his Apology against Rufinus. - - - -   15

404   End of the Contest. Review of its character.   16

CHAPTER VIII.

History of Universalism from A. D. 405, to A. D. 500.

A. D.   SECT.

405   Division of the Roman Empire. Disorders and
weakness of the state. Progress of the church
towards supreme power. Contest with the Donatists.   -   -   -   -   -   -   -   1

405   The Origenists find repose. Rufinus, Melania,
John of Jerusalem, Evagrius Ponticus, and Palladius of Galatia.   Theophilus grows attached
to   again to Origen's works. His death. Jerome,
too, avails himself of Origen's authority, though
he inveighs against the Origenists. States his
views of future punishment. Perhaps, in secret,
412   a Universalist still.   -   -   -   -   2

The orthodox of this age are divided into five
classes, in their notions of future punishment, and
of the final extent of salvation.   -   -   3

Universalists in Spain, under the two Avitus's,
410 to 415 Basil, &c. Their peculiar opinions. Augustine,
by request of the Spanish bishops, writes against
them. His criticism on the Greek word translated *everlasting*. His arguments against Universalism.   .   -   -   -   -   4

Augustine ; author of the doctrine of total depravity, irresistible grace, and sovereign, partial
election.   -   -   -   -   -   5

Unfavorable influence of that doctrine against
Universalism.   -   -   -   -   6

412   Account of its introduction : Augustine, in op-
to   posing Pelagius and Celestius, runs to the opposite
418   extreme.   -   -   -   -   -   7

413 to 420 Pelagius patronized by John of Jerusalem.
Death and character of the latter. Death of
Jerome.   -   -   -   -   -   8

420 to 428 Theodorus of Mopsuestia, a Universalist. His
life, character, and works.   -   -   -   9

430 to 450 Universalism prevails around Cesarea in Palestine ; but is not mentioned again, till the end of
this century.   -   -   -   -   -   10

400 to 500 Probable cause of this silence may be found in
the civil and ecclesiastical commotions, which
engrossed the public attention. Fall of the Western Empire. Nestorian controversy in the East.   11

About 500 Bar-Sudaili of Edessa, a Universalist.   -   12

Manicheans and Gnostics of this century.   -   13

CHAPTER IX.

Revival and progress of Origenism in Palestine ; and final condemnation of Universalism in the Fifth General Council.

View of the Solitude between Jerusalem and
the Dead Sea.   -   -   -   1

A. D.		SECT.

Lauras and monasteries in that region. St.

500 Sabas. Disaffection in his Laura ; the founding

501 to 507 of Nova Laura. - - - - 2

514 Nonnus, Leontius, and other Origenists admitted into Nova Laura. Their Universalism. Their

to expulsion ; and re-admission. Their doctrine spreads in the country. The affair introduced,

531 by Sabas, to the notice of the emperor Justinian. 3

Death of Sabas ; prosperity of the Origenists.

532 Domitian and Theodorus Ascidas, Universalists. They go to Constantinople, and are appointed archbishops. Their influence at Court ; and their patronage of their friends in Palestine. - 4

537 Gelasius, abbot of St. Sabas, expels the leading Origenists from the great laura ; but is obliged

538 to drive away, in turn, some of his orthodox monks. These go to Antioch, and lay the matter before Ephraim, patriarch of that city ; who calls a council of the bishops, and anathematizes the heresy. The Origenists, in revenge, attempt to procure the excommunication of Ephraim. Peter, bishop of Jerusalem, withstands them, and sends an account of their heresy and conduct to Justinian. - - - - - 5

539—540 Justinian publishes an Edict, commanding Origen's errors, among which is Universalism, to be condemned, together with their author and advocates. The bishops at Constantinople meet in council and approve the edict ; and the patriarchs of the Eastern and Western churches subscribe it. - - - - - - 6

540 But in Palestine, Alexander, a bishop, refuses to subscribe ; and the partizans of Nonnus prefer banishment from their cells. Peter, bishop of Jerusalem, is compelled to compromise, and re-

to store them. Their quarrels and combat with the orthodox monks. Gelasius goes, with a complaint, to Constantinople ; but is driven away by Theodorus Ascidas. The orthodox in Palestine

546 are dispersed ; and the Origenists take possession of the lauras and monasteries. Death of Nonnus and Leontius. The laura of Sabas falls into the hands of the orthodox ; while the Origenists gain the election of Macarius to the bishopric of Jerusalem. Dissention among them-

547 selves. - - - - - 7

546 Artful plan of Theodorus to revenge the late condemnation of Origen. He procures an edict

to from Justinian against the Three Chapters. Commotions which followed in the church. - 8

553

553 Meeting of the Fifth General Council, in which certain writings of Theodorus of Mopsuestia, Theodoret of Cyrus, and Ibas of Edessa, are condemned. The subject of Origenism is brought before the council; anathemas pronounced against the doctrine; and the works of Didymus of Alexandria, and of Evagrius Ponticus in favor of Universalism, condemned. - - - 9

553—554 Execution of the Council's decrees in Palestine; and consequent dispersion of the Origenists. - 10

APPENDIX.

Traces of the doctrine from the time of the Fifth General Council to the Era of the Reformation.

649 to 869 The first Lateran Council, and the seventh and and eighth General Councils repeat the condemnation of Origen, Didymus and Evagrius. Germanus writes against the Universalists. - 1

744 Clement, perhaps a Universalist, in France. 2

870 John Scotus Erigena, a Universalist. - - 3

850 to 1050 Age of darkness, in the church. Character of the clergy, and state of religion. - - 4

660 The Paulicians perhaps the remote occasion of the Reformation. Their character, manners, and

to doctrine. - - - - - 5

  Their History. Their dispersion over Europe,

1100 where they appeared under various denominations. - -- - - 6

1190 Raynold, abbot of St. Martin's, at Nevers, in France, accused of Universalism. - - 7

1200 to 1210 Amalric, or Amauri, perhaps a Universalist. His sentiments condemned at Paris and Rome. 8

1222 Salomon, bishop of Bassora, a Universalist. 9

1230 to 1234 Du Pin's account of the Stadings, in Germany. 10

1315, &c. Lollards in Germany. - - - 11

1368 Universalism taught in England, and condemned by a council at Canterbury. - 12

1400 to 1412 Men of Understanding, in Holland, Universalists. Ægidius Cantor, and William of Hildenissen. - - - - - 13

1480 to 1494 John Picus Mirandola, an Italian prince, denies the infinite demerit of sin; is accused of heresy, and makes his peace with the Pope. - - 14

1490 to 1498 Peter D'Aranda, a Spanish bishop denies purgatory and hell; is deposed on a false charge of Judaism, and condemned to perpetual imprison-

 - - - - 15

ANCIENT HISTORY

OF

UNIVERSALISM.

CHAPTER I.

[From A. D. 90, to A. D. 150.]

A. D. 90.] I. At the date with which this history begins, none of the apostles are supposed to have been alive, except St. John, who then resided, at a very advanced age, in the great city of Ephesus. St. Peter and St. Paul suffered martyrdom at Rome, more than twenty years before : and St. James the Great, and St. James the Less, at Jerusalem, still earlier. Of the deaths of the other apostles, nothing can be pronounced with confidence, notwithstanding the accounts given of their martyrdom by some ancient writers, and adopted by many of the moderns.

Nor must we pretend to define the extent to which Christianity had now spread ; since, on this subject, it is often impossible to distinguish the true from the fabulous accounts of early historians. It is probable, however, that some churches were already established in most of the Roman provinces, especially in the eastern. But the number of *professed* Christians must still have been very small, compared with the whole mass of community ; and it must have been composed, with some exceptions, of the lower classes of people. The rich and noble were, for the most part, attached to the ancient forms and institutions ; and the men of great learning, and those of refined taste, did not depart, as indeed they seldom do, from that popular course where they might find reward, or at least hope for admiration.

The Christians were, nevertheless, not an obscure sect. Their religion was so novel, so different from every other, and they were so zealous and successful in its cause, that it drew much attention wherever it was introduced. It was, indeed, greatly misunderstood by the public at large ; and still more misrepresented by its particular enemies. Of these, the most bitter were the heathen priests, who felt their long unmolested repose disturbed by the growing desertion of their temples, and neglect of their services.[1] Still it must be remarked, that the Christians had suffered very little persecution, except slander, since the death of Nero, more than twenty years before. But the time drew near, when they were to encounter proscription, danger, and even death, from the civil authorities : It was but four or five years afterwards, that the jealousy of the emperor Domitan revived the

[1] Plinii Epist. 97. Lib. x. and Taciti Annal. Lib. xv. cap. 44. Afterwards, or towards the year 150, we find the most outrageous calumny heaped upon the Christians : they were commonly called Atheists ; and all kinds of licentiousness, even such as cannot, with decency, be mentioned, were charged upon them. To refute and expose these slanderous falsehoods, was a grand object with several of the early Christian writers.

storm, which raged, with some considerable intervals, for more than two centuries, till the inauspicious conversion of Constantine gave to the church the kingdoms of this world, and the glory of them.

As to the system of doctrine held by the Christians, at this period, we can determine few of its particulars, if indeed it be proper to say that such a system then obtained. Their religion had not, as yet, been taught on any regular plan, like that of a body of divinity. Its fundamental truths, that Jesus Christ was the Messiah of the only true God, and the Saviour of men, and that he rose from the dead, necessarily engrossed the chief attention of its professors, since these were the important facts they were obliged, almost continually, to urge on the people, and to defend against opponents. It is extremely difficult for us, who are brought up in a state of society where Christianity is the original and universal religion, and where our disputes extend only to its particular tenets, to conceive of the simplicity in which the first preachers taught their faith, when, not the doctrine, but the truth itself, of that religion, was the principal point in dispute. When people were brought to acknowledge the mission of Christ, they were considered Christians, and, if their conduct became their profession, they were gladly received into the churches ; though further instructions were then given, or afterwards added, as opportunities offered.[2] Such being the liberal con-

---

[2] This was the practice of the apostles. See the abstracts and accounts of those discourses which they addressed to *unbelievers :* Acts ii. 14—41. iii. 12—26. iv. 8—12. v. 29—32. viii. 30—38. ix. 20—22. x. 34—48. xiii. 16—41. xvi. 30—33. xvii. 2—4. 18. 22—34. xxiii. 6. xxv. 18, 19. xxvi. xxviii. 23.

2*

ditions on which the churches were gathered, they, of course, admitted persons of different, and even of opposite sentiments, on many points of doctrine. Both the Jewish and Gentile converts retained many of their respective prejudices. The consequence was, that disputes had already arisen among them, particularly concerning the obligation of the Mosaic rituals, on óne hand, and the heathen schemes of philosophy, on another. The apostles themselves had, years before, interposed to decide these controversies ; but even their authority could not remove the prejudices of the parties, nor silence their contentions. Some of the Gnostic believers, in particular, had, perhaps, gone so far, even at this early period, as to separate from the other churches, and to form themselves into distinct bodies, which, however, must have been small and obscure. After all, we cannot suppose that the Christians, in general, had so soon obliterated from their faith the prominent features of the apostolic doctrine ; especially, when we consider that most of the books of the New Testament were now in circulation, and that St. John still lived to be consulted, and to give instructions.[3]

II. Proceeding, now, to the particular subject of our history, we shall, in the present chapter, produce all that can be known, with any degree of certainty, of the views entertained by the Christians, from this time till A. D. 150, in relation to a future state of punishment and the eventful salvation of the world.

[3]. The principal facts in this section are illustrated at large by Mosheim, Eccl. Hist. Cent. i ; and more particularly in his Commentaries on the Affairs of the Christians, before the Time of Constantine, &c. Vol. i. *Vidal's Translation.*

The only direct light that gleams, at intervals, through the obscurity of the course we attempt, is derived from the few Christian writings of this period, which are still extant. These are the productions of those commonly called the Apostolical Fathers, the first Christian authors, whose works have reached us, after the apostles themselves. They are the following : *The First Epistle of Clemens Romanus ;* seven *Epistles of Ignatius ; The Epistle of Polycarp ; The Epistle of Barnabas ;* and *The Shepherd of Hermas.* Among these, we should perhaps insert a *Relation of the Martyrdom of Ignatius.*[4] These writings, composed by men of little learning, and, for the most part, of as little judgment, are still valuable as they afford some notion of the state of the early Christians, and of their sentiments ; but whoever expects to find them instructive or edifying in other respects, will rise from their perusal in disappointment, if not with disgust.

III. The *Epistle of Clemens Romanus* A. D. 90, is distinguished for the respect it received —95 from the ancient churches, some of which caused it to be read, in public, with the books of the New Testament. It may be allowed, at least, the

[4] Of the *Second Epistle of Clemens Romanus,* so called, the genuineness is considered doubtful by Eusebius, Jerome, Du Pin, Mosheim, &c. and wholly denied by Photius, Archbishop Usher, Lardner, Brucker, Le Clerc, and others. Scarcely one admits it. There are other writings extant, ascribed to Clemens Romanus, but which are now universally considered forgeries, and of a much later date. I omit *The Acts of Paul and Thecla,* a forgery of the First Century, because our present copy is either a forgery upon that original one, or else so much interpolated that we cannot determine what is ancient. See Lardner's Credibility, &c. Chap. *Supposititious Writings of 2d Century.* The reason why I place *The Epistle of Barnabas,* and *The Shepherd of Hermas* last in this catalogue, will be given under the accounts respectively of those works.

commendations, that it is simple though diffuse, and that it contains but one instance,[5] of those absurd allegories which abound in the succeeding fathers. Clemens, who was bishop of the church at Rome, and perhaps the same person whom St. Paul had mentioned, (*Phil.* iv. 3.) wrote this Epistle to the Corinthian Christians for the purpose of dissuading them from their quarrels and seditions. Earnestly exhorting them to repent of their mutual envy and abuse, he adduces, among other considerations, the justice of God as a motive of fear, and the terrible destruction of Sodom and its neighboring cities, as instances of the divine judgements on sinners. But it is remarkable that, in the whole of this Epistle, about as long as St. Mark's Gospel, there is no expression which discovers whether he believed in any future state of punishment, nor whether he held the salvation of all mankind. There are, indeed, two passages,[6] which may naturally, not necessarily, be understood to intimate that those only who here serve the Lord, will hereafter be raised from the dead.

A. D. 94, to 100. In passing over the time at which St. John is commonly supposed to have written his *Gospel* and three *Epistles*,[7] we may remark that this last of the apostles died at

---

[5] Clemens Rom. Epis. §12. *Wake's Translation.* The date of this Epistle was probably between A. D. 90 and 95. Lardner places it at A. D. 94 or 95; Junius, at 98; Baronius and Cotelerius, at 92; Dodwell, Wake and Le Clerc, between 64 and 70.

[6] Clem. Rom. Epis. § 26 and 49. In these two passages, Clemens expressly mentions the resurrection of those who "religiously serve the Lord," and are "made perfect in love;" but nowhere does he *assert* the resurrection of others.

[7] Of the *Revelation*, the date has been a point of much dispute; but there seems, now, a general inclination to place it before the

Ephesus, about the year 100. He left the world at a period when old errors appear to have been spreading in the church, and springing up there, under new forms and modifications. They were chiefly of the Gnostic kind, derived from the Oriental or Persian philosophy ; of which we shall have a more particular account to give in the sequel.

A. D. 107, or 116. IV. We come next to the famous *Epistles of Ignatius ;* the genuineness of which has been attacked and defended with an immoderate zeal altogether disproportioned to their worth, or real weight in any cause whatever. Though the question is still involved in uncertainty, we shall follow, with some doubt, what appears the prevailing opinion, that the seven,[8] translated by Archbishop Wake, are, in the main, genuine. They were written, if by Ignatius, while he was conducted, partly by sea, and partly by land, on a tardy journey of two thousand miles,[9] from Antioch to Rome, for

destruction of Jerusalem. Of the date of St. John's other writings, various opinions are entertained : Dr. Witherspoon places the *Gospel* at A. D. 96, and the *Epistles* at 98 ; Lardner dates the Gospel at A. D. 68, and the Epistles at 80 and 85 ; by Le Clerc, the Gospel is assigned to the year 97, and the Epistles to 91 and 92 ; Dr. Owen places the Gospel at about A. D. 69 ; Jer. Jones, at 97 ; and DuPin, at about A. D. 100.

[8] Even of these there are two very different copies : the larger, which is generally supposed to be much interpolated ; and the shorter, which is followed by Wake, and almost universally preferred. Mosheim, however, (Comment. on the Affairs of the Christians, &c.) seems to doubt whether the larger be not the genuine, if indeed either be so.

[9] His route, real or fabulous, is traced from Antioch to Smyrna, Troas, over the Ægean, into Macedonia and through Epirus, across the Adriatic and Tyrrhene Seas, to the mouth of the Tiber, and thence to Rome. The date of his journey, and of course of his Epistles and Martyrdom, is placed at A. D. 107, by Du Pin, Tillemont, Cave and Lardner ; but at A. D. 116, by Pearson, Lloyd, Pagi, Le Clerc and Fabricius. If the *Relation of the Martyrdom of*

the execution of the sentence of martyrdom. He is said to have been bishop of the church in the former city, for about forty years, and to have been personally acquainted, in his younger days, with some of the apostles. His writings, however, are not always worthy of his advantages : they contain some puerile conceits,[10] betray a fondness for the eastern fables concerning the angelic world,[11] and abound with earnest injunctions of the most unreserved submission of reason, faith and practice, to the clergy ; whose authority is often likened, expressly, to that of God and Jesus Christ.

We cannot ascertain the author's views concerning the final extent of salvation ; and the following is all that seems to refer to a future state of punishment : " Those that corrupt families by adultery, shall not " inherit the kingdom of God. If therefore they, who " have done this according to the flesh, have suffered " death, how much more shall he die, who by his " wicked doctrine corrupts the faith of God, for which " Christ was crucified ? He, that is thus defiled, shall " depart into unquenchable fire, and so also shall he " that hearkens to him. "[12] In another place he says, in rather a disjointed paragraph, " Seeing, then, " all things have an end, there are these two indiffer- " ently set before us, life and death ; and every one " shall depart unto his proper place. "[13] In the same

---

Ignatius, which professes to be written by eye-witnesses, be genuine, this disputed date is fixed at A. D. 116. See § 3. *Wake's Translation.*

[10.] Ignat. Epist. to the Ephesians, § 9. *Wake's trans.* [11.] Ditto. § 19. and Epist. to the Trallians, § 5.

[12.] Epist. to the Ephes. § 26. [13.] Epist. to the Magnesians, § 5.

unconnected manner, he says again, " For what re-
" mains, it is very reasonable that we should return
" unto a sound mind, whilst there is yet time to return
unto God. "[14]   Some of these passages may, indeed,
have no allusion to a future state.   It must, however,
be remarked here, that the author evidently believed
that certain heretics, and perhaps the wicked in general, will not be raised from the dead, but exist hereafter as mere incorporeal spirits.[15]

The *Relation of the Martyrdom of Ignatius*, written by Christian eye-witnesses of his trial and sufferings, contains nothing to our purpose ; we, therefore,
proceed to

A. D. 108,
or 117.

V. *The Epistle of Polycarp ;* a piece
which evinces a more connected tenor of
thought, than most of the ecclesiastical
writings of that age.   The author is guilty of one exception to his usual moderation, when he exhorts his breth-
" ren to be subject to the elders and deacons as unto
" ' God and Christ."[16]   They who receive this epistle
as Polycarp's,[17] generally suppose it to have been written soon after the martyrdom of Ignatius, to which it
alludes.   Polycarp was a bishop of the church at
Smyrna, from about the year 100, till after the middle
of the second century.   He is said to have been the
disciple of St. John ; and he was certainly regarded,

14. Epist. to the Smyrneans, § 9.   15. Ditto § 2 and 7, compared
with Epist. to the Trall. § 9. and Epist. to the Romans, § 2.
   16. Polycarp's Epist. § 5. *Wake's trans.*   17. M. Daille and Blon-
del reject it, and Mosheim says it "has merely a questionable claim
to credit. "   But Lardner, on the contrary, asserts that " there is
scarce any doubt or question among learned men about the genuineness of this Epistle of Polycarp. "

after the death of that apostle, as the most eminent of the Christians of Asia.[18]

The following is all that his Epistle contains in relation to the particular subject of this history : " To " whom [Christ] all things are made subject, both " that are in heaven and that are in earth ; whom " every living creature shall worship ; who shall come " to be the judge of the quick and dead ; whose blood " God shall require of them that believe not in him."[19] Alluding, without doubt, to some of the Gnostic heretics, he says, " Whosoever does not confess that Jesus " Christ is come in the flesh, he is antichrist. And " whoever does not confess his suffering upon the " cross, is from the devil. And whosoever perverts " the oracles of the Lord to his own lusts, and says " that there shall be neither any resurrection, nor " judgement, he is the first born of Satan.[20] " There may also be a question, whether the author does not intimate that the future resurrection depends on faith and obedience in this life.[21]

VI. To these dates succeeds a period of several years, from which no Christian writings have descended to us, except a few passages that happen to have been quoted, by later writers, from Papias, Quadratus and

[18.] By some he is considered *the angel of the Church in Smyrna*, addressed in Rev. ii. 8. This, however, is doubtful, as it is probable that he was not ordained till after the Revelation was written. [19.] Polycarp's Epist. § 2.   [20.] Ditto. § 7.

[21.] Ditto. § 2 and 5. If Clemens Romanus and Polycarp, as well as Ignatius, really held a partial resurrection, that of the saints exclusively, the circumstance would seem to prove that the notion of the Jews, or rather of the Pharisees, on this point, had spread pretty extensively in the church,—from Asia Minor to Rome—at this early period. That such was the notion of the Pharisees, about the end of the first century, see Josephus, &c.

Agrippa Castor ; of which, however, we shall take no notice, as they throw no light upon our subject. But it is important to remark that Papias and Aristides (a writer of whom nothing whatever remains) contributed, undesignedly to pervert the simplicity of Christianity ; and that they serve, at the same time, to exemplify the manner in which corruptions grew up in the church. The former, who was bishop at

A. D. 116. Hierapolis, near Laodicea, is said to have devoted himself to collecting traditions of the apostolic doctrine and sayings ; but being very credulous and of a weak mind, he received, with little discrimination, whatever was related to him. Having thus formed a collection of idle tales and foolish notions, he published them to the world as the authoritative instructions of Christ and his apostles. Such was the character of the church, that his work appears to have been well received ; and it certainly met with considerable credit among the succeeding fathers, who adopted some of its fictions.[22] But whatever were the injurious effects of these pretended traditions, the cause of truth sustained a much greater detriment from the gradual incorporation of the Grecian philosophy. Aristides was probably the first professed philosopher from

A. D. 124, the Grecian schools, who took an active part in support of Christianity. But he —126 appears, unhappily, to have clothed it in the robe of the Academy ; for Jerome informs us that the *Apology*, which he presented to the emperor Adrian, in behalf of the persecuted Christians, was

[22.] Du Pin's Bibliotheca Patrum, Article, Papias. Papias is said to have flourished about A. D. 116.

full of philosophic notions, which were afterwards adopted by Justin Martyr.[23] The Grecian philosophy was nearly as incompatible with Christianity, as was the Oriental ; but the corruptions it introduced, flourished in the church, after a few years, as in a congenial soil ; and, in less than a century, gave a new appearance to the general mass of doctrine considered orthodox.

VII. *The Epistle of Barnabas* is the
A. D. 131. next, in order ; unless, as has been hitherto conjectured, it belong to the first century.[24] It was composed by some Jewish Chris-

[23.] Du Pin's Biblioth. Pat. Art. Quadratus and Aristides. The Apology of Aristides is supposed to have been written about A. D. 124, or 126.

[24.] It has been thought, by most of the learned, that the Epistle of Barnabas was written in the first century ; and, by many, that it was the work of that Barnabas who was the companion and fellow-traveller of St. Paul. The latter opinion, Mosheim treats as scarcely worthy of a refutation ; and though it has had some eminent advocates, it is now generally discarded. That the former opinion is also incorrect, I cannot but think sufficiently evident from the Epistle itself. The author, speaking of the temple of Jerusalem, says, " Again, he [Christ] speaketh after this manner : *Behold, they that destroy this temple, even they shall again build it up.* And so it came to pass ; for through their wars, it is now destroyed by their enemies ; and the servants of their enemies build it up." (Barnab. Epist. § 16. *Wake's trans.*) It will not be questioned that the author here speaks, 1, of the destruction of the temple after our Lord's ministry ; i. e. of its destruction by Titus ; and 2, of attempts at rebuilding it by the servants of the Romans, at the time of writing this Epistle. Now, it is well known that there was no attempt at rebuilding either the temple or the city, after their destruction by Titus, till the time of Adrian, who, in A. D. 130, or 136, sent a colony to Jerusalem to restore the city, and on or near the site of the former temple to erect a new one, which he afterwards dedicated to Jupiter. This circumstance appears to determine the date of the allusion quoted from Barnabas ; and I know of nothing that can be urged against the hypothesis. Irenæus, about A. D. 190, is the first who seems to have imitated any of the expressions of this Epistle ; and Clemens Alexandrinus, about A. D. 194, is the first who either mentioned it, or formally alluded to it. It is but just, however, to

tian, of mean abilities, for the purpose of representing the Mosaic law and other parts of the Old Testament as containing a hidden account of Christ and his religion. The allegorical and mystical interpretations, of which the Epistle mostly consists, present an extraordinary instance of blind stupidity aiming at discoveries.[25]

It is worthy of remark, that of all the Christian writings, after the sacred Scriptures, this Epistle is the first in which we find the word *everlasting*, or *eternal*, applied to suffering : Near the end, Barnabas represents two ways, that of light, over which the angels of God are appointed, and that of darkness, where

apprize the reader, that my hypothesis is not supported by the authority of the critics ; who, so far as I know, have taken no notice of Barnabas's allusion to the rebuilding of the temple. Mosheim supposes the Epistle to have been written in the first century ; and he agrees with Cotelerius, Brucker, Basnage and others, that its author was not the Barnabas who was the companion of St. Paul. Wake, Du Pin and Lardner, on the contrary, ascribe it to that Barnabas, and place its date about a. d. 71 or 72.

25. " Understand, children," says he, " these things more fully. " that Abraham, who was the first that brought in circumcision, " performed it, after having received the mystery of three letters, " by which he looked forward in the spirit, to Jesus. For the Scrip- " ture says that Abraham circumcised three hundred and eigh- " teen men of his house. But what, therefore, was the mystery " that was made known unto him ? Mark, first, the eighteen ; and " next, the three hundred. For the numeral letters of ten and eight, " are IH, [i.e. the Greek Eta, or long E,—IE are the first two letters " of the word Jesus.] And these denote *Jesus*. And because the " cross was that by which we were to find grace, he therefore adds " three hundred ; the numeral letter of which is T, [the figure of " the cross.] Wherefore, by two letters he signified Jesus, and by " the third, his cross. He who has put the engrafted gift of his " doctrine within us, knows that I never taught to any a more cer- " tain truth ; but I trust that ye are worthy of it. "—Barnabas's Epist. § 9. Such is one the important discoveries our author communicates ; and strange as it may seem, the later fathers, even those of undoubted learning, as Justin Martyr, Irenæus, Clemens Alexandrinus, &c. appear to have been by no means insensible to the charms of this kind of nonsense.

the angels of Satan preside ; and after describing the manner of walking in the way of light, he says, " But " the way of darkness is crooked, and full of cursing ; " for it is the way of *eternal* death with punishment, " in which they that walk meet with those things that " destroy their own souls. "[26]   He afterwards adds, that he who chooses this part, shall " be destroyed, " together with his works. For this cause, there " shall be both a resurrection and a retribution. "[27] Throughout his Epistle he says nothing of universal salvation ; and it appears from what we have quoted, that he believed in a future state of punishment.   But whether he thought it endless, cannot be determined ; since the word *everlasting* or *eternal*, was used, by the ancients, to denote indefinite rather than interminable duration.[28]

VIII. The last, as well as the longest,
A. D. 150.   of the works of the Apostolical Fathers,
          so called, is that effusion of second child-
ishness, *The Shepherd of Hermas.*[29]   It was written at Rome, by a brother of the bishop of that city ; but it betrays an ignorant and imbecile mind, in absolute

[26.] Barnabas's Epistle, *(Wake's translation,)* § 18, and 20.
[27.] Ditto, § 21.   [28.] See instances of this, in the next Chapter, Sect. iii. iv. xi. and in succeeding Chapters.
[29.] It had long been debated, by the learned, whether this work was composed in the first century, by that Hermas whom St. Paul mentions (Rom. xvi. 14.;) or in the second century, by another Hermas, brother to Pius, bishop of Rome. But the question was finally decided by a fragment of a work of the second century, brought to light by Muratori ; " Hermas, brother to Pius, bishop of the church in the city of Rome, " says this fragment, " wrote very lately, in our own time, *The Shepherd*, at Rome. " (See Mosheim's Commentaries on the Affairs of the Christians, &c. eccl. hist. of the first Cent. § liv. notes *n* and *o*; where may be found a full discussion of this point.) The date of *The Shepherd*, therefore, cannot be much earlier than A. D. 150 ; perhaps later.

dotage. Its object appears to have been to excite the professors of Christianity to more uprightness, zeal, and abstraction from the business as well as ordinary pleasures of life ; and this, the author strives to effect by relating pretended visions, and by introducing instructions from an angel, who occasionally appeared to him, as he asserts, in the habit of a *shepherd*. But the conversation he attributes to his celestial visitants, is more insipid than we commonly hear from the weakest of men.

Without extracting at full length, as in the case of former works, the several passages which seem to have relation to our subject, it is sufficient to observe, that Hermas has left nothing to determine his views of the final extent of salvation, unless it may be gathered, from the following, that he totally precludes some of the human race from all prospect of bliss : He teaches that a Christian, if he sin after his baptism, may possibly be allowed the privilege of one repentance, and of one only ;[30] but that for such as apostatize from the faith, and blaspheme God, there is no return. They have *forever* departed from God ; and, in the next world, they are to be burned, together with the heathen nations.[31] Strong as such language may seem, those acquainted with the style of the earliest fathers, will not, perhaps, account it altogether decisive in favor of endless perdition. We may here add, that Hermas supposed that the apostles, after their death, went and preached to the souls of those who had led pure and virtuous lives before Christ's

[30] Hermas. Book ii. Command. iv. § 3. compared with Book i. Vis. ii. § 2. *Wake's trans.* [31] Ditto, Book iii. Simil. vi. § 2.

3*

birth ; and that, when those spirits had thus heard the gospel, they received water baptism, in some way untold, and then entered the kingdom of God.[32] He also held an opinion, common during the remainder of this century, that the end of the world was near at hand.[33]

IX. We must now take our leave, for a while, of the orthodox believers, and go back to an account of a very different kind of Christians, concerning whom we have not even the feeble light hitherto enjoyed, to guide our investigations. No part of ecclesiastical history is involved in more uncertainty, than that of the Gnostic heretics of the first and second centuries. Their own writings, except a few unconnected fragments, are wholly lost ; and the only way of attaining to an acquaintance with them and their sentiments, is by comparing the faulty, and often abusive, representations of their zealous opposers, with the imperfect knowledge we have of that system of philosophy, the Oriental, which they amalgamated with Christianity.[34] That they believed in our Saviour as a messenger from the supreme God, and generally maintained their Christian profession, amidst the opposition of the heathens, and the obloquy of the orthodox, is certain. But it is now considered equally certain, that they believed, some of them, that Jesus Christ was an angelic being

A. D. 90,
to 150.

---

[32] Ditto. Book iii. Simil. ix. § 16.   [33] Ditto. Book i. Vis. iv. § 3.
[34] I, however, attempt only to follow our modern historian, Mosheim, (Ecclesiastical History ; and Commentaries on the Affairs of the Christians, &c.) with some help from Le Clerc, (Histor. Eccl. duorum primorum, a Christo nato, Sæculorum) from Beausobre, (Histoire de Manichee, &c.) and from the History of Heretics in Lardner's Works.

of the highest order, who came into our world with
only the visionary appearance, not the real body, of
a man; and others, that Jesus alone was a mere man,
with a human soul, into whom the Christ, a high celestial spirit, descended at his baptism in Jordan. As
to the object of our Saviour's mission, they are thought
to have been perfectly agreed, that it was, not to satisfy any vindictive justice in Deity, whom they considered infinitely good, but to deliver mankind from
the oppressive service of the degenerate gods of this
world, and to teach them how to subdue their passions,
and approximate the supreme God, the fountain of
purity and bliss. From the long-venerated, but chimerical, philosophy of the Persians, they retained the
notion, that the *material* world was formed, not by
the Self-Existent, but by the inferior gods, called Æons,
whose being was derived through a long and intricate
succession, as most of them thought, originally from
him.[35] This led them to regard the God of the Jews,
the Jehovah of the Old Testament, as but a secondary
being, the principal Maker of this world; and they
also concluded that he had apostatized, more or less,
from the divine allegiance, inasmuch as he had arrogated to himself the honors of worship, and as Christ
had been sent to annul his ancient covenant, and to
overthrow his institutions. From the same philosophy,
they also received the doctrine of the eternity of matter, and, especially, of its inherent, radical depravity.

[35] A few of them, *perhaps*, held two original, self-existent Beings, an evil, as well as a good, Deity. Such, it is conjectured,
was the opinion of the Saturninians, about A. D. 120, and of the
Marcionites, about A. D. 140. This is denied, however, in the
History of Heretics in Lardner's Works, and also by Beausobre.

Hence, they in general discarded the hope of the resurrection of the material body, which, in their view,
would but perpetuate the bondage and corruption of
the soul. With such dislike did most of them regard
the body, that they prescribed an excessively rigid discipline, a continual abstinence, in order to thwart all
its inclinations, and to weaken, as far as possible, its
power over the mind.

Such are the common outlines of their several systems, as laid down by the more judicious of modern
historians, who at the same time confess and lament
the impossibility of arriving at a satisfactory knowledge of the subject.   All the Gnostics were charged,
by their cotemporary orthodox adversaries, with being
abandoned to licentiousness : a scandal which the
heathens first poured forth, with unsparing liberality,
upon the orthodox themselves, and which these, in
turn, have as freely passed over, and doubtless from
nearly the same motives, to the successive orders of
heretics.[36]

[36] The licentiousness, alleged by the ancient orthodox against
the Gnostics, is in part denied, and in part admitted, by Mosheim ;
uniformly mentioned in terms of uncertainty, by Le Clerc ; and
wholly denied, by Beausobre ; as it likewise is, in the History of
Heretics, in Lardner's Works. The following remark deserves
more consideration than, I fear, most readers will allow it : " This
is certain, that as bad things were said of the primitive Christians,
as were ever said of the ancient heretics by the Catholics, [Or-
thodox.]   Modern Reformers have been treated just in the same
manner." (Hist. of Heretics, Book i. Sect. 8, Lardner's Works.)
Look into Roman Catholic writings, and see all kinds of immoral
tenets attributed to Luther, Calvin, and their associates ; turn to
the Protestant side, and see the charge retorted with, at least, equal
exaggeration ; hear the mutual criminations of our modern sects,
who accuse each other of principles of conduct which they never
thought of ;—and then judge how much credit should be given to
ancient calumnies of the same sort ! It is a curious circumstance,
that Mosheim, honored and admired, and standing on high ground

Some of the Gnostics, perhaps some of the earliest, believed in the endless exclusion of a part of mankind from the abodes of celestial light. But, among those who arose in Egypt, there were many, particularly the Basilidians, the Carpocratians and the Valentinians, who are supposed to have held an eventual restoration, or rather transmigration, of all human souls to a heaven of purity and bliss. But this tenet they appear to have involved in other notions, wild and chimerical enough to warrant the suspicion of lunacy, were it not for the antiquity, prevalence, and reputation of that whimsical philosophy from which they were derived.

X. The Basilidians and Carpocratians, About A. D. 120. it is said, believed that such souls as here follow the instructions of our Saviour, will, at death, ascend immediately to the happy mansions above; while, on the contrary, such as neglect and disobey, will be condemned to pass into other bodies, either of men or of brutes, until by their purification they shall be fitted to share the joys of the incorporeal blest; and so, all will finally be saved.

The Basilidians were the followers of Basilides, a Gnostic Christian and Egyptian philosopher, who flourished, at Alexandria, in the early part of the second century, and died there between the years 130 and 140. Though he believed in one self-existent, supreme, and infinitely glorious God, yet he also held that depraved matter had been, in one state or another,

in a national church, had never, himself, encountered the slander of bigotry; while Le Clerc, an odious Arminian from Geneva, and Beausobre, a Protestant refugee from France, had ample experience of its malignity and falsehood. The Unitarian Lardner was, in his own country, a heretic of the most obnoxious kind,

coeval with him. In the past ages of eternity, the Deity produced from himself certain Æons, who, in their turn, begat others, but of a rank somewhat inferior, and of a lower station ; and from these again proceeded a species still less exalted ; and so on, in succession, till the celestial hierarchy extended from the highest heaven down to the vicinity of chaotic matter. The lowest race of Æons, whose station was the nethermost heaven, undertook, at length, to reduce the immense material mass below them from its pristine state of disorder; and having formed it into a world, and made man with a body and a *material* soul, the Deity, approving their work, gave the creature a *rational* mind, and thus completed the undertaking. He then allowed these Æons to divide, among themselves, the government of the world they had formed. But they, swerving by degrees from their allegiance, arrogated at length divine honors from their creatures, grew ambitious of enlarging, each one, his dominion over the territory of the others, and for this purpose embroiled mankind in mutual wars, till the world became full of wretchedness and crime. Touched with compassion for the human race, God sent his Son, the first-begotten and noblest of all the Æons, to take up his abode in the man Jesus ; and through him to proclaim the supreme, but forgotten, Deity, teach mankind to abjure the authority of their tyrannical gods, especially of the God of the Jews ; and to instruct them how to subdue their own sinful propensities, by mortifying their bodies, as well as by governing their passions. The God of the Jews, alarmed for his dominion, excited the people to apprehend and crucify

Jesus ; but the Christ, the celestial Æon, had left his mortal associate, before the suffering man was nailed to the cross.

Basilides taught that God is perfectly good, or benevolent, in the real sense of those words ; but that he inflicts the proper punishment for every wilful transgression, whether of saint or sinner. Reformation and improvement are the grand objects, as he appears to have held, of. all punishment, and of all God's dealings with mankind. Though he treated the Old Testament with respect, as the revelation of that dignified Being who governed the Jews, he did not think it inspired by the supreme God ; and he is accused of having also rejected some parts of the New Testament ; which, though possibly a fact,[37] cannot be satisfactorily proved. He wrote a *Commentary*, in twenty-four books, *on the Gospels*, which was soon answered by Agrippa Castor, a cotemporary orthodox writer.

Basilides is thought to have been a grave and pious man, but bewildered by the fabulous theology of the East. He had a son, named Isidore, who wrote some books, long since lost, in illustration of their religious sentiments. His sect, though often assailed, and constantly opposed, both by the orthodox and the heathens, was for a long time numerous, chiefly in Egypt and Asia. After having continued about two hundred years, we find it broken and decreased in the fourth century ; and not long afterwards it probably became extinct, or perhaps coalesced with that of the Manicheans.

[37] Mosheim thinks it credible ; Beausobre sees no proof of it ; and in the History of Heretics in Lardner, it is disputed. Le Clerc says nothing about it.

XI. The Carpocratians, who arose at the same place with the Basilidians, and nearly at the same time, agreed with them in the final salvation of all souls, and did not greatly differ from them in the general system of their doctrine. Like them, they distinguished between the Deity and the inferior Æons who formed the world; like them they believed that matter had existed from eternity, and was unalterably corrupt. They, indeed, arranged the Æons in a little different order; and there is some reason to think that they considered our Saviour not a two-fold being, human and angelic, but a mere man, though of more than ordinary wisdom and divine intelligence. He was appointed by Deity to teach mankind the knowledge of the true God, and to abolish the dominion of the arrogant makers of the world.

This sect, which seems never to have been large, spread chiefly in Egypt and the adjoining parts of Asia; and disappeared, probably, in little more than a century after its rise, if indeed it had ever been altogether distinct from that of the Basilidians. Its founder was Carpocrates, a learned Egyptian, who flourished at Alexandria, about the year 130. His son, Epiphanes, was a youth of vast attainments and extraordinary promise; but he died (about A. D. 140) at the early age of seventeen, after having written several treatises on religious subjects.

Their ancient opponents accuse the Carpocratians of avowing the most infamous principles of moral conduct, and even of teaching that to arrive at heaven, we must devote ourselves to the perpetration of every vile and licentious abomination: a calumny which, by its manifest exaggeration and malice, reflects only on its authors. Some of the learned allow no credit whatever to any of the disadvantageous representations of their moral character; while others refuse to exculpate them entirely, at the consequent expense of their orthodox slanderers[38].

XII. A sect of Gnostics, still more About whimsical than either of the preceding, A. D. 130. was the Valentinians. Man, in their view, was a complex being, consisting, 1, of the outward visible body; 2, of another body[39] within this, composed of fluid matter, and imperceptible to the senses; 3, of an animated soul, the seat of life and sensation only; and 4, of a nobler, rational soul, of an angelic substance. The bodies, both outward and internal, were, they held, destined to perish; of the two souls, the animal or sensitive could be saved by its obedience, or by its negligence bring upon itself entire dissolution at death; but the rational, intelligent soul, will, in all cases, be admitted to the realms of bliss.

In the immediate habitation of Deity, a world of pure light, infinitely above the visible heavens, the Valentinians placed thirty Æons, divided into three

---

[38] Among the licentious tenets charged on the Carpocratians, some of the most moderate and judicious of the moderns consider that of the community of women, as well as of goods, justly imputed to them. But in the Hist. of Heretics in Lardner, (book ii. ch. iii. § 11,) this charge is, I think, fairly shown to rest on very uncertain authority, and to be, in itself, quite improbable. Mosheim, in his Commentaries, &c. has softened the features of the picture which he had drawn of the Carpocratians, in his Ecclesiastical History.

[39] At least, so asserts Mosheim, confidently; from whom, therefore, I dare not wander, though, in this particular, I follow him with much doubt.

4

orders. These were guarded by Horus, stationed on the extreme verge of the high abode, to prevent them from wandering off into the immense regions of chaotic matter, which lay around. The Æons, in process of time, grew envious of the distinguished and peculiar felicity enjoyed by the first and highest individual of their number, who alone was adequate to comprehend the supreme Father's greatness. The ardent desire to attain the same divine pleasure, grew stronger and stronger among them; until Wisdom, the youngest and weakest of all, became excessively agitated. From her ungovernable perturbations sprang a daughter, who was immediately expelled into the vast abyss of rude and unformed matter without. To allay the agitation thus raised in the celestial realm, the Deity produced two new Æons, who instructed the others to be content with their limited capacity, and to unite all their powers in giving existence to a being called Jesus, the noblest and brightest of all the Æons.

Scarcely was the tranquillity of the heavenly world thus restored, when the most violent commotions began to agitate the drear abyss without. The exiled daughter of Wisdom had caught some glimpses of the eternal radiance, and attempted to reach the glorious abode; but being continually repulsed by its watchful guardian, her passions of grief, anxiety and desire grew so violent, that the chaotic mass of matter, in which she was immersed, caught the strong contagious emotions, and became thereby separated into the different elements which exist in our world. By the assistance of Jesus, she formed a being who is the Maker and Governor of the material system. This Creator, having afterwards, with the same assistance, constructed the visible Universe, took up his abode in the lowest heaven, far from the refulgent habitation of the Deity ; and here his vanity at length transported him to fancy himself the only true God, and to call upon mankind by his prophets, especially by those he sent to the Jews, to worship him as such. To extricate mankind from this delusion, to reveal the Deity to them, to teach them piety and virtue, was Christ, one of the Æons, sent into the world. He had a real body, but unlike those of mortals, since it was composed of an etherial substance ; and when he was baptized in Jordan, Jesus himself, in the form of a dove, descended into him. Thus completely constituted, our Saviour proceeded, by means of instructions and miracles, to fulfil his ministry. The Maker of the world was enraged by his success, and procured his apprehension and crucifixion ; but not till both Jesus and the spiritual, rational soul of Christ, had ascended, leaving nothing but the sensitive soul and the etherial body to suffer. Like other Gnostics, the Valentinians denied the resurrection of the body, and thought the authors of the Old Testament to have been under the inspiration of the Maker of this world.

This sect sprung from, Valentine an Egyptian, who, after propagating his notions, for a while, in his native country, went, about A. D. 140, to Rome. Here, so many professors embraced his views, that the church became alarmed, and after thrice excommunicating him, succeeded in rendering his residence in Italy so uncomfortable, that he withdrew to the island of Cyprus. In this delightful and luxurious region, his sect flourished in quiet; and after his death, which occurred a little subsequent, perhaps, to A. D. 150, it was widely diffused throughout Asia, Africa and Europe, and excited considerable fear in the orthodox churches. It existed about a century and a half; when it seems to have sunk gradually into oblivion. Many of its sentiments, however, were then revived among the Manicheans, whom we shall consider in their proper place.

XIII. In closing our account of these Gnostic sects, it is important to remark, that while the orthodox fathers warmly and bitterly attacked their respective systems at large, it does not appear that they ever selected the particular tenet of the salvation of all souls, as obnoxious. What chiefly excited their resentment and animadversions, was, the distinction between Deity and the Maker of the world, the fables of the Æons, the views of our Saviour's person, the rejection of the Old Testament, and the denial of the resurrection and of a future judgement.

CHAPTER II.

A. D. 150.   I. It has been seen that heresies had multiplied to such a number, and spread to such an extent, as to become troublesome[1] to the regular and approved churches, and that several sects had established separate communities, in distinction from the common body. Most of these were of the Gnostic kind, already described ; but there was one which, though small, deserves particular mention, as consisting of that part of the original church at Jerusalem, which continued to adhere, with unyielding tenacity, to the practice of the Mosaic rituals. This was the Nazarene, or Ebionite, sect, which is said to have held the simple humanity of Jesus Christ.

But from the heretics, of all kinds, we return to a view of the doctrine and character of the orthodox. Many of the vulgar superstitions of the Gentiles prevailed among them, concerning magic, the demons, and the poetical regions of the infernal world ; and the Greek philosophy, which had begun to mingle with the doctrine of Christ, was rapidly modifying his religion to its own genius. The credulity of this age was rank, and the learning of the day, at least that of the fathers, was too superficial to prove either a pre-

---

1. This is also evident from the circumstance that Agrippa Castor wrote a book against the heretics some years before this period, and Justin Martyr a little after.

4*

ventive or remedy. Apostolical tradition also began to be urged as proof, when it was so far lost or corrupted, that even they who had been disciples of the apostles, adduced contrary traditions on one and the same point;[2] and yet upon this very precarious authority some whimsical notions[3] prevailed. To these shades in the picture we must add a still darker: the Christians, orthodox as well as heretics, appear to have employed, in some cases, known falsehood in support of their cause. This pernicious artifice they are said to have derived from the Platonic paradox, *that it is lawful to lie for the truth;* but one would suppose it to have been suggested by their own intemperate zeal, rather than by any maxims of philosophy. They had already begun to forge books in support of their religion, a practice which, it is thought, they borrowed from the heretics; and they now proceeded to propagate accounts of frequent miracles, concerning which, all the early writers, after the apostles, had been entirely silent.

II. In the works which we have hitherto had under examination, we can discover little that belongs to the Grecian literature, except the language. All their fanciful conceits, all their extravagances, are either of that peculiar character which denotes a Jewish, at least Asiatic, origin; or else are the natural effusions of a stupidity that needs not the aggravation of false

---

[2] For instance, Polycarp visited Anicetus, bishop at Rome, about A. D. 150, and held an amicable discussion with him on the proper time for holding Easter. Each, according to Eusebius (Hist. Eccl. lib. v. cap. 24,) alleged Apostolical tradition for his own time, in opposition to that of the other; and they parted, but in friendship, without coming to an agreement on the point. [3] The doctrine of the proper Millennarians. for instance.

learning to become ridiculous. But when we pass the *Shepherd of Hermas*, we enter immediately on a new series of ecclesiastical writings, in most of which the learning of the Athenian and Roman schools is divested of its elegance, and converted into Christianity. This, however, we shall have occasion to exemplify, in detail, as we pursue the course of our examination.

The works which have descended to us from the period embraced in this chapter, and which succeed those of the Apostolical fathers, are *The Sibylline Oracles, The Writings of Justin Martyr, A Relation of the Martyrdom of Polycarp, The Oration of Tatian, The Letter of the Churches of Lyons and Vienne, Two productions of Athenagoras, A Treatise of Theophilus,* and *The Works of Irenæus.*[4] Through these, successively, we shall now attempt to follow the traces of our general subject.

A. D. 150, &c.

III. It will be difficult to give the reader a just notion of the first work, *The Sibylline Oracles.* They were forged[5] by some Christian or Christians, generally supposed orthodox, for the purpose of convincing the heathens of the truth of Christianity. The Sibyls were regarded as very ancient prophetesses, of extraordinary inspiration among the Romans and the Greeks ; but their books,

---

[4] The book of one *Hermias* in ridicule of the heathen philosophers, though often mentioned among the ecclesiastical works of this period, is, by all, acknowledged to be of uncertain date, and by the best critics, considered the production of a later age.

[5] Cave thinks the larger part of them composed about A. D. 130, and the rest before A. D. 192. Du Pin places them at about A. D. 160. Lardner thinks they may have been completed before A. D. 169, though possibly not till A. D. 190. Justin Martyr repeatedly refers to them ; and Hermas probably alluded to them in Book i. Vis. ii.

if indeed they ever existed, had always been carefully
concealed from the public, and consulted only upon
emergencies, and by order of the government. The
great veneration in which these supposed, but unknown,
prophecies were held among the vulgar, induced some
zealots to fabricate, under the name of the Sybils, and
in the form of ancient predictions, a narrative of the
most striking events in sacred history, and a delineation of what was then considered the Christian faith.
This work, which we now have with some variations,[6]
in eight books of coarse Greek verses, was then sent
into the world, to convert the heathens by the pretended testimony of their own prophetesses. It appears to
have been seized with avidity by the orthodox Christians in general; and all their principal writers,[7] quoted
it as genuine, and urged its testimonies as indubitable
evidence. It is mortifying to relate, that not one of
them had the honesty to discard the fraud, even when
it was detected by their heathen opponents.

These books, though brought forth in iniquity, serve
to show what sentiments existed among the Christians;
which is, indeed, about all the utility of the genuine
productions of this period. They contain the earliest
explicit declaration extant of a restoration from the

6. So think Fabricius, Du Pin, Le Clerc, Lardner and Jortin.
Others speak of these now extant as wholly the same with the
ancient. Paley, who by calling them *Latin* verses, betrays his
ignorance of them, supposes they cannot be that ancient work, because such is the manifestness of their forgery, that these could
not have deceivéd the early fathers into a belief of their genuineness. (Evidences of Christian. Part. i. chap. 9, sect. xi.) But all
this he might have said, with equal propriety, of the very passages
which they actually quoted. They were probably aware of the
forgery.
7. Justin Martyr, Athenagoras, Theophilus of Antioch, Clemens
Alexandrinus, and the succeeding fathers.

torments of hell. Having predicted the burning of the universe, the resurrection of the dead, the scene before the eternal judgement-seat, and the condemnation and horrible torments of the damned in the flames of hell, the writer proceeds to expatiate on the bliss and the privileges of the saved ; and he concludes his account by saying that, after the general judgement, " the omnipotent, incorruptible God shall confer an- " other favor on his worshippers, when they shall ask " him : he shall save mankind from the pernicious fire " and immortal agonies. This will he do. For, hav- " ing gathered them, safely secured from the unwearied " flame, and appointed them to another place, he shall " send them, for his people's sake, into another and an " eternal life, with the immortals on the Elysian plain, " where flow perpetually the long dark waves of the " deep sea of Acheron. "[8]

This work is full of the fables of the Greeks concerning demons, the Titans or giants, and the infernal regions. The world was to be burned about the end of the second century ; and then all mankind were to be brought forth from the secret receptacle of the dead to judgement ; when the vicious and abominable should be condemned to an intense fiery torment, repeatedly called *everlasting*, and described nearly in the language of the heathen poets, and with many of the circumstances they employed: The righteous, on the contrary, were to be received into a heaven too nearly resembling the Elysian fields ;[9] and finally, at

[8.] Sibyll. Oracula, Lib. ii. p. 212. Edit. Opsopœi, Paris. 1667.
[9.] All these particulars may be found in Lib. ii.

their request, the damned were to be admitted to the like happiness.[10]

IV. We proceed to the writings of the
A. D. 150,   renowned Justin Martyr, the first professed
to 162.   scholar of the Grecian philosophy, whose
productions in favor of the Christian religion, have reached us.   He was a native of Neapolis,
the ancient Sichem, in Palestine.   Having sought, as
he says, for the knowledge of the true God, among all
the sects of heathen philosophers, he was at length
converted to Christianity by the conversation of an old
man ; but he never laid aside the peculiar habit nor
the profession of the Platonists.   He engaged, however, with great zeal and boldness in the Christian
cause, for which he wrote two *Apologies :* one, addressed to the emperor Antonnius Pius, about A. D. 150 ;
and the other, about A. D. 162, to the succeeding emperor, Marcus Antoninus, and to the Senate and People of Rome.[11]   It was in this city, where he had

[10.] The following prophecy of the final conflagration may amuse,
as a specimen of the author's descriptions : — Elijah, " the Thes-
" bite, shall descend from heaven, drawn in a celestial car, and show
" the whole world the three signs of the destruction of all life.   Woe
" unto them whom that day shall overtake oppressed with the bur-
" den of the womb ; woe unto them who shall nurse children at the
" breast, and unto those who shall dwell near the waters. Woe unto
" them who shall see that day ; for from the rising to the setting
" sun, and from the north to the south, the whole world shall be
" involved in the gloom of hideous night.   A burning river of fire
" shall then flow from the lofty heavens, and utterly consume the
" earth, the vast ocean with its cerulean abyss, the lakes, rivers,
" fountains, the horrible realm of Pluto, and the celestial pole.   The
" stars in heaven shall melt and drop down without form.   All
" mankind shall gnash their teeth, encompassed on every hand with
" a flood of fire, and covered with burning cinders.   The elements
" of the world shall lie forsaken : the air, the earth, the heavens,
" the sea, the light, and nights and days be confounded."   Lib. ii.
p. 201.
[11.] Cave, Pagi, Basnage and Le Clerc date Justin's First Apolo-

resided for many years, that he sealed his testimony by martyrdom, about A. D. 166.

His profession of philosophy, his extensive though cursory reading, together with his zeal and piety, secured him a great reputation and influence among the early fathers; who lacked the discernment to perceive his want of sober judgement, and to discover the frequent mistakes into which his carelessness and gross credulity betrayed him. His early heathen notions, so far from being dispelled by the light of truth, were only modified to his new religion, and the more fondly cherished, as they now formed part of a system he deemed sacred. Angels, he supposes, once descended to the earth, became enamored of women, and in their embraces begat the demons. These demons, learning from the prophets the principal events in Christ's life and administration, fabricated, in order to imitate them, the stories of the heathen mythology. They first instituted idolatry, and they still continue to allure men to practise it, by the mysterious tricks they perform for the purpose; and all this, out of a desire to feed on the fumes of the sacrifices and libations.[12] Nothing can be more wonderful than the varied part which the demons perform in this world, according to Justin's representations. They labored, however, under one essential disadvantage; for our author assures us, that the Christians, in his time, had the

gy at about A. D. 140; Massuet 145; the Benedictine Editors and Tillemont, Grabe, Du Pin, and Lardner, at 150. The Dialogue with Trypho was written certainly after the First Apology, but perhaps before the Second, which is generally placed at the year 162. Besides these three works, some attribute to him Two Orations to the Greeks, and the Epistle to Diognetus.

12. Justini. Apolog. Prim. p. 61. Edit. Paris.

miraculous gift of exorcising them at pleasure, whatever shape they assumed, or wherever they concealed themselves.[13]   The reader cannot be surprised that Justin applied and explained Scripture without the least regard to rational interpretation.

His opinion concerning the future state of mankind was, that all souls, after death, are reserved in a certain place, probably the *Infernum* of the Latins, till the general resurrection and judgement ; when the righteous, whether Christians, or virtuous heathens, such as Socrates and Plato, shall reign with Christ a thousand years upon the earth, and then be admitted to the celestial mansions ;[14] while the wicked shall be condemned to a punishment which he frequently calls *everlasting*.[15]   In another place, however, he states his opinion upon this last point more particularly, and intimates that the wicked will be, eventually, annihilated : " Souls, " says he " are not immortal . . . . . . " I do not say that *all* souls will die.   Those of the " pious will remain, [after death] in a certain better " place, and those of the unholy and wicked in a " worse, all expecting the time of judgement.   In this " manner, those which are worthy to appear before " God, never die ; but the others are tormented so " long as God wills that they should exist and be tor- " mented . . . .   Whatever does, or ever will, " exist, in dependance, on the will of God, is of a per- " ishable nature, and can be annihilated so as to exist " no longer.   God alone is self-existent, and by his

13. Apol. Secund. p. 45, and *passim.*   14. Compare Dialog. cum. Tryph. p. 223, 306. Apol. i. p. 71. Apol. ii. p. 83, &c. Edit. Paris. 1742.   15. Apol. Prim. pp. 57, 64, &c.

"own nature imperishable, and therefore he is God ;
"but all other things are begotten and corruptible.
"For which reason, souls both suffer punishment and
"die."[16]

A. D. 160, —170. V. It was about this period, that the venerable Polycarp closed an aged and pious life, amidst the flock he had long cherished in the great city of Smyrna. Exhausted nature was not permitted to expire in quiet decay : the persecuting heathens sought him out, and crowned him with the honors of martyrdom. *The Relation of his Martyrdom*, written,[17] if genuine, (of which there is some doubt,) by his own church at Smyrna, asserts that the martyrs hoped, by suffering the momentary torments of their cruel death, "to escape that fire "which is eternal and shall not be extinguished."[18] And Polycarp himself is represented, by these writers, as reminding the Proconsul, before whom he was arraigned and tried, of "the fire of future judgement, and "of that eternal punishment which is reserved for the "ungodly."[19]

This *Relation*, though composed apparently by plain, unlettered men, and manifestly free from the corruptions of the Greek philosophy, affords a moderate specimen of the hyperbolical genius of that age. When the flame, say the writers, had arisen to a great height around Polycarp at the stake, it made a sort of

[16.] Dialog. cum. Tryphone, pp. 222, 223. [17.] Probably very soon after the martyrdom it relates ; which is placed by Pearson in A. D. 147 ; by Usher and Le Clerc, in 169 ; and by Petit in 175, Polycarp visited Rome while Anicetus was bishop there ; to which office the latter is commonly supposed to have been chosen as late as A. D. 150. [18.] Relation of the Martyrdom of Polycarp, § 2. *Wake's trans.* [19.] Ditto. § 11.

5

arch, leaving him untouched in the midst ; while a
rich odor, as of frankincense, proceeded from his body,
and filled the air. The executioners, perceiving that
they could not destroy him by burning, struck him
through with a dagger ; upon which, there came from
him such a quantity of blood as extinguished the
flames ! so that it " raised an admiration in all the
" people to consider what a difference there was be-
" tween the infidels and the elect."[20]

VI. Tatian the Syrian, a convert from
A. D. 170. heathenism, and the scholar perhaps of
Justin Martyr, was a man of considerable
Greek reading, and the author of several works ; of
which only his *Oration against the Gentiles* is extant.
In this he represents that such souls as have not the
truth or knowledge of God, die with the body, and
with it rise to judgement, at the end of the world ;
when they are to undergo " a death in immortality."[21]
To the wicked demons he assigns the same final
doom.[22] It is sufficiently evident that Tatian was, at
this time, like his master, a follower of the Platonic
philosophy ; but towards the end of his life, he ran
into heresy, by prohibiting marriage, wine, and divers
sorts of meat, and by advocating certain Gnostic notions.

A. D. 173. VII. In order to embrace every thing
that relates to our subject, we must insert
a small fragment from an *Ecclesiastical History by*

---

[20] Ditto. § 15, 16. [21] Tatiani Assyr. Contra Græc. Orat. § 6
and 13. inter. Justini Martyr. Opp. Edit. Paris. 1742. This Oration is placed by Lardner between A. D. 165, and 172. [22] Ditto.
§ 14.

Hegesippus, an author whose works are lost, but who is suspected of having been a weak and credulous writer. He relates that when some of our Saviour's kindred were called before the emperor Domitian, and questioned on the nature of the kingdom they attributed to Christ, they answered that it was merely celestial, and would take place " at the consummation of " the world, when he should come in his glory, judge " the quick and the dead, and reward every man ac- " cording to his works. "[23] This is evidence of the opinion of Hegesippus ; but no historian would probably consider it as authority for the sentiments of the persons he mentions. The whole story, indeed, is now suspected to be fabulous.

VIII. *The Epistle of the Churches of* A. D. 177. *Lyons and Vienne,* generally supposed to have been written by the celebrated Irenæus, claims but a moment's attention. It gives an affecting, though perhaps exaggerated, account of the terrible persecution and martyrdom of the Christians in those two cities, during the reign of the philosophical emperor, Marcus Aurelius. Of one Byblias, who through weakness had at first recanted her profession, it is said, " that in the midst of her torments she return- " ed to herself, waking as it were out of a deep slum- " ber ; and, calling to recollection the everlasting " punishment in hell, she, against all men's expecta- " tions reproved her tormentors. "[24]

---

[23]. Eusebii Hist. Eccl. Lib. iii. cap. 20. Lardner dates Hegisippus's History at the year 173. [24] Eusebii Hist. Eccl. Lib. v. cap. 1. Lardner assigns this Epistle to the year 177.

IX. The next, in order, is Athenagoras, A. D. 178, an Athenian philosopher, and probably, for to 180. a while, master of that distinguished Christian seminary, the Cathetical School at Alexandria in Egypt. He addressed to the emperor Marcus Aurelius and to his son Commodus, an *Apology* for the Christians; and wrote a *Treatise on the Resurrection*, to remove the objections of the heathens, and to convince them, by philosophical reasonings, of the truth of that doctrine.[25] Though a learned and polite writer, little notice was paid him or his works, by the early fathers.

He asserts, as a manifest fact, " that the righteous " are not properly rewarded, nor the evil punished in " this life ; " and contends that there is no ground on which we can vindicate the ways of providence and maintain the justice of God, but by admitting a resurrection to a state of retribution. At the future judgement, says he, " rewards and punishments will be dis- " tributed to all mankind, as they shall have conducted " well or ill ; "[26] but of the duration of suffering, he has left us no intimation. He treats it as a conjecture not unreasonable, that the brutes may be raised from the dead, and afterwards remain in subjection to man.[27] As to the mode of governing the universe, he says that God has distributed the angels into different ranks and orders, and assigned to them the care of the elements, the heavens and the earth. But the angel presiding over matter, together with some others,

---

[25] His Apology is placed by Lardner at A. D. 178. His Treatise on the Resurrection was probably written soon afterwards.
[26] Athenagor. De Resurrec. *passim.* particularly the latter part.
[27] Ditto. near the beginning.

swerving from their allegiance, fell in love with women, and begat giants; and those rebellious spirits now wander up and down the earth, opposing God, exciting lust, and upholding idolatry, that they may refresh themselves with the blood and steam of sacrifices.[28]

X. Of Theophilus, bishop of the church A. D. 181. at Antioch, we have only one work remaining : a *Treatise* in defence of Christianity, addressed to *Autolycus*, a learned heathen. There are sufficient proofs that our author was a man of at least a moderate degree of learning ; but, like most of his cotemporaries, he was unhappily an admirer of the Greek philosophy, and a believer in the vulgar superstitions of the heathens. His views of future punishment may be discovered from his exhortation to Autolycus : "Do you also studiously read the prophetic "Scriptures, and you will have their safer light to "enable you to shun everlasting torments." Soon afterwards he says of the unbelieving and abominable, "to them there will be wrath and indignation, tribu- "lation and anguish ; and, at length, everlasting fire "shall be their portion."[29]

XI. We arrive, at last, to the writings of A. D. 180, that distinguished father, Irenæus. Born —190. and brought up in Asia Minor, he attended, in his youth, the discourses both of the venerable Polycarp, and of the weak, injudicious Papias ; and perhaps enjoyed some acquaintance with those who had personally conversed with the apostles.

[28]. Athenagoræ Legat. *passim.* [29]. Theophili Ad Autolycum Lib. i. cap. 14. inter Justini Martyr. Opp. Edit. Paris. 1742. Lardner places this work at A. D. 181.

5*

At a later period, he travelled into France, where his piety, his zeal and devotedness to the Christian cause, together with his acquirements, rendered him conspicuous, and at length elevated him to the bishopric of the church at Lyons. But notwithstanding his advantages, there are some things in his principal remaining work, that *Against Heresies*,[30] which show that he yielded to the whimsical and credulous turn of the age, if, indeed, that were not also his own character. Miracles, he says, even from raising of the dead, down to the casting out of demons, were, in his time, frequently performed by Christians ; so that it was " impossible " to reckon up all the mighty works which the church " performed, every day, for the benefit of the na- " tions. "[31] With the Greek philosophy he was not so thoroughly imbued as Justin Martyr ; but like his master Papias, he was an assiduous collector of apostolic traditions, and upon their authority advanced some very ridiculous notions.[32] Some of his allegorical interpretations[33] of Scripture, too, will almost vie, in contemptible absurdity, with those of Barnabas. We remark, once for all, that the principal writers, mentioned in this chapter, agreed in attributing to the

---

[30.] This is a large, and in many respects a valuable work. Lardner thinks it to have been published not long after A. D. 178; Tillemont, near 190.   [31.] Iren. Adv. Hæres. Lib. ii. cap. 57.

[32] In the Millennium, says he, " there shall grow vineyards, " having each ten thousand vine-stocks ; each stock ten thousand " branches ; each branch ten thousand twigs ; each twig ten thou- " sand bunches ; each bunch ten thousand grapes ; and each grape, " when pressed, shall yield twenty-five measures of wine. And " when any of the saints shall go to pluck a bunch, another bunch " will cry out, *I am better, take me, and bless the Lord through me.* " In like manner, a grain of wheat sown, shall bear ten thousand " stalks ; each stalk ten thousand grains ; and each grain ten thou- " sand pounds of the finest flour," &c. Ditto. Lib. v. cap. 32, 33.

[33.] Ditto. Lib. iv. cap. 42, and Lib. v cap. 8.

Scriptures a double meaning, a hidden and mysterious as well as the obvious.

With regard to the future state, Irenæus supposes that souls are, after death, reserved in some invisible place, the *Infernum* of the heathens, whither Christ went and preached after his crucifixion, delivering from sufferance those who then believed. At the end of the world, which was then very near at hand, all were to be raised, and brought to judgement, when the just should be admitted to a thousand years' reign with Christ upon earth, preparatory to endless bliss in heaven ; but the unjust should be sent into *inextinguishable* and *eternal* fire.[34] Here, he appears to think, they will be annihilated : he contends that souls, or spirits, like all other created things, depend entirely on the upholding providence of God, for their continuance in being, and that they can " exist only " so long as he wills. For, " says he, " the principle " of existence is not inherent in our own constitution, " but given us by God. He who cherishes this gift, " and is thankful to the Giver, shall exist forever ; but " he who despises it, and is ungrateful, deprives him- " self of the privilege of existing forever. Therefore, " the Lord said, *If ye have not been faithful in a* " *little, who will give you that which is greater ?* " (Luke xvi. 11,) signifying that he who is ungrateful " to him for this temporal life, which is little, cannot " justly expect from him an existence which is end- " less. "[35]

It is in Irenæus that we meet with the earliest at-

[34] Ditto. Lib. v. cap. 27, and *passim*. [35] Ditto. Lib. ii. cap. 64.

tempt at a formal summary of the faith, as held by the orthodox churches in general ; and, on this account, his compendium, or creed, is worthy of particular notice. In opposition to all the peculiar tenets of the Gnostics, he brings forward the system of doctrine which, he says, " the churches, though scattered into " all parts of the world, had received from the apostles " and their disciples, viz : To believe in one God, the " omnipotent Father, who made heaven, and earth, " and sea, and all things in them ; in one Jesus " Christ, the Son of God, incarnate for our salvation ; " and in the Holy Ghost, who by the prophets de- " clared the dispensation and coming of Christ, his " birth of a virgin, his suffering, his resurrection from " the dead, his ascension in his flesh into heaven, and " his coming from heaven, in the glory of the Father, " to gather together in one all things, and to raise the " flesh of all mankind ; that unto Jesus Christ, our " Lord, Saviour and King, according to the will of the " invisible Father, every knee shall bow, of things in " heaven, on earth, and under the earth, and every " tongue confess to him ; and that he shall pass a " righteous sentence upon all, and send wicked spirits, " and the angels who have transgressed, together with " ungodly men, into eternal fire, but give life to the " righteous who have kept his commandments and " abided in his love, either from the beginning or after " repentance, and confer on them immortality and " eternal glory. "[36]

[36.] Ditto. Lib. i. cap. 2. Any one, acquainted with the notions attributed to the Gnostics, will instantly perceive that almost every expression in this Creed was framed for the purpose of op-

XII. A great number of the early productions of the orthodox, and all those of the heretics, are lost, and with them, probably, some information upon the subject of our history. Thus far, however, we have carefully produced, in his own words, the opinion of every writer whose works are extant ; we have also presented the views of the heretics upon this subject, from the best authorities within our reach. To the reader belongs the privilege of such reflections as the whole case, now pretty fully laid before him, may suggest. We will, however, observe that of the orthodox writers, nearly all allude to, or expressly assert, a future judgement and a future state of punishment : seven[37] call it the *everlasting*, the *eternal* fire or torment ; but out of these there are three who certainly did not think it endless, since two of them believed the damned would be annihilated, and the other asserted their restoration to bliss. What were the views of the remaining four, upon this point, cannot be determined ; for the circumstance just mentioned shows that their use of the word *everlasting*, is no criterion. The others whom we have passed in review, are silent with regard to the duration of misery.

To these remarks we must add, that such of the Gnostic sects as are thought to have held the salvation of all souls, still flourished ; but their history, like that of all the heretic Christians, is obscure and uncertain.

posing them ; as, indeed, is intimated by the manner in which Irenæus introduces the passage.

[37.] Viz. Barnabas, Hermas, Sibylline Oracles, Justin Martyr, Relation of Polycarp's Martyrdom, Theophilus, and Irenæus in the Letter of the churches of Lyons and Vienne, and in his work Against Heresies.

Among the orthodox, it is curious to mark the seeming progress of sentiment concerning a future state of punishment. In their earliest writings, that of Clemens Romanus and those of Ignatius, it is either wholly omitted, or else expressed in the most indefinite manner. Afterwards, we find it introduced as a peculiar motive of terror ; and as such, it became more and more employed, even by those who expressly assigned it a limited duration. When the Greek philosophy and heathen superstitions began to prevail in the church, they soon succeeded in delineating the whole *topography* of the infernal realm, pointed out its divisions, described its regulations, and familiarly brought to light all its secrets.

XIII. In the succeeding parts of our work, we shall not detain the reader with a distinct paragraph for every ecclesiastical writer ; but direct our attention more specially to those authors and those parties who advocated the salvation of all mankind. In the mean time, however, we shall aim at such a representation as will afford a general view of the notions entertained by the church at large, in relation to that subject.

CHAPTER III.

[From A. D. 190, to A. D. 230.]

A. D. 190, to 196.
I. Of all the Christian fathers, before Origen, the most illustrious writer and the most renowned for extensive erudition, was Clemens Alexandrinus. That he was a Universalist, is alleged against him by some of the learned,[1] and sufficiently manifest from his works yet extant ; though he seldom affords us a direct and positive assertion to this point. He uniformly asserts, however, and illustrates, the universal goodness of God, the benevolent nature of justice, the salutary design and effect of punishment both here and hereafter, the purification of the damned in hell, and their deliverance from suffering and exaltation to bliss.

[1.] The learned and orthodox Daille says "It is manifest, throughout his works, that Clemens thought all the punishments that God inflicts upon men, are salutary, and executed by him only for the purpose of instruction and reformation. Of this kind he reckons the torments which the damned in hell suffer . . . . . . From which we discover that Clemens was of the same opinion as his scholar Origen, who every where teaches that all the punishments of those in hell are purgatorial, that they are not endless, but will at length cease, when the damned are sufficiently purified by the fire." Dallæi De Usu Patrum Lib. ii. cap. 4.

Archbishop Potter, having spoken of Origen's belief in the salvation of all the damned, and of the devil himself, adds, "from which opinion Clemens does not appear to have differed much, as he taught that the Devil *can* repent, and that even the most heinous sins are purged away by punishments after death." V. Not. in Clem. Alexand. Strom. Lib. vi. p. 794. Edit. Potter 1715

"The Lord," says he, "does good unto all, and "delights in all ; as God, he forgives our transgres-"sions, and as Man, he teaches and instructs us that "we may not sin.   Man is, indeed, necessarily dear "to God, because he is his workmanship.   Other "things he made only by his order ; but man he form-"ed by his own hand, and breathed into him his dis-"tinguishing properties.   Now, whatever was created "by him, especially in his own image, must have been "created because it was, in itself, desirable to God, or "else desirable from some other consideration.   If man "was made because he was in himself desirable, then "God loved him on account of his being good ; and "there certainly is in man that lovely principle, called "the breath or inspiration of God.   But if it was on "account of some other desirable end that he was "made, then there could be no other reason why God "should create him, than that God could not otherwise "be a benevolent Maker, nor his glory be displayed "to the human race. . . . . And, indeed in either "case, man may be said to be, in himself considered, "a being desirable to God, since the Almighty, who "cannot err in his undertakings, made him just such "as he desired.   He therefore loves him.   How in-"deed is it possible that he should not love him, for "whom he sent his only begotten Son from his own "bosom ?"[2]

There are some,[3] says Clemens, who deny that the Lord is good, because he inflicts punishments and en-

[2] Clem. Alexand. Pædagog. Lib. i. cap. 3, pp. 101, 102, Edit. Potter.   [3] Clemens here alludes to the Marcionites, a Gnostic sect.

joins fear. To this he replies, that "there is nothing "which the Lord hates ; for he cannot hate any thing "and yet will that it should exist ; nor can he will "that any thing should not exist, and at the same time "cause it to exist. Now as the Lord is certainly the "cause of whatever exists, he cannot, of course, de- "sire that any thing which is, should not be ; and "therefore he cannot hate any thing, as all exist by his "own will." And, continues our author, "if he hates "none of his works, then it is evident that he loves "them all, especially man above the rest, who is the "most excellent of his creatures. Now whoever loves "another, wishes to benefit him ; and therefore God "does good unto all. He does not merely bless them "in some particulars, yet neglect all care over them ; "he is both careful for them, and solicitous for their "interests." Consistently with this, Clemens adds, that God's "justice is, of itself, nothing but goodness ; "for it rewards the virtuous with blessings, and con- "duces to the improvement of the sinful. There are "many evil affections which are to be cured only "by suffering. Punishment is, in its operation, like "medicine : it dissolves the hard heart, purges away "the filth of uncleanness, and reduces the swellings of "pride and haughtiness ; thus restoring its subject to a "sound and healthful state. It is not from hatred, "therefore, that the Lord rebukes mankind."[4]

"It is the office of salutary justice," says he, in another place, "continually to exalt every thing to-

---

[4]. Pædagog. Lib. i. cap. 8, pp. 135—140. N. B. I have attempted in this paragraph to compress the argument which Clemens, in his diffuse style and rambling method, spreads over two or three folio pages.

"wards the best state of which it is capable.   Inferior
"things are adapted to promote and confirm the salva-
"tion of that which is more excellent ; and thus, what-
"ever is endued with any virtue, is forthwith changed
"still for the better, through the liberty of choice, which
"the mind has in its own power.   And the necessary
"chastisements of the great judge, who regards all with
"benignity, make mankind grieve for their sins and
"imperfections, and advance them through the various
"states of discipline to perfection."[5]   " Even God's
"wrath, if so his admonitions can be called, is full of
"benevolence, towards the human race ; for whose
"sake the word of God was made man."[6]

The same means which are employed upon earth
for the salvation of the living, are introduced, he thinks,
among the dead, for the restoration of such as died,
either in sin, or in ignorance and unbelief of Jesus
Christ : " Wherefore, our Lord," says he, " preached
"also in the regions of the dead; for says the Scrip-
"ture, *the Grave saith to Destruction, His counte-*
"*nance we have not indeed beheld, but we have heard*
"*his voice.* (Job xxviii. 22.)   It is not the *place*,
"however, which thus speaks, but its inhabitants,
"who had delivered themselves to destruction.   They
"heard the divine power and voice.   And, indeed,
"who can suppose that souls [which departed igno-
"rant of Christ] are indiscriminately abandoned, the
"virtuous and the vicious, to the same condemnation,
"thus impeaching the justice of providence ?   Does
"not the Scripture inform us that the Lord preached

" the gospel even to those who perished in the deluge,
" and were confined in prison?[7] We have already ·
" shown that the apostles also, as well as their Master,
" preached the gospel to the dead. . . . . . Wherefore,
" since the Lord descended to hell for no other pur-
" pose than to preach the gospel there, he preached it
" either to all, or only to the Jews. If to all, then
" all who believed there, were saved, whether Jews or
" Gentiles. And the chastisements of God are salu-
" tary and instructive, leading to amendment, and pre-
" ferring the repentance to the death of the sinner;
" especially as souls in their separate state, though
" darkened by evil passions, have yet a clearer dis-
" cernment than they had whilst in the body, because
" they are no longer clouded and encumbered by the
" flesh."[8] Again he says, " Now all the poets, as well
" as the Greek philosophers, took their notions of the
" punishments after death, and the torments of fire,
" from the Hebrews. Does not Plato mention the
" rivers of fire, and that profound abyss which the
" Jews call Gehenna [hell,] together with other places
" of punishment, where the characters of men are re-
" formed by suffering?"[9] It would, however, far exceed our limits, to transcribe the passages of this kind,
scattered through his writings.

[7] In another place Clemens says, " If, therefore, the Lord
" preached the gospel to those in the flesh, lest they should be
" unjustly condemned, was it not necessary, for the same reason,
" that he should preach also to those who had departed this life
" before his advent? And as all sinful flesh perished in the de-
" luge, we must believe that the will of God, which has the pow-
" er of instructing and operating, confers salvation upon those
" who are converted by the punishments inflicted on them."
Stromat. Lib. vi. cap. 6, p. 766.   [8] Stromat. Lib. vi. cap. 6, pp,
763, 764.   [9] Ditto. Lib. v. cap. 14, p. 700.

With regard to the actual salvation of all, the following are, perhaps, his fullest and most pointed expressions: " How is he a Saviour and Lord, unless he " is the Saviour and Lord of all?   He is certainly the " Saviour of those who have believed; and of those " who have not believed, he is the Lord, until by be- " ing brought to confess him, they shall receive the " proper and well adapted blessing for themselves."[10] " The Lord," says he, " *is the propitiation, not only* " *for our sins*, that is, of the faithful, *but also for the* " *whole world:* (1 John, ii. 2,) therefore he indeed " saves all; but converts some by punishments, and " others by gaining their free will; so that he has " the high honor, *that unto him every knee should* " *bow, of things in heaven, on earth, and under the* " *earth;* that is, angels, men and the souls of those " who died before his advent."[11]

It is remarkable that Clemens, unlike the other ancient fathers who believed in Universalism, appears to have avoided the use of such epithets and phrases as *everlasting, forever and ever*, &c. in connexion with misery.[12] Nor does he seem to have considered the torments of the future state very intense, as he never represents them in terrific colours, nor dwells upon them in a way to agitate the mind with fear. When the virtuous Christian dies, he enters upon a mild and

---

[10] Stromat. Lib. vii. cap. 2, p. 833.   [11] Fragmenta. Adumbrat. in Epist. I. Johan. p. 1009.

[12] The only place I recollect in all his writings, where any of these controverted words is applied to suffering, is Pædagog. Lib. i. cap. 8, *end*, p. 142. " When the soul has ceased to " grieve for its sins, it is not, even then, a time to inflict upon it " a deadly wound, but a healthful one, that by a little grief it may " escape *eternal death*."

grateful discipline, which, by purifying his remaining faults, and supplying his imperfections, elevates him by degrees from glory to glory, till he arrives at perfection ; but the soul of an obstinate and vicious infidel must, before it can begin this sublime progression, be overcome by severe chastisement, instructed in the knowledge of the truth, and brought to control its passions.

II. Like all the early fathers, Clemens held the entire and permanent freedom of the human will, contrary to the present orthodox doctrines of predestination and irresistible grace. Original sin and total depravity were unknown in his day ; as was also the modern notion of a mysterious and counter-natural conversion.

We may now complete the sketch of his general system of doctrine : God, infinitely and unchangeably good, created man upright, though not entirely[13] perfect, and designed him, and all his posterity for happiness. But Adam, being left to his own free will, yielded to temptation ; and so, in a greater or less degree, have all mankind, after him. As the world thus began to grow up in ignorance of God, in the indulgence of vice, and under the dominion of evil demons, the Almighty gave, as a partial remedy, the Law to the Jews, and Philosophy to the Gentiles, in order to restrain and enlighten them in some measure, till the coming of Christ. Both the Law and Philosophy were preparatory to the Gospel ; and so far as the Hebrews on the one hand, and the Heathens on the

13. Stromat. Lib. iv. cap. 23, p. 632.

6*

other, preserved and practised their respective systems
in their pristine purity, they were justified; though
they still needed evangelical faith to prepare them for
heaven. At length, God was pleased to grant the
world a full and perfect revelation; and for this purpose sent his Son, the Jehovah of the Old Testament,
who was a divine agent, begotten of the Father. He
came, not to appease God, whom Clemens thought
originally and immutably good, but to crush the power of the evil demons, to impart the knowledge and
commend the love of God to mankind, to instruct them
in religion, and to set before them a perfect example
of piety and virtue. That these means may become
effectual to the salvation of the world, the whole system of divine providence and government is constantly
directed to induce mankind to believe and obey their
Saviour. To this end, the Almighty urges them by
threatenings and punishments, and allures them by
promises and rewards; and if they die impenitent or
unbelieving, a similar course is pursued with them after
death, until they are brought to submission. After
all, faith and obedience depend both here and hereafter, on the free will of the creature; though God, by
his holy spirit, communicates impulses to all, and, by
his grace, assists those who strive to obey. Such were
his views.

He was a hearty champion of the orthodox church
against the heretics, particularly against all the Gnostics; and he has had the good, or indifferent, fortune,
that notwithstanding his manifest Universalism, his
doctrine was reprehended by none of his cotemporaries, nor his standing ever impeached, even in after

ages, when the works of Origen came to be anathematized, partly on account of the same sentiment.

III. Titus Flavius Clemens, usually called Clemens Alexandrinus, or Clement of Alexandria, is thought, by some, to have been a native of Athens, and by others, of Alexandria in Egypt, where he certainly spent the most memorable part of his life. The precise dates of his birth and death are unknown; and not the slightest account is preserved of his childhood and youth. It appears that, after travelling through many countries in pursuit of philosophical and religious knowledge, he sat down at last under the instructions of the learned Pantænus, a Christian philosopher in Egypt. Here, Clemens studied, in conformity with the plan of his master, to extract from all the schemes of philosophy then in vogue, from the Oriental as well as the Grecian, what he deemed their original principles, and to form a system for himself out of all these combined; though he gave a decided preference to the tenets of the Stoics. About the year 195, he was ordained a presbyter in the church at Alexandria; and, near the same time, was appointed, in the absence of Pantænus, to supply his place as President of the famous Catechetical School in that city. In addition to the cares and labors which necessarily devolved upon him from these two offices, he composed, it is thought, at about this period, those of his works which are yet extant.[14]

14. These are—1, *His Exhortation to the Gentiles*, designed to confute the notions of the heathens, and to convince them of the truth of christianity; 2, his *Pædagogue*, written to instruct new converts, and to train them up to a holy and truly Christian life; 3, his *Stromata*, a miscellaneous work, containing a more particular illustration of the Christian doctrine, together with confutations both of the heathen religions, and of the heretical opinions, par-

Alexandria, next to Rome, the most populous and frequented city of that age, was then the great emporium of literature, philosophy and religion. The splendor of learning, which had once beamed so full upon Athens, seemed returned, though with many fantastic colours, to shine upon the native land of letters and of science. Some of the celebrity, and many of the advantages, which the capital of Egypt now enjoyed, arose, undoubtedly, from its immense library, the largest the world had ever seen. Seven hundred thousand manuscripts, deposited in two sections of the city, offered to the inquisitive geniuses who assembled from every region, all the treasures of ancient wisdom and folly.

Ever since the days of the apostles, the Christians of this city had supported a school, founded, it is said, by St. Mark ; but it had always been obscure, and kept in rather a private manner, till the time of Pantænus. When he succeeded to its care, he brought it into public notice, and soon rendered it the first in character and renown, of all the ancient Christian seminaries.

While Clemens presided here, with distinguished reputation, he had the honor of instructing some who

ticularly those of the Gnostics ; 4, his *Tract*, entitled, *What rich man shall be saved :* 5, his *Epitome of the Oriental Doctrine of Theodotus ;* and 6, his *Comments* on some of the Epistles of the New Testament. These Comments were formerly thought supposititious ; but they are now generally considered fragments from his *Hypotyposes*, a work which is lost. His exhortation to the Gentiles, Pædagogue and Stromata, are supposed to have been written between A. D. 193, and 195 ; (Dodwell. Dissert. iii. in Irenæum, and Dissert. de. prim. Pontif. Roman. successione. Mosheim. Dissertationes ad Hist. Eccl. vol. 1, pp. 34—38.) his Hypotyposes perhaps earlier.

arose to eminence in the church, particularly Alexander, afterwards bishop of Jerusalem, and the celebrated Origen. But about A. D. 202, the persecution under the emperor Severus, which spread death and terror through the church at Alexandria, drove Clemens from the city. It is supposed that he embraced this opportunity to revisit the eastern countries ; and we find him, in the year 205, at Jerusalem, in company with his scholar, Alexander. From this place we trace him to Antioch ; whence he returned, it is thought, to Alexandria, and in connection with Origen, resumed for a while, the care of the school. He died not far, probably, from A. D. 217.[15]

IV. So imperfect is the account preserved of this distinguished father. Of his learning the ancients uniformly speak in terms of admiration. His reading was certainly extensive, almost universal : history, poetry, mythology and philosophy, seem perfectly familiar to him ; and the sacred Scriptures, together with all that related to the concerns of the church, were treasured in his memory. With his great learning and piety, the placid benevolence of his disposition must have conspired to render him esteemed and beloved. If we may judge from the character of his writings, his passions were naturally moderate, his heart benignant and incapable of sourness and severity. Impartiality obliges us, however, to remark, that like the rest of the early fathers, he wanted sober judgement : he was credulous, fanciful and incorrect, ignorant of rational criticism, and delighted with allegorical interpretations

15. For his life, see Cave's Lives of the Fathers, and Lardner's Credibility, &c. Chap. Clement of Alexandria.

of Scripture. His fondness for the heathen systems of
philosophy was extravagant ; and it is thought that
his example had the pernicious influence to recommend those systems to a more general admiration in
the church. He was naturally of a poetical genius ;
his style often runs into metre, and his works abound
with quotations from the ancient poets and philosophers, as well as from the Scriptures. His method
of writing is careless, feeble and sometimes very rambling.

V. Passing over several writers of little note, we
shall now make some observations on the only succeeding fathers of eminence, before Origen. Cotemporary
with Clemens, but belonging to the Western or Latin
church, was the celebrated Tertullian, a
A. D. 200,   presbyter of Carthage in Africa : a man
to 204.   of extensive learning, of strong and vehement genius, but severe and morose, su-
perstitious and fanatical, even when compared with
those of his own age. He is thought to have been
the first Christian writer who expressly asserted that
the torments of the damned will be of " *equal* [16] duration " with the happiness of the blest. This circumstance is, indeed, no proof that the same opinion had
never been entertained before ; but we may safely say
that, of all the early fathers, there was none with whose
natural disposition the doctrine of endless misery better

[16.] Tertulliani Apologet. cap. 18. At the general resurrection
and judgement, says he, " God will recompense his worshippers
" with life eternal ; and cast the profane into a fire *equally* per-
" petual and unintermitted." See *Whiston on the Eternity of Hell
Torments*, p. 86. N. B. Tertullian's Apology was written about
A. D. 200.

accorded, than with Tertullian's : "You are fond of your spectacles," said he, in allusion to the pagans ; "there are other spectacles : that day disbelieved, "derided, by the nations, that last eternal day of "judgement, when all ages shall be swallowed up "in one conflagration — what a variety of spectacles "shall then appear ! How shall I admire, how laugh, "how rejoice, how exult, when I behold so many kings, "worshipped as gods in heaven, together with Jove "himself, groaning in the lowest abyss of darkness ! "so many magistrates who persecuted the name of the "Lord, liquefying in fiercer flames than they ever kin- "dled against Christians : so many sage philosophers "blushing in raging fire, with their scholars whom "they persuaded to despise God, and to disbelieve "the resurrection ; and so many poets shuddering be- "fore the tribunal, not of Radamanthus, not of Minos, "but of the disbelieved Christ ! Then shall we hear "the tragedians more tuneful under their own suffer- "ings ; then shall we see the players far more sprightly "amidst the flames ; the charioteer all red-hot in his "burning car ; and the wrestlers hurled, not upon the "accustomed list, but on a plain of fire."[17] Such is the relish with which his fierce spirit dwells on the prospect of eternal torments. His gloomy and en-thusiastic disposition soon led him to abandon the reg-ular churches, as not sufficiently austere and visionary, and to join himself to the fanatical sect of Montanists.

VI. Next to Tertullian is Minucius Fe-
A. D. 210. lix, another writer of the Western church, either a Roman or an African, a lawyer

[17] Tertull. De Spectaculis, cap. 30. Written about A. D. 203, or 204.

by profession, and a man of considerable learning. His *Dialogue*, the only work he has left us, is a popular disputation, elegantly written, in defence of Christianity against paganism ; but its beauty is somewhat sullied by a mixture of heathen superstitions, and its force impaired by frequent declamation instead of argument. The author seems to assert the strict eternity of hell-torments, and to represent that his was the common opinion of Christians, on the subject. In allusion to the Grecian fable of the tremendous oath of the gods, he says that Jupiter swears by the broiling banks of the river of fire, and "shudders at the tor- "ments which await him and his worshippers : torments "that know neither measure nor end. For there the "subtile fire burns and repairs, consumes and nourish- "es ; and as lightenings waste not the bodies they "blast, and as Etna, Vesuvius and other volcanoes "continue to burn without expending their fuel, so "these penal flames of hell are fed, not from the dimi- "nution of the damned, but from the bodies they prey "upon without consuming."[18] The objector to Christianity is, in another passage, represented as saying that Christians threaten all but themselves "with tor- "ments that never shall have an end."[19]

VII. Clemens, Tertullian, and Minucius Felix, in treating of the infernal region and its torments, frequently adopt the language, and some of the views, of the ancient heathen poets. Ever since Justin Martyr, it had been a common opinion among the orthodox

---

[18] Minucii Fel. Dialog. cap. 34. Lardner dates this Dialogue at A. D. 210; some critics have assigned it to an earlier period, and others to a later, even to the year 230. [19] Ditto. cap. 11.

fathers, that at death all souls, both the righteous and the wicked, descended to the *Hades* of the Greeks, or *Infernum* of the Latins; which was a subterranean world consisting of two general divisions, the mansions of the just, and the abodes of the guilty. Here the separate spirits dwelt, either in joy or suffering, according to their different characters and deserts; undergoing various courses of discipline and purification, as was thought by some; or, fixed in their respective stations, awaiting the decision of the approaching general judgement, as was represented by others. Some of the fathers,[20] however, do not seem to have believed in the conscious existence of the soul in the interval between death and the general judgement; but the latter event, they all agreed, was near at hand, when the world should be destroyed by fire, Tertullian says, in the end of his own age.

VIII. In concluding this chapter, it may be proper to give, as far as practicable, a succinct account of the state of Universalism, at the period now under consideration. It appears, then, that of the orthodox Christians, some believed the eventual salvation of all mankind, after a future punishment for the wicked; while others, again, held the doctrine of endless misery. This diversity of opinion, however, occasioned no divisions, no controversies nor contentions among them; and both sentiments existed together in the church without reproach. If we may hazard a conjecture, the generality of the orthodox had not any fixed nor definite opinion on the subject. That there

20. Viz. Tatian, and perhaps Minucius Felix.

7

was a future state of suffering, they all agreed; but whether it were endless, or would terminate in annihilation, or whether it would result in a general restoration, were probably points which few inquired into. Such, we may suppose, was the case with the orthodox churches.

But we must not here forget the Universalists among the Gnostic Christians. The Basilidians, Carpocratians and Valentinians were now thinly scattered over all christendom, and abounded in some places, particularly in Egypt and the adjacent countries. Though they agreed with the Universalists among the orthodox, in the simple fact of the ultimate salvation of all souls, yet their denial of the resurrection and of a future judgement, their views concerning the creation of this world, and, in short, the mass of Oriental fables which they held in common with the rest of the Gnostics, deprived them of all intercourse with their brethren, except as opponents. They were Gnostics, and the others were Orthodox: these were the terms of distinction. As Universalism, on either side, was not a subject of abuse, so it was not an occasion for special favor and friendship; and the striking difference between their views on almost every particular in the whole circle of divinity, occasioned a perpetual altercation, in which the few instances of their mutual agreement were overlooked or forgotten. The entire body of the orthodox, whether Universalists or not, stood in uniform array against the Gnostics of all kinds; and these, in their turn, united their various sects, in the struggle against their common adversaries.

CHAPTER IV.

[Origen.]

I. Meanwhile, the attention of the A. D. 230. Christian world was directed to an extraordinary genius who had arisen in the church. The name of Origen Adamantius had awakened an interest among heathens as well as believers, from Egypt and Greece eastward to the remotest provinces of the Roman empire. As a doctor in the church, and as a philosopher[1] among the learned, he stood alone, without either rival or competitor, and enjoyed, while living, such a reputation as few, in any age, have ever acquired.

It was about the year 230, that he published, at Alexandria, among other works, his books *Of Principles*, in which he advocated, at considerable length, the doctrine of Universal Salvation. This work has come down to us only in the Latin translation by Rufinus, who altered it in many places, especially in

---

[1] He became a philosopher, as many a one does, not by original discoveries, nor by his own investigations into the nature of things; but by a thorough acquaintance with the philosophic principles and maxims he had learned from his preceptors, and by his surprising, though not always happy readiness in illustrating and tracing them, and in accommodating them to every case and subject which occurred. In one word, he was a philosopher of the schools, not of nature. Mosheim (De Reb. Christian. Ante Constant. pp. 611, 612,) has drawn his character, as a philosopher, in strong, but not unfaithful colours.

what related to the Trinity, in order to accommodate its doctrine to the faith of the fourth century. This circumstance throws a shade of uncertainty, in some respects, upon the original character of the treatise. But that it contained, in its first, as well as in its present state, the doctrine in view, is beyond a question; since ancient writers,[2] who lived while the genuine Greek copies were yet extant, referred to them, and quoted their language, for the purpose of exciting the indignation, or calling forth the anathema, of the church, against the memory of the illustrious author, for having asserted the restoration of every fallen, intelligent creature.

II. Taking, then, the translation of Rufinus for our authority, where we can obtain no better, it appears that Origen introduced the doctrine of Universalism and that of the Pre-existence of souls, together: "Whoever," said he, "would read and acquaint him-"self with these subjects, so difficult to be understood, "should possess a mature and well instructed under-"standing. For if he be not accustomed to such "topics, they may appear to him vain and useless; "or if his mind be already established in opposite "sentiments, he may hastily suppose, through his own "prejudice, that these are heretical and contrary to "the faith of the church. Indeed, they are advanced "by us with much hesitation, and more in the way of "investigating and discussing them, than as pronounc-"ing them certain and indisputable.

. "The end and consummation of the world will take place, when all shall be subjected to punishments

[2] Viz. Jerome, Justinian, &c.

" proportioned to their several sins ; and how long
" each one shall suffer, in order to receive his deserts,
" God only knows. But we suppose that the good-
" ness of God, through Christ, will certainly restore
" all creatures into one final state ; his very enemies
" being overcome and subdued. For thus saith the
" Scripture : *The Lord said unto my Lord, sit thou*
" *at my right hand, until I make thine enemies thy*
" *footstool.* (Ps. cx. 1.) To the same purport, but
" more clearly, the apostle Paul says that Christ *must*
" *reign till he hath put all enemies under his feet.*
" But if there be any doubt what is meant by *putting*
" *enemies under his feet,* let us hear the apostle still
" further, who says, *for* ALL *things must be subjected*
" *to him.* (1 Cor. xv.) What, then, is that subjec-
" tion with which *all* things must be subdued to
" Christ ? I think it to be that with which we ourselves
" desire to be subdued to him ; and with which also
" the apostles and all the saints who have followed
" Christ, have been subdued to him. For the very
" expression, *subjected to Christ,* denotes the salvation
" of those who are subjected : as David says, *shall*
" *not my soul be subjected to God ? for from him is*
" *my salvation.* (Ps. lxii. 1.)

" Such, then, being the final result of things, that
" all enemies shall be subdued to Christ, death the
" last enemy be destroyed, and the kingdom be deliv-
" ered up to the Father, by Christ ; let us, with this
" view before us, now turn and contemplate the be-
" ginning of things. Now, the beginning always re-
" sembles the end ; and as there will be one common
" end or result to all, so we should believe that all

7*

"had one common beginning. In other words, that
"as the great variety of characters and different orders
"of beings which now exist, will, through the good-
"ness of God, their subjection to Jesus Christ, and
"the unity of the Holy Spirit, be finally restored to
"one and the same state; so were they all originally
"created in one common condition, resembling that
"into which they are eventually to be recalled. All
"who are, at last, to bow the knee to Jesus Christ,
"in token of subjection, that is, all who are in heaven,
"all on earth, and all under the earth, (by which three
"terms is comprehended the whole intelligent crea-
"tion,) proceeded, at first, from that one common
"state; but as virtue was not immutably fixed in
"them, as in God, they came to indulge different
"passions, and to cherish different principles. They
"were therefore assigned to the various ranks and
"conditions they now hold, as the reward or punish-
"ment of their respective deserts,"[3] &c. &c. The
same subject he introduces repeatedly, with various
illustrations, in the course of this work.

III. Our author was, at this time, about forty-five
years old. From his childhood, the greatest expecta-
tions had been entertained of him; and in his case,
mature years did not disappoint the hopes which pre-
cocious genius had inspired. Origen, afterwards surnamed Adamantius, was born
in the city of Alexandria, A. D. 185, or
186. Under his father, Leonidas, he was, while very

A. D. 185,
to 203.

---

[3]. Origen. de Principiis, Lib. i. cap. 6. N. B. The reader will
find our author's notion of Pre-existence more plainly described,
in Sect. vi. of this chapter.

young, well instructed in all the rudiments of learning, and assiduously trained to the study of the sacred Scriptures. Of these; it was his daily task to commit a portion to memory; but with his characteristic passion for speculative inquiry, he refused to be content with their obvious meaning, and often perplexed his father by an inquisitive desire after a hidden, mysterious sense of the passages which struck his attention. This imaginary sense was then the great object of investigation, among all who aspired to superior attainments in religious knowledge; and therefore his son's inquiries, at so early an age, were hailed by Leonidas with secret rapture, though he seemingly checked his too manly researches, and admonished him to confine his thoughts to subjects more within the reach of his infantile powers.

When a little more advanced in years, Origen was sent to the Catechetical School, where he studied divinity under Clemens Alexandrinus. Here his pursuits were at length interrupted, in the seventeenth year of his age, by the persecution under Severus; which began at Alexandria in A. D. 202, and soon obliged his master to flee from the city. His father was seized and imprisoned for his religion; and many others shared the same fate. But, undismayed by the gathering dangers, the eager spirit of the youth contemplated them with the strange delight of an enthusiast. He would have thrown himself into the hands of the persecutors, in hope of obtaining the prize of martyrdom, had he not been prevented by his mother, who hid his clothes, and thus, by the sense of shame, confined him to his house. Fearing that his father's constancy would yield to anxiety for his family's welfare, he entreated him, by letter, to persevere: "Be "steadfast, my father," said he, "and take heed that "you do not renounce your profession, on our ac- "count." Animated by his son's exhortation, he remained inflexible to the last, and courageously suffered martyrdom.

On the execution of the father, the estate was confiscated, and the family reduced, at once, to extreme poverty; but a rich lady of Alexandria, either from compassion, or respect, took Origen into her own house, and freely gave him a support. There lived with her, at the same time, a famous heretic, whom she had adopted as her son, and who held public lectures under her patronage. With him though Origen was obliged by his situation to converse, yet not even gratitude to their common patroness could overcome his constant, perhaps bigoted refusal to unite in prayers; and he took every method to express his abhorrence of heresy, little thinking that future ages would repay this detestation two-fold upon his own head. Whether his benefactress began to withdraw her favor, or whether he resolved of himself to spare her charity, it appears that, in about a year he threw himself upon his own exertions for a livelihood. Having been engaged, ever since his father's death, in the study of the sciences, he now (A. D. 203,) opened a grammar school, from which he had the prospect of deriving a support. But his attention was immediately called to other subjects: some of the heathens applying to him for religious instruction, he gladly acceded to their request; the number of his scholars and converts increased; and Demetrius, bishop at Alexandria, appointed him, though but eighteen years old, to the care either of the great Catechetical School, or perhaps, at first, to a more private one of the same kind.

IV. Placed in a station so congenial A. D. 203, with his taste, all his talents and attain- to 216. ments were devoted to the discharge of its duties. In order to abstract his attention from other studies, as well as to secure himself a maintenance, he sold that part of his library which treated of science and literature, and received from the purchaser an obligation to supply him daily with *four oboli,* about five pence, as an income for his subsistence. From this period, his life was one of the most rigid abstinence and laborious study. The day he spent partly in fasting and other religious exercises, and partly in the duties of his office; the night he passed in the study of the Scriptures, reserving a little time for sleep, which he seldom took in bed, and generally on the bare ground. A sort of monkish austerity had grown to high repute in the church; consequently, Origen's self-denial increased the fame of his sanctity, and conspired, with his eloquence and extensive learning, to draw from every quarter a great number of disciples. They did not dishonor their master: Of their constancy in the faith, he soon had an opportunity of witnessing a full, though painful, proof; for, in a furious persecution which some of the Roman magistrates set on foot at Alexandria, several of his scholars undauntedly sealed their professions with their lives. He himself was often attacked with

showers of stones, while going to the place of execution to exhort and encourage the martyrs ; and as no
dangers ever deterred him from this practice, the exasperated heathens at length beset his house, and
obliged him to secrete himself, in order to escape their
rage. About this time, A. D. 206, in his twenty-first
year, the excessive rigor of his discipline led to an act
which became an occasion of self-regret, and of much
reproach, in future life : understanding our Saviour to
recommend emasculation,[4] he made himself a eunuch,
not only for the kingdom of heaven's sake, but also
from prudential considerations ; his instructions being
sought by both sexes. Demetrius, his bishop, ap-
plauded it, at first, as an act of the greatest Christian
heroism ; though he, afterwards, alleged it against
him as an inexcusable offence.

Such, at length, was the increase of his school, that
its cares engrossed too much of his thoughts, leaving
him no time for reflection and improvement. He
therefore committed the younger pupils to his friend
Heraclas, one of his earliest converts ; and employed
the leisure, which this arrangement afforded, in various studies and occupations. He applied himself to
the Hebrew, a language then but little known ; next
he began, it is thought, that astonishing monument of
application and labor, the *Hexapla* or *Octapla*, a
Polyglott of the Old Testament ; and it was, perhaps,
not far from this period,[5] that he attended the lectures
of the ingenious and subtle Ammonius Saccas, whose

[4.] Matt. xix. 12.   [5.] So thinks Lardner ; other biographers,
however, refer his attendance at the School of Ammonius, to an
earlier period.

darling study it was to harmonize all the different systems of philosophy and religion, heathen as well as Christian, by combining their leading principles, and by rejecting from each, or turning into allegory, whatever was absolutely discordant with his general design. Under him, Origen became master of the Platonic, Pythagorean, Stoic, and Oriental notions; which, together with his previous acquirements, rendered him so expert in the whole circle of ancient literature and science, that many of the learned, even among the heretics and the heathens, came to make trial of his skill, or to be instructed by him. Of these, there was one who preserved his own name from oblivion, by the zeal with which he assisted Origen, and the success with which he drew forth his talents. The name of Ambrosius will frequently occur in this biography. He was a wealthy nobleman of Alexandria, who had followed the Valentinian and Marcionite heresies; but on being convinced by attending the school of Origen, (A. D. 212,) he joined the orthodox church, and became the great patron and benefactor of his master. Not far from the year 213, Origen's curiosity led him to visit Rome. Here, however, he tarried but a short time, and then returned to Alexandria. Soon afterwards, he went into Arabia, on the request of some leader of the wandering tribes, who had earnestly entreated him to come and instruct him in the Christian religion. Scarcely was he re-established in Alexandria, when the emperor Caracalla (A. D. 216,) threw the whole city into consternation by an indiscriminate massacre, in revenge for the jeers and scoffs he had received from some of the inhabitants; and to escape the terrible confusion, Origen retired to Cesarea in Palestine. Here, the bishops of the province persuaded him, though never ordained, to expound the Scriptures publicly to the people.

V. This appointment, so honorable to A. D. 216, Origen, was but the forerunner of an into 230. veterate, and at length fatal, persecution from his own bishop at Alexandria. Demetrius instantly addressed a letter of complaint to his brethren in Palestine, asserting that it was a thing unheard of, that a layman should preach in the presence of bishops ; but Alexander bishop of Jerusalem, and Theoctistus, bishop of Cesarea, answered him, by showing that the practice had been sanctioned in the church by several precedents. Demetrius, however, remained dissatisfied, and sent some deacons to Origen, with an order for his immediate return to Alexandria. He came accordingly and resumed the care of his school. This he seems to have prosecuted, in quiet, for five or six years ; when an event occurred, which serves to show, at once, the superiority of his reputation, and the influence it had in recommending Christianity to the favorable notice of the great. The princess Mammæa, mother of Alexander, the reigning emperor, sent for Origen to visit her at Antioch, and furnished a military guard to escort him thither. Having given her a general illustration of the Christian doctrine, he returned, with her permission to his charge at Alexandria.

At the earnest solicitation of Ambrosius, he now began his *Commentaries*. He was furnished, by this devoted patron, with every convenience for the purpose : seven notaries stood ready to record as he dictated ; and a number of transcribers received their hasty notes, and wrote them out, in a plain and elegant hand. In this manner he was engaged, till A. D. 228 ; when he was sent into Achaia, on some ecclesiastical affairs, with letters of recommendation from Demetrius. Passing through Palestine on his journey, he was ordained *Presbyter*, by the bishops of that province. Demetrius warmly resented this procedure of foreign prelates, without his leave ; and wrote letters against Origen to the churches, declaring him disqualified for the priesthood, by the act performed in his youth, and alleging that it was unlawful to ordain the Principal of the Alexandrian School, without his knowledge and concurrence. In the midst of this ferment, Origen, having accomplished his business in Greece, returned to Alexandria, finished the first five books of his *Commentaries on St. John*, those *on the Lamentations*, on some of the *Psalms*, and on part of *Genesis*, and published them, A. D. 230, together with his work entitled *Stromata*, and his book *Of Principles*.

VI. These were, perhaps, his first publications. From the last mentioned work, we have already seen that, in connexion with Universalism, he held the doctrine of Pre-existence. His opinion was, that in the past ages of eternity, God created, at once, all the rational minds which have ever existed, whether of angels or men, gave them the same nature and the same powers, and placed them all in one celestial state. Accordingly, they were all, at first, exactly alike in rank, capacity and character. But as they all had perfect freedom of will, they did not long continue in this state of equality; for while some improved themselves more or less, others degenerated proportionally, till an infinite diversity of character and condition began to take place among them. In consequence of this, the Almighty at length formed the material Universe out of pre-existent matter, and appointed those spirits to different ranks and conditions in it, according to their respective deserts; elevating some to the angelic order, consigning others to the infernal abodes as demons, and sending the intermediate class, as occasion might require, into human bodies. Origen supposed, also, that the Sun, Moon and Stars were animated by certain spirits who had attained to great moral splendor, dignity and power, and who might, with justice, claim those bright and glorious spheres as their own appropriate bodies.

As all these intelligent beings, whatever their character and station, still retain their original freedom of will, and are therefore capable of returning from their former transgressions, of forfeiting their honors, or of rising to still higher degrees of excellence, their present conditions are not only the allotments of retributive justice for the past, but are also states of discipline adapted to reclaim the degenerate, and to encourage the virtuous. To this end, indeed, are all the appointments of providence, and all the administrations of the divine government, constantly directed; and justice itself steadily pursues the same gracious design,[6] in all its severe, but salutary, inflictions. Such

[6.] Many of the Gnostics held that Justice is opposed to Goodness, and that it is therefore an attribute of the stern Creator of

are the views we may gather from Origen's books *Of Principles*, and his other works published at this period.

this world, and not of the benevolent Deity. Against these Origen says, "Let them consider this : if Goodness is a virtue, as "doubtless they will confess it to be, what will they say of Jus- "tice ? They will not be so stupid, I think, as to deny that Jus- "tice is a virtue. If Goodness then is a virtue, and Justice also "a virtue, there is no question but that Justice is Goodness. But "if they still assert that Justice is not Goodness, it remains that it "is either evil or indifferent. Now, I suppose it would be folly "to reply to any who should say that Justice is evil ; for how can "that be evil, which renders blessing to the good, as they them "selves confess that Justice does? But if they assert that it is "indifferent, [neither good nor evil,] then it follows that together "with Justice, every other virtue, as sobriety, prudence, &c. must "be considered indifferent. And how then should we under "stand St. Paul, who says, *If there be any virtue, any praise,* "*think on these things which ye have both learned and received,* "*and heard, and seen in me.* (Phil. iv. 8, 9.) Let them, there- "fore, learn by searching the Scriptures, what are the several "virtues. And when they allege that the God who rewards "every one according to his deserts, renders evil to the evil, "let them not conceal the principle : that as the sick must be "cured by harsh medicines, so God administers, for the purpose "of emendation, what for the present appears to produce pain. "They do not consider what is written concerning the hope of "those who perished in the deluge ; of which hope, St. Peter "says, in his first Epistle, that Christ was *put to death in the flesh,* "*but quickened by the Spirit ; by which also he went and preached* "*to the spirits in prison, which sometime were disobedient, when* "*once the long-suffering of God waited in the days of Noah, while* "*the ark was a preparing, &c.* (1 Pet. iii. 18, 19, 20.) Let them "also consider the instances of Sodom and Gomorrah : as they "believe the prophecies are the word of that God, the Creator, "who is said to have rained fire and brimstone upon them ; what, "we ask, does the prophet Ezekiel say of them? *Sodom*, says "he, *shall be restored to its former state.* (Ezek. xvi. 55.) Now, "he who afflicts those who deserve punishment, does he not afflict "them for their good? He says also to Chaldea, *thou hast coals* "*of fire ; sit upon them ; they will be a help to thee.* (Isa. xlvii. "14, 15.) Let them also hear what is said, in the Psalms, of "those who fell in the desert : *when he had slain them, then they* "*sought him.* (Ps. lxxviii. 34.) It is not said, that when some "were slain, the rest sought God ; but that such was the end of "those who were slain, that when dead, they sought him." De Princip. Lib. ii. cap. 5, § 3.

N. B. Whenever the early fathers quote from the Old Testament, they make use of the Septuagint version, which, in many passages, differs considerably from our translation.

The language in which he defines, or involves, his notions of the Trinity, is not always such as would now be judged orthodox, though it was probably regarded as sufficiently so, in his own age. Of the *fall of man,* he has no other view than that it consisted in the descent of the celestial soul to the prison of an earthly body, in consequence of its transgressions ; it is evident that he made no distinction between the natural state of Adam, and that in which all mankind have since been born. He holds that none can ever be happy, or miserable, but by the right or wrong use of their own free-wills ; and that even what are now called the gracious influences of the Holy Spirit, are imparted to creatures only in proportion to their previous deserts. After death, the souls of the faithful may perhaps remain awhile upon earth, under a course of purification ; then be taken into the air, and at length elevated, by degrees, to the highest heaven. In the resurrection, mankind will come forth with bodies, not of gross earthly matter, but of an aerial substance ; and then the whole human race, both good and bad, will be subjected to a fiery ordeal in the general conflagration, with different degrees of pain, according to their moral purity or corruption. The righteous will quickly pass through this trial into the enjoyments of heaven ; but the wicked will then be condemned to the punishments of hell, which consist both of inflicted pain, and of the remorse of conscience. These sufferings, though he calls them *everlasting,*[7] Origen held, would be apportioned, in length and severity, to every one's wickedness and hardness

[7] Proem. Lib. De Principiis. and Lib. ii. cap. 10, § 1 and 3.

of heart : for some, they would be shorter and more moderate ; but for others, especially for the devil, they would necessarily be rendered intense, and protracted to an immense duration, in order to overcome the obstinacy and corruption of the guilty sufferers. At last, however, the whole intelligent creation should be purified, and God become all in all.[8]

VII. But nothing is more remarkable, in these early publications, than the rule they set forth for the interpretation of Scripture. We have already seen that the allegorical method had long been in vogue ; and that it had, now, become almost universal. Strange as it may seem, Origen pursued this farther than even his predecessors, and reduced it to a sort of system, unequalled in absurdity, except by that of the famous Baron Swedenborg. To the sacred writings in general, he attributed three distinct senses : 1, the *literal*, which in no case is of great importance, and sometimes entirely useless ; 2, the *moral*, superior in value to the former, teaching us to consider every historical account as an allegorical representation of certain virtues or vices in our own hearts ; as, when the Scripture relates that Joseph

[8.] Huet, Du Pin, and others, represent Origen to have held a perpetual change of character and condition among all classes of rational creatures ; so that not only the damned will, in time, ascend to happiness, but also the blest may, at length, fall into sin and misery ; and joy as well as suffering come to an end. It is true, he holds the perpetual freedom of the will, and seems to to admit, in consequence, the probability of a fall hereafter, from heaven, at least in individual cases. But if I do not greatly mistake, he contemplates a distant period, beyond all revolutions, when every intelligent nature will have become so thoroughly taught by experience and observation, and so intimately united to God, as to be in no more danger of defection. See De Princip. Lib. ii. cap. 3, § 5, and Lib. iii. cap. 6, § 6.

8*

being dead, the children of Israel increased in number, we learn,[9] by the moral sense, that if we receive the death of Christ, our spiritual Joseph, into our sinful members, the children of Israel, that is, the graces of the spirit, will be multiplied within us ; 3, the *mystical* or *spiritual* sense, the most excellent of all: by which the more enlightened can trace in all the Scripture narratives, of whatever sort, a latent history of Christ's church ; and by which also they can discover, in every account of earthly things, some representations of that celestial, invisible world, of which the present is but a faint and imperfect image.   There, souls are the inhabitants, and angels the rulers ; and there the *ideal* regions and the order of events correspond, in some degree, to those on earth.   Ridiculous as was this system of interpretation, it met the taste of his times ; though, even then, there were some who rejected it, at least in part, and raised their feeble voice against its extravagance.   But they themselves often ran into other notions nearly as chimerical.

VIII. While Origen was engaged in A. D. 230, preparing and publishing the works now to 245. mentioned, the storm which his bishop had raised against him, continued, increasing in violence.   Wearied out, at length, with contention, he took a private and final leave of his native country, (A. D. 231,) and retired to Palestine, where he was cordially received by his old friends,

9. Homil. i. in Exod. § 4. I have taken this *illustration* from one of Origen's later works; but in the books *Of Principles*, the nature and use of the moral sense are abundantly explained.

Alexander of Jerusalem, and Theoctistus of Cesarea.
Immediately on his retreat, Demetrius assembled all
the Egyptian bishops, and such of the presbyters as
he thought in his own favor, with the hope of procuring the condemnation of his victim. In this, however, he was disappointed : the council decreed only
that Origen should be deprived of his office in the
Catechetical School, and of the privilege of teaching
at Alexandria ; but that he should still enjoy his character of presbyter. This not satisfying his wrath,
Demetrius called another council (probably in A. D.
232,) composed of such bishops only as he saw fit to
select from his own province. With these he succeeded : they ordained that Origen should be deposed
from his sacerdotal dignity, and excommunicated from
the church. When this sentence was thus formally
passed upon him, he could not, according to the ecclesiastical Constitution and Canons, be received in
any church, nor by any bishop, under the Catholic jurisdiction ; nevertheless the bishops of Arabia, Palestine, Phœnicia, and Achaia, his personal acquaintan-
ces, hazarded the experiment of supporting him, at
the expense of non-conformity to the established regulations. But in the West, and particularly at Rome,
the sentence of excommunication was readily confirmed.

That it was not for error in doctrine that Origen
was condemned, is expressly asserted by some of the
ancients,[10] and evident from the silence of all the rest.
It is not incredible, indeed, that his adversary adopted

10. Jerome. Apud Ruf. Invect. ii. inter Hieronymi Opera.

the usual expedient in ecclesiastical persecution, and in order to increase the odium, represented some opinions he had advanced, as worthy of reproof. But if this were the case, it cannot have formed a prominent ground in the prosecution, since there is no trace of it left, in all antiquity. What were the principal charges alleged against him, we can only conjecture:[11] The consciences of an angry prelate, and his select minions, could not be very scrupulous in the choice of matter for condemnation; and it is thought to have related only to some informality in his ordination, and to some disregard of the customary claims of his bishop. Demetrius, however, did not long enjoy his revenge, as he died, probably, this year. After his decease, the rage of opposition appeared to subside; but still Origen was considered, by the Egyptian Christians, as an excommunicated person; and such was their respect for the ecclesiastical canons, that the sentence of Demetrius was never revoked by his successors, Heraclas and Dionysius, though they had been disciples of Origen,

---

[11.] As for the story we find in Epiphanius (Hæres. lxiv. 2,) that before Origen left Alexandria, he consented to hold incense over the altar in honor of an idol, rather than be unnaturally defiled by an Ethiopian, it is generally thought by the moderns to have been one of Epiphanius's fables, or perhaps an interpolation in his works. Nicephorus appears to have taken the same account, with some alteration, from Epiphanius. Some later writer, in order to continue the story, has forged a piece entitled *The Lamentation of Origen*, or *Origen's Repentance*, in which he is made to bewail, in the most extravagant manner, his having sacrificed to idols. See Huet. Origenian Lib. i. cap. 4, § 4, and Append. ad Lib. iii. § 8, Cave's Lives of the Fathers, Art. Origen, &c. Du Pin's Bibliotheca Patrum, Art. Origen, Note *n;* and Mosheim. De Reb. Christian. Ante Constant, p. 676. *The Lamentation of Origen* may be found in Dr. Hanmer's English translation of Eusebius, Socrates and Evagrius.

(the former, his assistant,) and though they both still retained the greatest veneration and the warmest affection for him.

At Cesarea he was again appointed to expound the Scriptures to the people; and the bishops of Palestine, themselves, often sat under his instructions, as though he were their master. This city, at that time the largest in the Holy Land, and the capital of one of its divisions, might be classed, perhaps, with the Roman cities of the third rank in Asia, inferior not only to Antioch, the queen of the East, but also to Ephesus and Smyrna. It rose on a gentle acclivity from the shore of the Mediterranean, about mid-way between Joppa and Ptolemais; and its white marble buildings, its magnificent amphitheatre, and, higher than all the rest, its splendid heathen temple, met the view of the distant voyager as he coasted along, or approached the harbor.[12] Here, Origen opened a school, somewhat on the plan of that at Alexandria, for the study of literature and religion; and his fame soon drew scholars both from the adjacent province, and from remoter regions. From Cappadocia, he received Firmilian, who afterwards returned to his native country and became the most eminent bishop there. Still farther to the north, from Pontus on the shore of the Euxine, came Gregory Thaumaturgus and his brother Athenodorus.

Meanwhile, Origen proceeded with his *Commentaries* on St. John's Gospel, and began those on Isaiah

---

12. Josephus Antiq. Book xv. chap. 9, § 6, and Reland. Palæst. Illustrat. Lib. iii. Art. Cesarea. The city was 62 miles N. W. of Jerusalem.

and Ezekiel. Thus constantly engaged either in his school, or in preaching, or writing, he seems to have passed about four years, in quiet, till A. D. 235; when the barbarous Maximin, on coming to the throne, instituted a persecution against the more distinguished of the Christians, out of a fearful suspicion that they cherished, with too grateful a regard, the memory of his murdered predecessor. Among others, Protoctetus, a presbyter of Cesarea, and the generous Ambrosius, were thrown into prison, and tortured with various cruelties. To them Origen wrote and dedicated his book *On Martyrdom;* but concealed himself, the meanwhile, in a private family in the city, and some time afterwards, retired across the seas to Athens. Here he finished his *Commentaries* on Ezekiel, and went forward with those upon Canticles. From this place, it is thought he made a visit to his friend Ambrosius; who, on being released from his sufferings in Palestine, had gone, with his family, to the city of Nicomedia, on the north-east of the Propontis. Returning at length to Cesarea, about A. D. 240, his next journey, it seems, was to the city of the same name in Cappadocia, the metropolis of that province, whither his former scholar, Firmilian, now elevated to the bishopric there, had importuned him to come, in order to instruct his churches in the knowledge of the Scriptures. About A. D. 243, he went into Arabia, on the request of a council convened against Beryllus of Bostra, a bishop of that country, who differed somewhat from the popular faith concerning the trinity. With him Origen's conversation effected, what the council had been unable to attain, the renunciation of his supposed error; and with such grace was this accomplished, that Beryllus became the lasting and ardent friend of his victorious opponent. It was a little after this, perhaps the next year, that he wrote, at the solicitation of Ambrosius, his books *Against Celsus*, a heathen philosopher of the second century, who had hoped, by a labored treatise, to overthrow Christianity. To this learned and witty enemy of the Gospel, Origen's work is generally esteemed a candid and thorough answer; though some of the more judicious and impartial have detected in it a few instances of the prevailing disingenuousness and sophistry of the times. He was soon called again into Arabia, by another council of bishops, in order to reclaim some Christians there, who held that the soul dies with the body, and with it awakes to consciousness at the resurrection. On his arrival, he contended so successfully against the obnoxious sentiment, that its advocates changed their opinion, and returned to the cordial fellowship of the church. This was under the reign of Philip, to whom, perhaps, more properly belongs the distinction, commonly allowed to Constantine, of having been, though secretly, the first Christian emperor. Be that as it may, Origen appears to have been honored with his correspondence, and with that of the empress.

A. D. 245, to 253. IX. Notwithstanding the multiplicity of his pursuits, the variety of his situations, and the changes of his fortune, he seems never to have neglected the *Hexapla* or *Octapla*,[13] that great work, which alone would have im-

---

13. It was called *Tetrapla*, *Hexapla*, or *Octapla*, according as the copy contained *three*, *six*, or *all* of the columns.

mortalized his name. At what time it was completed, is unknown ; probably, however, not far from this period. In its entire state, it consisted of the Hebrew text of the Old Testament, placed in the first column ; the same, but written in Greek letters, in the second ; the translation of Aquila, in the third ; that of Symmachus, in the fourth ; the Septuagint in the fifth ; the version of Theodotion in the sixth ; two other versions of the prophets, in the seventh and eighth ; together with a translation only of the Psalms. Wherever he found the Septuagint to depart from the Hebrew text, he affixed different marks to denote what was omitted, or what was added ; and, by similar means, he distinguished the various *readings* of the Original itself, according to the countenance each one received from the several translations. This is supposed to have been the first attempt at a Polyglott, or critical compilation of the Scriptures in different languages. In the great uncial letters of ancient manuscripts, it must have swelled to an enormous bulk, amounting, as Montfaucon thinks, to at least fifty volumes of a very large size. Mosheim says, that " though almost entirely destroyed by the waste of " time, it will even in its fragments, remain an eter- " nal monument of the incredible application with " which that great man labored to remove those ob- " stacles which retarded the progress of the gospel. "

But neither the services he had rendered the church, nor the veneration with which his name was generally regarded throughout the East, could stifle a strong disaffection, in many Christians of that day, towards some of his extravagances. We may perceive, in his later writings, allusions to the complaints of such as reprehended his perpetual use of heathen philosophy, and of those who animadverted on his allegorical system of interpreting the Scriptures. And we occasionally discover that he felt and lamented, what is the common misfortune of greatness, that the unbounded praises lavished upon him by his personal admirers, had awakened, in others, a spirit of envy and abuse. An invidious hostility, once excited, could never be at a loss, amidst the prodigious number of his writings, to select some wild notions, many unguarded expressions, which would seemingly justify the clamors of passion, and the cold discountenance of more prudent malignity ; and it is said that Origen, at length, judged it expedient to write a letter to Fabian, the bishop of Rome, in vindication of his impeached orthodoxy.[14]

14. Eusebius (Hist. Eccl. Lib. vi. cap. 36,) barely mentions that Origen wrote a letter to Fabian concerning his own orthodoxy ; but Jerome, who is not the best authority, says, (Hieron. Epist. xli. vel. 65, ad Pammach. p. 347,) that Origen therein lamented that he had written those things for which he had been censured, and that he also cast upon Ambrosius the blame of having circulated those writings which contained them, and which he himself had intended only for private use. How much of this improbable account is true, cannot be determined, as the letter is lost. It is natural, here, to ask, *Was Universalism one of those tenets which then gave offence?* But to this interesting question no certain answer is to be found. Circumstances, however, would lead us to hazard an answer in the negative : 1, Origen continued to advocate that doctrine even in his latest publications, (See note *s*, to § xi. of this chapter,) without an intimation that it was censured ; 2, in all the succeeding controversies concerning his orthodoxy, which began to rage in about forty years after his death, we never find that doctrine involved, till after the contention had lasted a century ; (See chapters vi. and vii.) and it is not likely that a doctrine of so much consequence, had it once been pointed out as a subject of complaint, would have been forgotten, as such, both by his adversaries and his apologists.

It does, indeed, appear, from an expression in his Letter to his

Though now above sixty years of age, (A. D. 246,) he appears to have subjected himself to as great exertions as at any former period ; proceeding in the composition of some large works, and at the same time delivering daily lectures to the people of Cesarea. These, though extemporaneous and unprepared, were nevertheless so highly esteemed, that, with his consent, transcribers were now employed, for the first time, to take them down as they were delivered, and then to publish them under the title of Homilies. At length his *Commentaries* on St. Matthew's Gospel, those on the twelve minor Prophets, and on the Epistle to the Romans, were finished in succession, having employed him till near the year 250. At this date the terrible persecution under the emperor Decius broke out ; and Origen was seized at the city of

Alexandrian friends, as explained by Jerome, that a Valentinian heretic endeavored to stigmatize him with holding the salvation of the devil. But we have only a part of the Letter, and that only in the translations of Rufinus (De Adulterat. Librorum Origen.) and of Jerome (Apolog. adversus Rufin. Lib. ii. pp. 413, 415 :) both of whom are well known to have taken considerable freedom with Origen's language. There is some difference in their versions of this passage ; but much more in the light in which they leave the subject. According to the former, Origen incidentally observes that his enemies accused him of asserting the salvation of the devil, " which," adds he, " no one can assert, unless trans- " ported, or manifestly insane. " According to Jerome, who corrects the misrepresentations of Rufinus, Origen barely alludes to the cavils of a certain Valentinian concerning the salvation of the devil ; " which, " continues he, " none could avow, unless insane. " What is unaccountable in these two translations, is, not their difference, but the point in which they agree, viz. that they both make Origen pronounce the salvation of the devil a tenet which none could assert, unless insane ; when he himself had asserted and illustrated it (De Principiis Lib. i. cap. 6, and Lib. iii. cap. 6, § 5,) and continued to do so in his latest works (Tom. xiii. in Matt. and Homil. in Josh.) As neither Rufinus nor Jerome had this sentence particularly in view, we may suspect that they have given it a false construction.

Tyre, cast into prison, and loaded with irons. Here he suffered the most excruciating torments: his feet were kept in the stocks, distended to the utmost extremity, for several days ; he was then threatened with being burned alive ; and when it appeared that threats could not shake his constancy, he was racked with several kinds of torture. At length his executioners, tired with the infliction of unavailing cruelties, or more probably prevented by the death of Decius, (A. D. 251,) suffered him to escape alive. After this, he held several conferences, and wrote many letters, in all which he evinced a soul worthy of the life he had led. He died, at Tyre, about A. D. 253, in the sixty-sixth or sixty-seventh year of his age ; and a splendid tomb, erected in that city, declared to future times the grateful veneration which the church paid to his memory.[15]

X. Nothing but a frame like iron could so long have held out under his rigid privations and unremitted labors. Employed, for the most of his life, in the numerous duties of a public and daily instructer, he still found time to perfect himself in the whole circle of human knowledge, such as it then was, and after all, to become one of the most voluminous[16] writers

[15] For the *Life* of Origen, I have had recourse to the moderns, instead of attempting to collect, arrange and illustrate the original accounts scattered through Eusebius and other ancient writers. See Huetii Origeniana, inter Origenis Opera ; Cave's Lives of the Fathers ; Du Pin's Bibliotheca Patrum ; Lardner's Credibility of the Gospel History ; and Delarue's Notes and prefatory Remarks, (Edit. Origenis Operum Delarue,) and Mosheim's Criticisms (De Rebus Christian. Ante Constantinum.) These authors, though they agree in every thing important, differ somewhat in dates and in the order of events.

[16] He published, some say, six thousand volumes, many of which, however, must, of course, have been very small. The

that ever lived.   The wonder, with which the ancients regarded his various achievements, was but
natural ; and it was with some propriety that they
surnamed him Adamantius, to intimate the invincible
strength of a constitution that sustained toils which
would have worn out several ordinary lives.   With
regard to his native talents, there is a striking, though
not singular contrariety in his character : Endued with
a perception the very quickest, and with a memory
the most retentive, but deficient in the more substantial gifts of cool judgement and good sense, he appears, by turns, the brightest of geniuses, and the
wildest of visionaries.   As a moral and religious man,
however, his character is consistent, and his reputation
without a blot.   Both his friends and his enemies
agree in attributing to him the most illustrious virtue,
ardent piety, and the purest zeal.   Austere, but not
morose, he never spared himself, and amidst all the
abuse he suffered, seldom showed the least severity
against others.   Naturally of a meek and unassuming
temper, he endured, unmoved, the admiration of the
world, with no apparent vanity, and without that more
treacherous symptom of pride, the affectation of hu-
mility.   As a writer, his style is simple, clear and
fluent ; but careless, redundant, and often incorrect.
To conclude his character in the words of one of the
most learned and discriminating of ecclesiastical historians, he was " a man of vast and uncommon abilities,
" and the greatest luminary of the Christian world,

remains of this astonishing mass, are collected in four volumes
folio, besides two additional volumes containing the fragments of
the Hexapla.

" which this age exhibited to view. Had the justness
" of his judgement been equal to the immensity of his
" genius, the fervor of his piety, his indefatigable pa-
" tience, his extensive erudition, and his other eminent
" and superior talents, all encomiums must have fallen
" short of his merit. Yet such as he was, his virtues
" and his labors deserve the admiration of all ages ;
" and his name will be transmitted with honor through
" the annals of time, as long as learning and genius
" shall be esteemed among men. "[17]

XI. We have as yet quoted only one of his testimonies in favor of Universalism. It was, with him, a
favorite topic ; and he introduced it, not only in his
earliest, but also in his latest publications, in his popular discourses, or *Homilies*, as well as in his more labored and systematic treatises.[18] Passing over his

[17.] Mosheim, Eccl. Hist. Cent. iii. Part 2, chap. ii. § 7.

[18.] I do not attempt to point out *all* the passages in which Origen introduces this doctrine ; but however imperfect, the following table of references to Delarue's splendid edition of his works,
may afford some notion of its frequent occurrence, and assist the
inquiries of such as wish to consult the original. The dates here
affixed to the respective works, are those assigned by the learned
editor.
De Principiis, A. D. 230. Lib. i. cap. vi. and vii. § 5. Lib. ii. cap. i.
2. cap. iii. 3, 5, 7. cap. v. 3. cap. x. 5, 6. Lib. iii. cap. v. 5, 6, 7, 8.
cap. vi. 1, 2, 3, 4, 5, 6, 8, 9. Lib. iv. cap. 21 and 22 and 25.—
Homilia in Lucam. Perhaps about A. D. 230. Homil. xiv.—*Com-
mentariorum in Johannem* Tom. i. cap. 14. About A. D. 230.—*De
Oratione.* After A. D. 231. Cap. v. p. 205. cap. xxvii. pp. 250, 251.
cap. xxix. pp. 261 to 264.—*Comment. in Johan.* Tom. xix. cap. 3.
About A. D. 234.—*Tract xxxiv. in Johannem.*—*Commentarii in
Matthæum.* About A. D. 245. Tom. x. and xiii. and xv.—*Tract
xxiii. and xxx. and xxxiii. in Matthæum.*—*Commentarii in Epist.
ad Romanos.* About A. D. 246. Lib. v. cap. 7. Lib. viii. cap. 12.—
Homiliæ. Between A. D. 245 and 250. Homil. in Liviticum vii.
cap. 2, p. 222. Homil. viii. cap. 4, p. 230. Homil. in Numeros vi.
cap. 4. Homil. xi. cap. 5. Homil. xxvi. cap. 4, &c. Homil. in i.
Lib. Regum ii. cap. 28, pp. 494 to 498. Homil. in Lib. Jesu Nave
viii. cap. 4. p. 416. Homil. in Jeremiam ii. cap. 2 and 3. pp. 138,
139. Homil. xvi. cap. 5 and 6, pp. 232, 233. Homil. in Ezekielem

9*

books *Of Principles,* and many other works, in which
this doctrine abounds, we shall transcribe only a passage or two from one of his last productions, which is
still extant in the original Greek.

Celsus, the heathen philosopher, had accused the
Christians of representing God as a merciless tormen-
tor, descending, at the end of the world, armed with
fire. To this charge Origen replied, that " since the
" scoffing Celsus thus compels us to go into subjects of
" a profounder nature, we shall first say a few things,
" enough to give the readers a notion of our defence
" on this point, and then proceed to the rest. The
" sacred Scripture does, indeed, call *our God a con-*
" *suming fire,* (Deut. iv. 24,) and says that *rivers*
" *of fire go before his face,* (Dan. vii. 10,) and that *he*
" *shall come as a refiner's fire and as fuller's soap,*
" *and purify the people.* (Mal. iii. 2.) As, therefore,
" God is a consuming fire, what is it that is to be con-
" sumed by him ? We say it is wickedness, and
" whatever proceeds from it, such as is figuratively
" called wood, hay and stubble. These are what God,
" in the character of fire, consumes. And as it is evi-
" dently the wicked works of man which are denoted by
" the terms wood, hay, and stubble, it is, consequently,
" easy to understand what is the nature of that fire by
" which they are to be consumed. Says the apostle,
" *the fire shall try every man's work of what sort it*
" *is. If any one's work abide, which he hath built,*
" *he shall receive a reward. If any one's work be*

iv. and v. and x.—*Contra Celsum.* About A. D. 248 or 249. Lib.
iv. cap. 10, p. 507. cap. 13, p. 509. cap. 28, p. 521. Lib. v. cap. 21,
p. 594. cap. 15 and 16, pp. 588, 589. Lib. viii. cap. 72, pp. 795, 796.

"*burned, he shall suffer loss.* (1 Cor. iii. 13—15.)
" What else is here meant by the work which is to
" be burned, than whatever arises-from iniquity ? Our
" God is, accordingly, a consuming fire, in the sense I
" have mentioned. *He shall come* also *as a refiner's*
" *fire*, to purify rational nature from the alloy of wick-
" edness, and from other impure matter which has
" adulterated, if I may so say, the intellectual gold
" and silver. Rivers of fire are, likewise, said to go
" forth before the face of God, for the purpose of
" consuming whatever of evil is admixed in all the
" soul."[19]

Again : Celsus had treated, as very extravagant,
the expectation of Christians that all the nations of
the earth should at length agree in one system of belief and practice. On this, Origen observed, " it is
" here necessary to prove that all rational beings, not
" only may, but actually shall, unite in one law.
" The Stoics say that when the most powerful of the
" elements shall prevail, then will come the universal
" conflagration, and all things be converted into fire ;
" but we assert that the Word, who is the wisdom of
" God, shall bring together all intelligent creatures,
" and convert them into his own perfection, through
" the instrumentality of their free will and of their
" exertions. For, though among the disorders of the
" body there are, indeed, some which the medical
" art cannot heal, yet we deny that of all the vices of
" the soul, there is any which the supreme Word can-
" not cure. For the Word is more powerful than all

19. Contra Celsum Lib. iv. cap. 13, p. 509.

" the diseases of the soul ; and he applies his remedies
"to every one, according to the pleasure of God.
" And the consummation of all things will be the ex-
"tinction of sin ; but whether it shall then be so
" abolished as never to revive again in the universe,
"does not belong to the present discourse to show.
" What relates, however, to the entire abolition of sin
" and the reformation of every soul, may be obscurely
" traced in many of the prophecies ; for, there we
" discover that the name of God is to be invoked by
" all, so that all shall serve him with one consent ;
" that the reproach of contumely is to be taken away,
" and that there is to be no more sin, nor vain words,
" nor treacherous tongue.   This may not, indeed, take
" place with mankind in the present life, but be ac-
" complished after they shall have been liberated from
" the body."[20]

XII. In all his works, Origen freely uses the expressions *everlasting fire, everlasting punishment, &c.*
without any explanation, such as our modern prepos-
sessions would render necessary, to prevent a misun-
derstanding.   It should also be particularly remarked,
that among the numerous passages in which he ad-
vances Universalism, there is not an instance of his
treating it in the way of controversy with the orthodox ; and that, on the other hand, they themselves
did not, so far as we can discover, censure or oppose
it.   Sometimes he avails himself of its peculiar principles to vindicate Christianity from the reproaches
or witticisms of the heathens, and to maintain the be-

[20] Contra Celsum Lib. viii. cap. 72, pp. 795, 796.

nevolence of the one God against the objections of
the Gnostics. Sometimes, again, he states and defines
it, in a formal and labored manner; but in most cases
he introduces it incidentally, either as the natural result of some well-known Christian principle, or as the
positive doctrine of particular Scriptures.[21]

[21.] I subjoin the *principal* texts that he adduced in favor of
Universalism. Those from the Old Testament are translated according to the Septuagint version, which Origen, like all the ancient fathers, followed.

Ps. xxxi. 19. How great is the multitude of thy favors, Lord,
which thou hast laid up in secret for those who shall fear thee!—
Ps. lxxviii. 30—35. Even while their meat was yet in their mouth
the anger of God came up against them, and slew them in their
fatness, and crippled the chosen ones of Israel. In all this they
still sinned, and belived not his wondrous works : therefore their
days passed away in vanity, and their years, with speed. *But
when he had slain them, then they sought him, and returned, and
came quickly to God; and they remembered that God was their
helper, and that God the Most High was their redeemer.*—Ps. cx.
1, 2. The Lord said unto my Lord, Sit thou at my right hand,
till I make thine enemies thy footstool. Out of Zion the Lord
will send thee a rod of power; rule thou in the midst of thine
enemies.—Isa. iv. 4. For the Lord shall wash away the filth of
the sons and of the daughters of Zion, and cleanse the blood from
the midst of them by the spirit of judgement and by the spirit of
burning.—Isa. xii. 1, 2. And in that day thou wilt say, I bless
thee, O Lord; for though thou wast angry with me, thou hast
turned away thy fury and pitied me. Behold, God is my Saviour; I will trust in him and not be afraid; because the Lord is
my glory and my praise, and hath saved me.—Isa. xxiv. And
the Lord shall bring his hand upon the host of heaven, even upon the kings of this land; and they shall gather the congregation
thereof to the prison, and shall shut them up in the strong hold.
*Their visitation shall be for many generations. But the brick shall
melt, and the wall shall fall;* because the Lord shall reign from
Zion and from Jerusalem, and be glorified in the presence of the
elders.—Isa xlvii. 14. Behold, they shall all be burned in the fire,
as stubble, and they shall not deliver their soul from the flame.
*Thou hast coals of fire; sit upon them; they will be a help to
thee.*—Ezek. xvi. 53—55. And I will restore their apostacies,
even the apostacy of Sodom and of her daughters; and I will
restore the apostacy of Samaria and of her daughters; and I will
restore thine apostacy in the midst of them, that thou mayest bear
thy punishment, and be put to shame for all thou hast done to
provoke me to anger. And thy sister Sodom and her daughters
shall be restored as at the beginning; and thou and thy daughters

In two or three places, however, he represents the salvation of all men as belonging, in some sense, to the Christian mysteries, which should not be too free-ly divulged. But we must observe that, in this, he only applied a rule which the orthodox of his age

shall be restored to your former state.—Hosea xiv. 3, 4. We will no more say to the work of our own hands, Ye are our Gods. He who is in thee shall have mercy on the fatherless. *I will heal their habitations; I will love them openly; for he hath turn-ed away my wrath from himself.*—Mich vii. 8, 9. Exult not over me, O mine enemy; though I have fallen, I shall rise, though I should sit in darkness, the Lord will give me light. I will sus-tain the anger of the Lord, until he justify my cause, for I have sinned against him. He will *do me justice*, and bring me into light, and I shall behold his righteousness.—Malachi iii. 2, 3. Who shall abide the day of his coming? or who shall be able to endure his appearance? For he cometh as the fire of a re-finer's furnace, and as the soap of the fullers. He shall sit as a refiner and purifier of silver and of gold; and he shall purify the sons of Levi, and melt them as gold and silver. Then shall they present to the Lord an offering in righteousness.—Matt. v. 26. Verily I say unto thee, thou shalt by no means come out thence till thou hast paid the uttermost farthing.—Matt. xviii. 12, 13. [*Parable of the Lost Sheep.*]—John x. 16. And other sheep I have, which are not of this fold: them also I must bring, and they shall hear my voice; and there shall be one fold and one shepherd.—Rom. viii. 20—23. For the creature was made sub-ject to vanity, not willingly, but by reason of him who hath sub-jected the same in hope; because the creature itself also shall be delivered from the bondage of corruption, into the glorious liberty of the children of God. For we know that the whole creation groaneth and travaileth in pain together until now; and not only they, but ourselves also, which have the first fruits of the spirit, even we ourselves groan within ourselves, waiting for the adoption, to wit, the redemption of our body.—Rom. xi. 25, 26. For I would not, brethren, that ye should be ignorant of this mystery, (lest ye should be wise in your own conceits) that blindness in part is happened to Israel, until the fulness of the Gentiles be come in; and so all Israel shall be saved.—Verse 32. For God hath concluded them all in unbelief, that he might have mercy upon all.—1 Cor. iii. 13—15. Every man's work shall be made manifest; for the day shall declare it, because it shall be revealed by fire; and the fire shall try every man's work, of what sort it is. If any man's work abide which he hath built thereupon, he shall receive a reward. If any man's work shall be burned, he shall suffer loss; but he himself shall be saved, yet so as by fire.—1 Cor. xv. 24—28. Then cometh the end, when he shall have delivered up the kingdom to God, even the

held with respect to several points in their common faith. They used much caution in avowing some of their tenets, particularly concerning Antichrist and the near approach of the end of the world. Even the form of their creed, and the rites of the Lord's supper, were concealed, as mysteries, from the uninitiated.[22] Indeed, within the church itself, there was a series of doctrines appropriated to the maturer believers, and withheld from the less disciplined members. This will help to account for the caution which Origen sometimes recommended in promulgating Universalism. Commenting on that text in Romans (xi. 26, 27,) where St. Paul denominates the salvation of all

Father; when he shall have put down all rule, and all authority, and power. For he must reign till he hath put all enemies under his feet. Death, the last enemy, shall be destroyed. For He hath put all things under his feet. But when he saith, all things are put under him, it is manifest that he is excepted which did put all things under him. And when all things shall be subdued unto him, then shall the Son also himself be subject unto him, that put all things under him, that God may be all in all.—Verse 54. So when this corruptible shall have put on incorruption and this mortal shall have put on immortality, then shall be brought to pass the saying that is written, Death is swallowed up in victory.—Eph. i. 9, 10. Having made known unto us the mystery of his will, according to his good pleasure which he hath purposed in himself: that in the dispensation of the fulness of times he might gather together in one all things in Christ, both which are in heaven, and which are on earth, even in him.—Eph. ii. 7. That in the ages to come, he might show the exceeding riches of his grace in his kindness towards us, through Christ Jesus.—Eph. iv. 13. Till we all come in the unity of the faith and of the knowledge of the Son of God, unto a perfect man, unto the measure of the stature of the fulness of Christ.—1 Tim. iv. 10. For therefore we both labor and suffer reproach, because we trust in the living God, who is the Saviour of all men, specially of those that believe.—1 Pet. iii. 19, 20. By which, also, he went and preached unto the spirits in prison, which sometime were disobedient, when once the long-suffering of God waited in the days of Noah, &c.—1 John ii. 1, 2. If any man sin, we have an Advocate with the Father, Jesus Christ, the righteous: and he is the propitiation for our sins; and not for ours only, but also for the sins of the whole world.

22. Mosheim. de Reb. Christian. ante Constant. pp. 304, 305.

Israel, and of the Gentile world, a *mystery*, he takes particular notice of this term, and then says, "the "word of the gospel in the present life, purifies the "saints, whether Israelites or Gentiles, according "to that expression of our Lord, *now ye are clean* "*through the word I have spoken unto you.* (John "xv. 3.)   But he who shall have spurned the cleans- "ing which is effected by the Gospel of God, will "reserve himself for a dreadful and penal course of "purification ; for the fire of hell shall, by its tor- "ments, purify him whom neither the apostolic doc- "trine nor the evangelical word has cleansed : **as it is** "written, *I will thoroughly purify you with fire.* "(Isa. i. 25.)   But how long, or for how many ages, "sinners shall be tormented in this course of purifica- "tion which is effected by the pain of fire, he only "knows to whom the Father hath committed all "judgement, and who so loved his creatures that for "them he laid aside the form of God, took the form "of a servant, and humbled himself unto death, that "all men might be saved and come to the knowledge "of the truth.   Nevertheless, we ought always to re- "member that the apostle would have the text now "under consideration, regarded as a *mystery ;* so that "the faithful and thoroughly instructed should conceal "its meaning among themselves, as a mystery of God, "nor obtrude it every where upon the imperfect and "those of less capacity.   For says the Scripture, *it is* "*good to keep close the mystery of the king.* (Tobit. "xii. 7.)"[23]   Such is his suggestion.

[23] Coment. in Epist. ad Rom. Lib. viii. cap. 12. The other passage of this kind, is Contra Celsum Lib. v. cap. 15.

It may be difficult to reconcile it with the undeniable fact that he himself was in the habit of publishing this *secret* doctrine in his works, and of proclaiming it in his sermons, or homilies, before indiscriminate congregations. Of this species of inconsistency, however, there are remarkable instances, not only among the ancients, but also among the moderns; who sometimes declare, in public, the secret will of God, and proclaim the doctrine of universal decree, which they contend, the meanwhile, should be rather withheld than divulged.

10

CHAPTER V.

[Origen's Scholars and Cotemporaries.]

I. With the account of Origen naturally belongs a view of the extent to which Universalism prevailed in his time, together with some notice of the more eminent of its believers among his cotemporaries. But, here, the clear light of history forsakes us. In the lapse of ten or fifteen centuries, every document, if such there was, which might have pointed out the state of the doctrine, has perished; and we are left to the uncertainty of conjecture, guided only by a circumstantial evidence, scanty and indistinct.

In attempting to gather some general opinion out of this obscurity, we must place no great reliance on any supposed effect which the plain testimonies of Scripture ought to have had upon the common belief of that time; for ecclesiastical history shows that, in every age, Christians have taken their sentiments from other sources than immediately from the Bible. Nor must we adopt the convenient axiom of some enthusiasts, that every essential Christian truth, or what we deem such, has found an uninterrupted succession of adherents, from Christ to the present time; for when we assume this ground, we forsake, at once, the region of history, for that of mere hypothesis. We must, in the present case, judge what is *probable*, only from what is known; and remember, the meanwhile, that we may still err in our conclusions.

It would certainly be unreasonable to suppose that the great authority of Clemens Alexandrinus, and the vast influence of Origen, could have failed to secure many believers in all their prominent tenets. Were we to take into our account all their disciples, patrons and admiring friends, or even those of the latter alone, we should have the main body of the bishops and churches throughout all the East. Those of Arabia regarded him as the great and successful champion of the faith; in Palestine and Phœnicia, his authority in doctrine was almost absolute; in Cappadocia, his instructions were eagerly sought and followed; and in the remote province of Pontus, his scholars stood first among the bishops; Greece had long esteemed and revered him; and even in Egypt, notwithstanding the quarrel of Demetrius, it is evident that the churches, together with the presbyters in general, and many of their bishops, were warmly attached to Origen. But to reckon all these, barely on this account, as Universalists, would certainly be extravagant: Many of his advocates probably regarded him only for his astonishing genius, his universal erudition, his illustrious virtue, or the services he had rendered the church; some, perhaps, considered him merely as a persecuted man, and, overlooking his harmless peculiarities, felt it their duty to defend him against injustice. It must also be remarked, that as his Universalism was not made a matter of complaint, we can draw but little evidence of an agreement in that particular, from mere friendship and adherence to him; but this circumstance, at the same time, leads us strongly to suspect that a doctrine, so momentous and yet unimpeached, prevailed among his adversaries as well as among his followers.

Without attempting, then, the impracticable task or exploring the real extent of the doctrine at this period, I shall only select from the Eastern or Greek churches, which were the principal sphere of Origen's influence, some eminent individuals, whose intimacy with him, veneration for his opinions, and peculiar regard for his expositions of the Scripture, can hardly be taken into view without producing a conviction that they were Universalists.

II. Among these, the venerable Alexander, bishop of Jesusalem, holds a distinguished place. Somewhat older, probably, than Origen, he had already studied with Pantænus, when the former became his schoolfellow under Clemens Alexandrinus. In this situation, the two scholars formed a friendship which was to endure through life. After the interruption of their studies by the persecution under Severus, we find Alexander in prison at Jerusalem, in A. D. 205; at which time, his faithful sufferings were cheered, for a while, by a visit from his late master Clemens, whom he always regarded with great respect. The exact period of his release is not known; but within a few years he was chosen bishop of some place in Cappadocia, perhaps of the metropolis. He returned, however to Jerusalem, about A. D. 212; and, on his arrival, was unanimously elected colleague with Narcissus, the superannuated bishop of that city. From this time, we hear nothing of him, till Origen visited Pal-

estine, about A. D. 216; and the affectionate deference he then paid his early friend, together with the
faithful support he afterwards gave him, has been already mentioned. He and Theoctistus appear to
have taken the lead in the promotion and defence of
their illustrious guest. Regarding him as their own
master, they resigned to him, in their respective
churches, the authority of publicly expounding the
Scriptures, and instructing the people in religion.

To Alexander belongs the honor of having established, at Jerusalem, the first ecclesiastical library of
which there is any account. Though a bishop of
some eminence, he seems to have written nothing, except common-place letters; a few sentences only of
which are extant. In the general persecution under
Decius, he was arraigned at Cesarea, and again cast
into prison, where he soon died, A. D. 250.[1]

Of Theoctistus, we have only to add, that after
presiding with reputation for many years, in the metropolitan bishopric of Cesarea in Palestine, he died
not far from A. D. 260.[2] It does not appear that he
left any writings whatever.

III. Perhaps we ought here to mention Heraclas,
the successor of Demetrius, in the bishopric of Alexandria. He was one of those heathens who were
converted to Christianity in the year 203, by Origen's
instructions; and who then entered the great Catechetical School under his care. Heraclas was soon

---

[1] Cave's Lives of the Fathers, Chap. Clem. Alexand. § 4 and
5; and Chap. Origen, § 22; and Chronol. Table, Ann. 212. Also Euseb. Hist. Eccl. Lib. vi. cap. 14. I have omitted, in this account, a vision or two.   [2] Euseb. Hist. Eccl. Lib. vi. cap. 46,
and Lib. vii. cap. 14.

10*

called to witness the sacrifice of his own brother, a fellow-convert and disciple, among the early martyrs with which this seminary was honored. Pursuing his studies, he seems to have become the favorite of his master, since he was at length selected as his assistant, when Origen found the increasing duties of the school too numerous for his sole management. On the flight of the latter from Alexandria, in A. D. 231, Heraclas succeeded him in the presidency; and about a year afterwards, on the death of Demetrius, he was promoted to the Alexandrian bishopric, the second for dignity and influence, in all christendom. Here he continued to govern the churches, till his death, in A. D. 247, or 248; when Dionysius the Great, another disciple and friend of Origen, succeeded him.

Heraclas seems to have been of a quiet and philosophic disposition. He had the reputation of extensive learning, particularly in secular literature, for which he, perhaps, entertained a decided partiality; for on his elevation to the bishopric, he adopted, and ever afterwards wore, the philosopher's robe as his distinguishing habit.[3] He has left no writings.

IV. Ambrosius, the convert, patron, and familiar friend of Origen, can hardly be refused, by the most skeptical, a place among the believers in Universalism. It was at his request, and by his pecuniary aid, that Origen composed several of the works in which that doctrine is found. So zealous was he to perfect himself in the whole system of his master, that during some years in which they were almost constantly together,

[3] Euseb. Hist. Eccl. Lib. vi. cap. 3, 15, 20, 26, 31, 35.

he suffered scarcely a leisure moment to escape without additional instruction from him on religion. Their meals and their walks, their morning and their evening hours, were devoted to investigations of the Scriptures, and to the solution of difficult questions. We have only to add, that he was ordained deacon in the church of Alexandria, and that he died before Origen. It is said that some of his *Letters*, extant in Jerome's time, but long since lost, except a short fragment, evinced considerable genius.[4]

V. Firmilian, who, after returning from his studies, presided with celebrity over the churches of Cappadocia, entertained so warm an affection for his former master, and so great a regard for his doctrine, that he made several journies into Palestine, in order to enjoy his society, and attend his instructions. At length he prevailed on Origen to visit Cappadocia, in turn, and to gratify the common wish of the churches there, by imparting to them those treasures of religious knowledge which he himself had so much admired, and which they were so desirous to obtain.

Cesarea, the metropolis of Cappadocia, stood on the northern declivity, at the foot of Mount Argæus; which, rising to the south above the clouds, looked down on the whole province, and from its summit of everlasting snow, afforded indistinct views, in opposite directions, of the remote waters of the Euxine and the Mediterranean. In this great city, of perhaps four hundred thousand inhabitants,[5] Firmilian was chosen

[4.] Cave's Lives, &c. Chap. Origen, § 10; and Historia Literaria, cap. Ambrosius. Also Du Pin's Bibliotheca Patrum, Art. Ambrose and Tryphon.

[5.] D'Anville's Ancient Geography. And Rees' Cyclopedia, Art. Cesarea.

bishop, not far from A. D. 234, over the churches in that region. He soon became eminent and considerably known throughout christendom, by his extensive correspondence, and the active part he took in the general concerns of the church. On the famous question, which began to be agitated about A. D. 253, concerning the validity of baptism administered by heretics, he, like the churches of Asia in general, maintained the negative ; and in the violent contention which raged upon that point, between the two western bishops, Stephen of Rome, and Cyprian of Carthage, he accordingly sided with the latter. Soon after this, at the numerous synod held in Antioch, A. D. 264, against the unitarian Paul of Samosata, Firmilian is thought to have presided, and to have prevented his condemnation, being either favorable to his sentiment, or perhaps deceived with the evasions practised by the accused. As the matter was not put to rest, he was called to a second council, held there on the same subject, and finally to a third ; in going to which he died on the way, at the city of Tarsus, A. D. 269 or 270. He has left no writings, except a long *Letter*, on the rebaptizing of heretics, addressed *to Cyprian.* In this, we discover that Firmilian entertained the common notion of that period, that baptism, administered by proper authority, conferred remission of sins and the spiritual new birth ; that he held the prevailing faith respecting the mysterious tricks of demons, and their ordinary interference with the concerns of life ; and that the good man was capable of sarcasm, and boisterous invective, which he pours out profusely against Stephen of Rome. The subject, however, leads to no discovery of his sentiments concerning endless punishment, or universal salvation.[6]

VI. The last, whom I here mention, are the two brothers, Gregory Thaumaturgus,[7] and Athenodorus. Born of a rich and noble family at Neocesarea, the capital of Pontus, they were brought up in a manner suitable to their birth and fortune, and instructed in heathenism, the common religion of the place. When Gregory was about fourteen years old, their father died, and their mother, assuming the care of their education, placed them successively under different masters, with whom they studied Rhetoric, the Latin language, and the Roman laws. At length their sister removing to Palestine, the Governor of which had appointed her husband one of his assessors or counsellors, the brothers accompanied her as far as Berytus in Phœnicia, where was a celebrated school for the study of law. This happened about the time of Origen's flight from Egypt, in A. D. 231 ; and the youths, eager to see and converse with a man of his renown, went to visit him at Cesarea. Here they were at length prevailed upon, by his entreaties, to apply themselves to the study of philosophy, the introduction, as he considered it, to the science of religion ; and when they had made sufficient progress, he led them to the study of the Scriptures, explaining to them, as they proceeded, the obscure and difficult

---

[6.] Firmiliani Epistola ad Cyprianum, is the Epist. lxxv. inter Cypriani Opera. Edit. Baluzii. For his life, see Cave's Lives, &c. Chap. Origen, § 16; and Hist. Literaria. cap. Firmilianus. Consult also Lardner's Credibility, &c. Chap. Firmilian. [7.] His name originally was Theodorus.

passages. In this way, he trained them up to a systematical knowledge and ardent love of christianity, which they had, indeed, begun to regard with a favorable eye when they left Pontus. It is worthy of remark that in the early part of their residence in Palestine, Firmilian was their fellow student, with whom they then formed an acquaintance, which the future circumstances and events of their lives must have cherished.

Having remained with Origen about five years, they were recalled to their native country. At their departure, Gregory pronounced in public his *Panegyric on Origen*, yet extant, in which he lavishes the most extravagant praise on the genius and doctrine of his master, recounts the history of their acquaintance with each other, and laments, with fulsome declamation, the necessity that tore them asunder. On the return of the brothers to Neocesarea, it is said that the inhabitants entertained so high an expectation of Gregory's talents and acquirements, that, though heathens, they desired him to reside among them as a public instructer of philosophy and virtue. He soon received, also, a letter from Origen, commending his abilities, and urging him to prosecute his study of the Scriptures and of the Christian religion. But, disliking the cares of a public life, or modestly distrusting his qualifications, he complied neither with the request of the citizens, nor with the evident wishes of his late master, and withdrew to some obscure retreat, in order to lead a solitary and contemplative life. A certain bishop of that country, however, pursued him with unwearied solicitations to devote himself to the public service of Christianity ; and overcoming at length his reluctance, ordained him about A. D. 240, or 245.

Neocesarea, an inland place, of considerable size,* on the river Lycus, had scarcely been visited, as yet, by the light of the gospel ; but when the popular Gregory entered on his ministry there, things assumed a new aspect. His success was surprising. A large congregation was soon gathered ; the number of his converts rapidly increased ; and eventually a stately church, or Christian temple, was erected : the first of the kind, of which we have any distinct account in ecclesiastical history. In the general persecution of A. D. 250, he and his people fled to caves and deserts for safety ; but when the brief, yet violent, tempest subsided, he returned with such of his brethren as had survived. About ten years afterwards, an irruption of the northern barbarians carried universal desolation and distress through Pontus and other Roman provinces ; and the heathen inhabitants, though sufferers in common with the christian, seem to have taken advantage of the general confusion which ensued, to indulge their malice. Many of the believers having denied their faith in order to save their lives, and others having committed depredations on the property of those who had fled, Gregory was per-

*It now bears the name of Niksar ; and stands in a luxuriant and delightful valley, through which, to the west of the city, flows the river, called Kelki Irmak, from south to north. Around, but at some distance, rise the mountains, covered with forests of the wildest growth, and presenting the most romantic and picturesque views. It is thirty miles north east of Tocat ; and is placed on the map at about eighty miles from the shore of the Black Sea. (Morier's Journey through Persia, Armenia, and Asia Minor, pp. 332, 334. Philadelphia, 1816.)

suaded, at the request of a neighboring bishop, to address them a *Canonical Epistle*, yet extant, consisting of authoritative rules to regulate their conduct and discipline in those lawless times. In A. D. 264, he and Athenodorus, who also was an influential bishop of some place in Pontus, assisted at the council of Antioch against Paul of Samosata. Having returned to Neocesarea, Gregory soon afterwards died in peace, with the satisfaction of leaving but few heathens in the city, where, at the beginning of his ministry, Christianity had scarcely an advocate.[8] He was reckoned among the most eminent bishops of the time ; but his reputation unfortunately increased and grew monstrous after his death, when miracles the most ridiculous and incredible were attributed to him, so that his name went down to posterity with the significant appellation of Thaumaturgus, or Wonder-worker. Besides his *Panegyric on Origen* and his *Canonical Epistle,* we have his brief *Paraphrase on Ecclesiastes,*[9] but none of these being of a doctrinal character, they throw no light on his views concerning the final extent of salvation, or the nature and result

[8] In the account of Gregory Thaumaturgus and Athenodorus, I have generally followed Lardner, who allows but little credit to Gregory Nyssen's legendary tale. Du Pin, also, seems to have discarded it. But Cave and some others, adopt the whole, miracles and all, with veteran credulity.

[9] Some attribute to him the short *Creed*, relating solely to the Trinity, which Gregory Nyssen says was brought to him from heaven by St. John and the Virgin Mary. It is probable, however, that Gregory Thaumaturgus never saw it. (See Lardner's Credibility, &c. Chap. Gregory Thaumat.) The *Brevis Expositio Fidei*, which Cave, in his Lives of the Fathers, had ascribed to Gregory, is allowed, in his Hist. Literaria, to be supposititious ; in which he agrees with Du Pin, Fabricius, Tillemont, and Lardner.

of future punishment. An ancient writer,[10] however, intimates, if I mistake him not, that Gregory Thaumaturgus was well known to have held, with his master, the doctrine of Universal Restoration.

VII. With him ends our select catalogue of Origen's cotemporary followers. It may serve, at least, to point out some of the circumstances, which, together with the general diffusion of his writings, tended to spread his sentiments widely through the East. What other particular causes operated to diffuse or cherish Universalism among the orthodox of this period, it is in vain to enquire ; but we have no reason to believe that it was confined exclusively to his adherents.

As to the different bodies of heretics, it is probable that among the Gnostics the doctrine remained in the same state as formerly ; and among those of other kinds, it may have found some believers and advocates.[11]

[10.] Rufinus (Invect. in Hieronym. Lib. i. *prope finem*, inter Hieronymi. Opp. Tom. iv. Part. i. p. 406, Edit. Martianay) alludes to the fact, as notorious, that Gregory Thaumaturgus erred with Origen ; and it is of Universalism that he is speaking.

[11.] The author of the anonymous book called *Prædestinatus*, attributed by some to Prismasius an African bishop of the sixth century, but considered, by others, of uncertain date and origin, says that one " Ampullianus, a heretic of Bithynia, avowed the " following error : *that all the guilty, together with the devil and* " *the demons, will be thoroughly purified in Gehenna, or hell, and* " *come out thence wholly immaculate ;* and when he had raised " the whole church against himself, on this account, he corrupted " the works of Origen, especially the books Of Principles, that he " might sanction his own sentiments by their authority." (Prædestinat. Lib. i. Hæres. 43, inter Simondi Opera, Tom. i.) When this Ampullianus lived, he does not inform us ; nor is his name so much as mentioned by any other ancient writer. But though the account of his having inserted the alleged error in Origen's works, is demonstrably untrue, and universally disregarded, there yet may be a question whether there was not a heretic of that name

VIII. Turning our eyes, for a moment, from the Greek churches, to a hasty survey of the Western or Latin, it may be remarked that here the influence of Origen, as well as of the other Greek fathers, was partial and feeble, on account of the difference of language, which prevented intimacy. There was, also, a peculiarity in the customs, manners, and general turn of thought which distinguished the Christians of the West. We perceive no certain[12] traces of Universalism among them at this period. Indeed, the materials for determining, with precision, their sentiments on a number of points, are rather scanty. Though they had several bishops and writers of temporary renown, there was but one who still holds any distinguished place in ecclesiastical history. This was the eloquent,

in Bithynia, sometime during this century, who held the doctrine of Universal Restoration. At any later period he could not well have escaped the notice of other writers, whose works are extant; and indeed it seems difficult to account for their profound silence, in any way whatever, short of denying the whole story.

12. Novatus, or as he is often called, Novatian, an eminent presbyter of Rome, who contested the bishopric of the church there with Cornelius, advanced something like Universalism. He extolled in the highest, though in general terms, the unbounded goodness of God; (De Regula Fidei, cap. ii. *prope finem.* Edit. Jackson. Lond. 1728. pp. 23—25.) and maintained that the wrath, indignation, and hatred of the Lord, so called, are not such passions in him as bear the same name in man; but that they are operations in the divine mind which are directed solely to our purification. (De Regula Fidei cap. iv.) In short he asserted the peculiar principles of Universalism; but whether he pursued them out to their necessary result, does not appear.

Novatus flourished from A. D. 250, onwards, for several years. After his contest for the bishopric, in which he was once elected, he was condemned by his more fortunate rival, and excommunicated for obstinately refusing to admit to the communion such members as had once fallen from their purity or steadfastness, however penitent they might become. A considerable party attached itself to him, which maintained his opinion and practice, on this point, till the seventh century, and which was therefore occasionally treated as heretical, and at other times merely as schismatical.

the active and resolute Cyprian, who presided in the bishopric of Carthage, from about A. D. 249, till his martyrdom in the year 258. Formerly a heathen professor of Rhetoric, he became, on his conversion, one of the most zealous advocates of the Christian cause, sold his large estate to supply himself with the means of charity, and devoted all his time and all his powers to the service in which he had engaged, so late in life. As a prelate, he must always stand distinguished by his enterprizing and commanding talents ; and as a writer, he evinces considerable ability, though no extraordinary learning. His study, however, was not doctrine, but discipline, the art of governing his churches, and particularly the management of the ecclesiastical concerns in times of great perplexity and danger. For this difficult task he was qualified by a genius of ready resource, a bold decision, and a vehemence approaching to enthusiasm, which often carried him through the execution of his designs with surprising promptness, though at the expense of perpetual contention. We may lament, rather than wonder, that he had the faults natural to such a character, — ambition and a strong propensity to domineer ; and that his conduct appears sometimes dictated by self-will and passion. While he sternly opposed the arrogance of the Roman bishop, he himself cherished extravagant notions of episcopal authority, and unwarily promoted that ecclesiastical tyranny which was, at length, to enslave the Christian world. But a worse fault than all these, at least in moral principle, aside from its general consequences, was

A. D. 249, to 258.

his knavish assertion of visions and immediate revelations from God, as his authority and justification, whenever he encroached on the rights of others, or resorted to unpopular measures.

As he seems to have had little acquaintance with the Greek fathers, except Firmilian, and perhaps none with Origen, his views of the future state may be regarded as, in some degree, a specimen of those that prevailed in the West. He held a temporary and mild purgatory for the less deserving saints ;[13] but for impenitent unbelievers an endless punishment.[14] And it is too manifest that he indulged, at times, the spirit of a doctrine so congenial with the hot African temper : " O what a glorious day, " says he, " will " come, when the Lord shall begin to recount his peo- " ple and to adjudge their rewards, to send the guilty " into hell, to condemn our persecutors to the per- " petual fire of penal flames, and to bestow on us the " reward of faith and devotedness to him ! What " glory, what joy, to be admitted to see God, to be " honored, to partake of the joy of eternal light and " salvation with Christ the Lord your God ; to salute " Abraham, Isaac and Jacob, and all the patriarchs " and prophets, apostles and martyrs, to rejoice with " the righteous, the friends of God, in the pleasures of " immortality ! When that revelation shall come, " when the beauty of God shall shine upon us, we " shall be as happy as the deserters and rebellious will " be miserable in inextinguishable fire. "[15]

[13] Cypriani Epist. ad Antonianum lii. p. 72. Edit. Baluzii, Paris. 1726. [14] Cypriani Lib. contra Demetrian. p. 224. And Epist. ad Clerum, p. 13 and *passim*.
[15] Cypriani Epist. ad Thibaritanos, lvi. fine pp. 93, 94. Milner

Cyprian frequently imitates Tertullian, and sometimes borrows from him ; and, it is said, he was so partial to that stern and gloomy enthusiast, that he daily read his works, habitually calling out, as he sat down, *Give me my Master.* His confident expectation of the immediate end of the world, and near approach of the general judgement, conspired, with his naturally warm temper, to cherish a high degree of devotional fervor ; and of all the earthly fathers, there was none whose general form of expression approached so near that of the more enthusiastic or fanatical of the modern orthodox. Yet his opinions are by no means reducible to any creed approved at present : He was a trinitarian, but ignorant of predestination and irresistible grace ; he held that remission of sins, and spiritual regeneration were imparted by the minister to the candidate in the rite of water baptism ; that true converts might afterwards utterly fall from grace ; that good works, particularly prayers, tears, fasting and penance, make satisfaction to God for our sins ;

the orthodox historian, whose translation I have here adopted, says *seriously*, on quoting this passage, that " The palm of heav- " enly mindedness belonged to these persecuted saints ; and I " wish, with all our theological improvements, we may obtain a " measure of this zeal, amidst the various good things of this life " which, as Christians, we at present enjoy." (Church Hist. Cent. iii. chap. 12.) A general collection of these heavenly-minded exultations, over the anticipated torments of the damned, would have satisfied our visionary, that latter ages can boast genuine instances of Tertullian's and Cyprian's zeal. Had he considered, too, that there was some earthly feeling of revenge to inspire the joy of the ancients in the damnation of their persecutors, he must have adjudged the *palm* to the more disinterested moderns ; who, without the aid of provocation, indulge a much more difficult satisfaction in expecting the agonies, not of their oppressors, but of their supporters, their kindest benefactors, and of their own families.

11*

and that matrimony is but a sort of tolerated prostitution.

IX. In these particulars, however, he had the agreement of a large proportion of his cotemporaries throughout the East as well as the West. Christianity had already assumed many of the peculiar features it now wears in the Romish religion. Salvation, it was represented, could be secured only within the pale of the orthodox church ; and all the heretics, the excommunicated and the dissenters, were exposed equally with the heathens, to the torments of hell. These separate sects, in their turn, however, usurped, at times, the same terrible prerogative, and retorted on the catholics their own favorite admonitions. At the head of the true church, the clerical body, and particularly that of the bishops, possessed, when united, an influence uncontrolable, and powerful even when divided by their frequent discords. Some of the prelates began to affect the splendor and magnificence of secular nobility, though the sword of persecution hung over their heads, and often fell upon them in ruthless extermination. The ecclesiastical ceremonies and ordinances, to which extravagant spiritual efficacy was generally attributed, were losing their pristine simplicity in pomp and tedious parade. Nor was the morality of the gospel less perverted : though downright monachism had not been introduced into the church, yet acts of mortification and penance were regarded as superior to ordinary virtue, and a life of rigid abstinence as the favorite institution of heaven. But, as might be expected, the manners of the time approach-

A. D. 250, to 270.

ed, at once, the two extremes of austerity and licentiousness : some who professed the abstinence of celibacy, even indulged, to the great scandal of the better sort, in the possession of concubines from among those who had vowed perpetual chastity.

Amidst this scene of growing corruption, a jealous zeal was cherished against all supposed error ; and the church exhibited the striking, though not singular, spectacle, of rage for soundness of faith, in proportion to the common degeneracy. While the destructive persecutions of the heathens, urged at this time with unprecedented violence, were drenching the earth with Christian blood, the believers, both in the East and the West, seemed to devote the intervals of repose, to a mad search for non-conformity in doctrine and discipline, which they hunted into every corner, and condemned with little discrimination. In the West, Novatus and his followers were excommunicated, for their factious conduct, and for their obstinate exclusion of the lapsed ; and Cyprian and the bishop of Rome were engaged in a quarrel about rebaptizing heretics. In the East, Noetus and Sabellius on the one hand, and Paul of Samosata on the other, were arraigned and condemned for opposite departures from the indefinable and wavering standard of trinitarianism. Between the East and the West, a controversy was kept up, concerning the proper days for fasting, and the time for the celebration of the Paschal Feast. In a word, so universal was the passion for censure, that scarcely an individual of eminence, escaped reproach from one quarter or another. This circumstance will serve to introduce us to the subject of the next chapter; which returning from our excursion among the cotemporaries of Origen, takes up the history of his doctrine, from the time of his death.

~~~~~~~~

APPENDIX TO CHAPTER V.

I. But in order to avoid an unseasonable interruption in that narrative, we must defer the history of Origen's doctrine, till we shall have brought into notice a new kind of Gnostic Christians. The sect of Manicheans began to appear, in the East, about this time; and though small at first, it became, eventually, the most famous of all the parties of *oriental* heretics that ever arose. By gradually drawing into itself the older bodies of Gnostics, it swelled, at length, to a formidable magnitude; the number of its converts, and the talents of some of its members, gave it an alarming respectability; and, so widely were its sentiments, under various modifications, diffused throughout christendom, that its influence disturbed the church for many succeeding centuries, and reached even down to the remote era of the Reformation.

The author of this heresy was one Mani, a Persian philosopher, who appears to have combined a daring imagination and a most fertile genius with the austerest life and manners. Though educated in the schools of the Magi, and thoroughly instructed in the religion and studies of his country, he abandoned the ancient established faith of Zoroaster, and embraced Christianity. Like many other converted philosophers, he attempted an accommodation between the gospel and his former theology. His history is deeply involved in contradiction, and mixed with fables; but if we

About
A. D. 265.

may adopt the most probable account, he was, on his conversion, ordained Presbyter in the city of Ahwaz, about seventy miles north of the mouth of the Euphrates. As his general system of doctrine was too manifestly inconsistent with the tenor of the Scriptures, as well as repugnant to the faith of the few Christians already in his country, he announced himself an apostle of Jesus Christ, inspired by heaven to complete the imperfect revelation of his Master, by declaring the remaining truths which he had not divulged, and by fulfilling his ancient promise of a Comforter. But whether this was the assumption of sincere fanaticism, or the impious pretence of designing imposture, cannot be absolutely determined.

Removing, afterwards, to the capital cities of Ctesiphon and Ecbatana, he converted, to his religion, the Persian king, the renowned Sapor, and obtained, perhaps, the place of tutor to the young prince, Hormizdas. Emboldened by the royal patronage, and growing zealous with the increasing number of his followers, he prosecuted a public attack on the old religion of the kingdom, in order to substitute his own. The ancient and numerous priesthood of Zoroaster was alarmed at this daring innovation within the very court; the Magi, crowding around the monarch, soon succeeded in alienating him from the apostate, and in rousing him to avenge the violated faith of his people. Mani perceived the change; and with the more faithful of his disciples, fled from the impending blow, into Mesopotamia. But on the death of Sapor, in A. D. 273, he returned to the Persian court, under the favor of the new king, his former pupil; and took up his residence in a strong tower, built for his security against his numerous and enraged enemies. Meanwhile, his disciples taught his doctrine, with success, in various parts of the country, and, perhaps, carried it eastward into India. The flattering prospect of safety and patronage, however, was suddenly blasted. The faithful Hormizdas died in the second year of his reign ; and his son, Varanes, on ascending the throne, soon yielded to the entreaties or warnings of the Magi. Having by a specious pretence, enticed the destined victim from his strong hold, he seized and put him to death, about A. D. 277. Thus fell Mani, probably in middle life ; but the blood of the martyr only quickened the growth of his cause.[1]

II. Like some other Gnostics, the Manicheans held two Original, Self-existent Principles, the primary causes of all things. From the depths of past eternity, the Universe existed in two separate and adverse regions : the pure and happy world of Light, on the one hand, and on the other, the world of Darkness, where all was corruption, turbulence and misery. Over the realm of Light, which was much the larger of the two, reigned the true God, self-existent, all-wise, omnipotent, completely blessed, and therefore perfectly good. Innumerable angels, emanating from him, filled his tranquil dominion, and partook of his uninterrupted enjoyment. In the deep centre of the opposite world of primeval darkness, was the abode of Hyle, or Satan, the loathsome prince of evil, without beginning, but stupid and feeble, though unceasingly engaged in malicious craft ; and the countless demons he had produced, swarmed through his hideous and boisterous realm, waging mutual warfare, and profoundly ignorant, like their king, of the existence of the world of light.

In the eternal lapse of ages, however, an accident at length occurred, by which a partial mixture took place between the two original substances, hitherto distinct. In one of the intestine quarrels which continually raged in the kingdom of Hyle, a van-

---

[1.] Mosheim (De Rebus Christian. &c. pp. 737—740,) has manifested his usual good sense in gathering from the confused stories of antiquity, a probable narative of Mani's Life.

quished party of demons fled to the very confines of that world ; and from its mountainous borders, caught their first view of the neighboring realm of light. Struck with admiration at its splendor and beauty, they paused ; their pursuers arrived ; and all, forgetting their mutual hostility, consulted how to gain possession of the glorious world before them. An expedition was immediately undertaken ; but the all-seeing Deity, beholding their approach, despatched a body of celestial powers under the command of an appointed leader. In the conflict that ensued, the forces of darkness were at first partially victorious ; and, though eventually repulsed, they succeeded in carrying into captivity a sufficient quantity of light and divine intelligence, to give them new capacities, and to produce a manifest change in their world. Fearing, however, that Deity would liberate and withdraw that portion of light now in their kingdom, they contrived to retain it. For this purpose, they made, out of evil matter, a human body, like that of the late leader of the celestial forces, whose form they remembered ; gave this body a soul merely animal, like their own ; and then drew into it the captive substance of light, which became a rational soul allied to heaven. Thus completely constituted, the creature was called Adam, the first of the human race. Afterwards, Eve was created in a similar manner, and with the same diversity of souls ; and it is from this diversity that arises the perpetual conflict between the sensual and heavenly natures of man.

The Deity, however, did not relinquish his design of reclaiming the celestial substance from the world of darkness. In order to provide a suitable dwelling-place for man, that his soul might be brought to spurn the soft enticements of the body, and return to its native mansion, he created our world, midway between the primeval spheres of light and darkness, out of matter furnished from both of these regions. The

sun he made of pure fire, and the moon, of uncon-
taminated water; the stars and the atmosphere, of a
substance somewhat tinctured with evil; and our
earth, of a matter almost wholly depraved.   Here
was the appointed habitation of Adam; who, possess-
ing a large share of celestial nature, persevered awhile
in rectitude.   But the influence of his corrupt constitution increasing, he yielded, at length, to the bland-
ishments of Eve, and so transgressed the divine law.
The superior, rational souls of the first pair, were
instantly overshadowed and obscured with darkness,
and their affections enslaved by the body; their evil
propensities gained entire ascendency; and all their
posterity, born in the same fallen condition, are free,
by nature, to do only evil; or rather, have lost the
knowledge how to employ their will effectually to
what is good.[2]

[2.] After a long discussion of their notions concerning free-will,
Beausobre comes to the following conclusions: " 1, The Mani-
" cheans allowed the soul to be free in its origin, and during its
" state of innocence.   For it had power to resist evil, and to
" overcome it.   2, After its fall it had not absolutely lost that
" power, but it had lost the use, because it was ignorant of its
" nature, and of its origin, and of its true interests; and because
" concupiscence, which has its seat in the flesh, carries it away
" by an invincible force to do, or allow what it condemns. 3, The
" gospel of Jesus Christ delivers the soul from that servitude, and
" gives it sufficient power to subdue sin and to obey the law of
" God, provided it make use of the helps therein afforded."   Af-
" terwards he adds: " Finally, I allow that the ancient fathers in
" general say that the Manicheans denied free-will.   The reason
" is, that the fathers believed and maintained, against the Mar-
" cionites and Manicheans, that whatever be the state man is in,
" he has the command over his own actions, and has equally
" power to do good and evil.   Augustine himself reasoned upon
" this principle, as well as other catholics, his predecessors, so
" long as he had to do with the Manicheans.   But when he came
" to dispute with the Pelagians, he changed his system.   Then,
" he denied that kind of freedom which he had before defended;
" and so far as I am able to judge, his sentiment no longer dif-
" fered from that of the Manicheans, concerning the servitude of
" the will.   He, however, ascribed that servitude to the corrup-
" tion which original sin brought into our nature; whereas, they
" attributed it to an evil quality eternally inherent in matter."

In order to promote the comfort of man, while on earth, but chiefly to aid the work of his restoration, the Deity, after the creation of this world, produced from his own being two peculiar existences, called Christ and the Holy Ghost, who, with himself, constitute a trinity. Christ, the brightness of eternal light, holds his throne in the resplendent orb of the sun, and extends his influence to the moon ; the Holy Ghost resides in our atmosphere, mollifying its asperity, cherishing the universal principle of vivification, and operating on the minds of men.

When, for many ages, God had attempted, with little success, to reclaim mankind through the ministry of angels and inspired saints, he at length sent Christ from his abode in the sun, to visit our world, not as a vicarious sufferer, but as an infallible Teacher. Assuming only the visionary appearance of a human body, the Saviour entered on his mission, instructing our fallen race how to forsake the service of the prince of darkness, to embrace that of the true God, and to subject the body to the government of the soul by a life of rigid virtue and extreme austerity. He only introduced, without perfecting, the system of Christianity, so that his first apostles knew but in part, and prophesied but in part; but, near the close of his ministry, and just before his *seeming* apprehension and suffering, he promised his disciples to send a Comforter, who should lead them into all truth. Accordingly, in due time, Mani the Comforter appeared; and not only completed his Master's revelation, but also restored that doctrine which Christ had already taught, to its original simplicity, by exposing the many corruptions introduced by his followers.

Those souls, who here obey the instructions of Christ, ascend, on the death of the vile body, to their

Hist. de Manichee, Tom. ii. pp. 447, 448. These conclusions are adopted by Lardner, Credibility of the Gospel Hist. part ii. chap. lxiii. sect. iv. 13.

native sphere; but they who neglect, are then sent into other bodies of men, brutes, or plants, to repeat their mortal course of discipline, until they are fitted for heaven. Such, however, as fight against the truth and persecute its adherents, are first driven into the dominions of the prince of darkness, to be tormented awhile in flame, before they transmigrate again upon earth.

At length, in the fulness of times, when all souls, or nearly all, shall have been reclaimed, and the captive particles of light won back to the kingdom of Deity, the whole of this world shall be destroyed by fire. Some of the Manicheans, perhaps, held the restoration of all souls;[3] but none of them, the salvation of Hyle and his demons. These were independent powers, over whom, so long as they remain in their own sphere, the true God claims no jurisdiction. After the end of our world, they are to be forever restricted to their original empire of darkness, unblest with the least mixture of the good substance; and if any human souls shall be found utterly irreclaimable, they will be stationed, as a guard, on the frontiers of that realm, to keep the evil hosts within their rightful dominions.

Like other Gnostics, the Manicheans denied the resurrection of the body. We have only to add that they rejected the Old Testament, pretended that many parts of the New, especially of the four Gospels, had been interpolated, either by ignorant or designing men; and that they received the writings of Mani, as of canonical authority.[4]

[3] Beausobre, Hist. de Manichee, Tom. ii. pp. 569—575. And Lardner's Credibility, &c. Chap. Mani and his followers, Sect. iv. 18.

[4] The sources whence I have drawn this short account of Manicheism, are Moshemii De Rebus Christianorum &c. pp. 728—903; Beausobre's large work, Histoire de Manichee et du Manicheisme; and Lardner's Credibility of the Gospel Hist. Part ii. Chap. lxiii. Of Beausobre, however, I have made but little

III. To us their scheme of doctrine appears almost too monstrous for conception ; but to those brought up in the oriental philosophy, it was an ingenious system, the fundamental principles of which accorded with all their prejudices and habits of thinking. Nor was it so utterly shocking to the more simple-minded Greeks ; and the advantages it was supposed to offer, in accounting for the introduction of evil without implicating the purity and goodness of God, counterbalanced weighty objections, in the opinion of many. When it had spread in Persia and other oriental countries awhile, it began to appear among the Christians in the eastern part of the Roman empire, as early, probably, as A. D. 280 ; but, here, its progress was, at first, undoubtedly slow, as the orthodox fathers do not seem to have taken any notice of it, till thirty or forty years afterwards.

use, except what may be derived from Lardner's remarks, extracts and references.

CHAPTER VI.

[From A. D. 254, to A. D. 390.]

I. Throughout the long period, of nearly a century and a half, to be surveyed in this chapter, there is not an intimation found that Origen's Universalism gave any offence in the church, notwithstanding his writings, the meanwhile, underwent the severest scrutiny, and were frequently attacked on other points. In order to give a full view of the state of that doctrine in this age, we must attempt a narration intricate and often digressive, stating not only the opinions of all the principal fathers concerning future punishment, but likewise all the complaints and controversies that arose on Origen's sentiments.[1] As we proceed we shall dis-

---

[1.] Huetii Origeniana, (inter Origenis Opera) particularly Lib. ii. cap. 4. directs to nearly all the materials for a history of Origen's doctrine. By his *doctrine*, we mean, of course, not his Universalism in particular, but his general religious system, or rather the whole body of his peculiar tenets. Whoever has perused Huet's work, will scarcely be repaid for reading the smaller and less critical treatise, " Histoire de l'Origenisme, par le P. Louis Doucin," published at Paris, 1700, in one volume, small 12mo. of 388 narrow pages ; but even this contains much more information than Bishop Rust's " Letter of Resolution concerning Origen, and the Chief of his Opinions, which may be found in the first volume of *The Phenix*, a miscellaneous work begun at London in 1707. I have seen the following titles, but not the works : " Joh. Hen. Horbii Historia Origeniana, sive de ultima origine et progressu Hæreseos Origenis Adamantii." Franc. 1670 ; and " Berrow's Illustration and Defence of the Opinions of Origen." 4to.

cover, what is a very important fact, that even the few who treated his name with indignity, and bitterly censured various parts of his doctrine, uniformly passed, in silence, over the prominent tenet of Universal Salvation.

It was but a few years after his death that some of his views appear to have been, for the first time, *publicly* impeached; though in this instance, without mentioning his name. Origen had combatted, even in his earliest publications, the prevailing notion of Christ's personal reign on earth for a thousand years; and his successive attacks, which he continued to urge against this point with more than his wonted spirit, had eventually brought it into disrepute, to the great dissatisfaction of the few who still adhered to it. A. D. 257, Towards the year 260, as is supposed, to 263. Nepos, bishop of some place in Egypt, published in its defence, a *Confutation of the Allegorists :* a title which aimed, undoubtedly, against Origen and his followers. This book, now lost, was well received in some parts of Egypt, particularly in the district of Arsinoe, south of the lake Mœris ; where the doctrine of the Millennium began to revive, and in the course of a few years, involved several churches in schism. But Dionysius the Great, formerly a scholar of Origen, and now bishop of Alexdria, happening in the infected district, about A. D. 262, succeeded in bringing over all its advocates to his own opinions.[2]

II. It will be readily believed that so obscure and

[2] Cave's Lives of the Fathers, Chap. Dionysius, § 15. And Mosheim, De Rebus Christian. &c. pp. 720—728.

momentary a disturbance could not affect the renown
of Origen. Accordingly, we find that,
A. D. 280, twenty or thirty years afterwards, to call
— 290. an author by *his* name, was generally
esteemed a peculiar honor ; and it appears that he was imitated by some Egyptian writers,
particularly by the learned Pierius, a presbyter of Alexandria, and by Theognostus, president of the Catechetical School in that city,— the works of both of
whom have perished.[3] But though his memory was
held in general veneration, it seems, nevertheless, that
the division, originally occasioned by Demetrius, still
continued, in some degree, among the Egyptian
churches.[4]

And in Asia, a public attack, more di-
A. D. 290, rect and hostile than that of Nepos, was,
— 300. about this time, made upon several points
of his doctrine. Methodius, bishop at
first of Olympus in Lycia, and then of Tyre, became,
from some cause unknown, bitterly prejudiced against
his memory, and sought every means to render it
odious. He published, professedly against him, a
treatise *On the Resurrection*, another *On the Pythoness* or *Witch of Endor*, and a third *on Created
Things* ; in all which, as well as in some other
pieces, he inveighed against his opinions, and sometimes treated his name with angry abuse. In the first,
he directed his attacks against such of Origen's notions
as may be comprised under the following heads, viz.

---

[3] See the accounts of Pierius and Theognostus, in Du Pin,
Lardner, &c. [4] Petrus Alexandrinus, apud Justiniani Epist. ad
Menam, quoted by Du Pin.

1, That mankind will rise from the dead with aerial, instead of fleshly, bodies ; 2, That in the ages of eternity, the saints will become angels ; 3, That human souls have existed and sinned in a former state of being ; 4, That Adam and Eve were, before their transgression, incorporeal spirits ; and 5, that the garden of Eden, so called, was an abode in heaven, belonging to the pre-existent state. The second work, now lost, is said to have been a stricture upon some of Origen's notions concerning the Witch of Endor, and the apparition of Samuel ; and the third, of which only a fragment remains, was a refutation of an opinion, attributed, perhaps falsely, to him, *that the world had no beginning*, as well as of another, which in some sense he doubtless advanced, *that the world existed long before the six days of creation mentioned in Genesis.* With these seven or eight particulars, there are some points more trivial which Methodius selected as obnoxious ; but in all his search for errors, Universalism escaped without a censure.[5] After these attacks, it seems, he grew more favorably disposed towards the object of his late enmity ; and at length joined in the general admiration of his talents and virtues.[6] He was a writer of no great celebrity.

[5] Du Pin's Biblioth. Pat. Art. Methodius. And Lardner's Credibility &c. Chap. Methodius. And Epiphanii Panarium, Hæres. lxiv. where most of Methodius On the Resurrection, is preserved. Also, Photii Bibliotheca, Cod. 234, 235. Some have said that Methodius's treatise on Free-will, was against Origen ; but it was against the Valentinians.

Lardner thinks that Methodius was made bishop about A. D. 290, and martyred in the year 311, or 312. It is suspected that his malicious treatment of Origen, was the reason of Eusebius's remarkable omission of his name in his Ecclesiastical History.

[6] Huet. Origenian. Lib. ii. cap. 4, sect. i. § 2, inter Origenis Opera, Edit. Delarue ; cum Not. in loco.

While this was transacting in the East, Origen's writings appear to have found a professed admirer in the West : Victorinus, who was probably a Greek by birth and education, but now bishop of Petabium on the Danube in Western Germany, is said to have imitated him in his *Commentaries,* though he disagreed with him in some of his views, particularly on the Millennium.[7]

III. In the numerous and influential churches of ˙Alexandria, we discover that the troubles which arose on his expulsion, seventy or eighty years before, had not yet subsided.   Among his adversaries, now, was Peter, the bishop ; the first, probably, of that class, who had presided there, since the time of Demetrius. About this time, or a little after, Peter publicly opposed the notion of pre-existence, though incidentally, perhaps, and without ascribing it to Origen.   But he certainly betrayed his prejudice by unjustly stigmatizing him as a-schismatic, merely for having disobeyed his passionate and domineering bishop.[8] There is reason to suspect that the dissensions at Alexandria, never ceased till they at length produced, as we shall hereafter see, two avowed parties, both in the orthodox churches there, and in the monasteries of the Egyptian deserts.

IV. As we are now arrived, however, at the age of two eminent fathers of the Western church, who explicitly stated their opinions of future torments, we

[7.] Hieronymi Epist. xxxvi. ad Vigilant. p. 276, Edit. Martianay. And Cave, Hist. Literaria, Art. Victorinus Petavionensis.   [8.] Petrus Alexandrinus apud Justiniani Epist. ad Menam, quoted by Du Pin, Biblioth. Pat. Art. Peter of Alexandria I.   Yet Eusebius mentions Peter with praise.

shall here avail ourselves of their representations.
Arnobius of Sicca, about seventy or eighty miles
southwest of Carthage in Africa, wrote his large work
Against the Heathens, probably about A. D. 305 ; in
which he asserted that the wicked will, hereafter, " be
" thrown into torrents of fire, amidst dark caverns and
" whirlpools, where they shall at length be annihilated
" and vanish in perpetual extinction," while the righteous on the other hand, shall reign in life eternal ;
" for," says he, " souls are of such a middle nature
" that they can be exterminated when they have not
" the knowledge of the God of life, and can also be
" preserved from destruction by taking heed to his
" threatenings and his mercies."[9]   So thought Arnobius.   But his own scholar, the celebrated Lactantius,
who, after going to Asia Minor, wrote his *Institutes*,
perhaps about A. D. 306,[10] asserted the endless misery,
instead of the annihilation, of unbelievers.   Having
mentioned certain events to precede the end of the
world, he says, " After these things the secret place
" of the dead shall be laid open, and they shall rise.
" And on them the great Judgement shall set, con-
" ducted by that King and God, to whom the supreme
" Father shall give full power both to judge and to
" reign . . . .   Nevertheless, not the whole Universe,
" but only such as have professed the divine religion,

9. Arnobius Adversus Gentes, Lib. ii. pp. 52, 53, Edit. Lugduni
Bat. 1651.   It has been said that this work was written soon after
his conversion, while he was only a Catechumen ; but Lardner
shows, satisfactorily I think, from the book itself, that the author
must have been in full communion.   See Lardner's Credibility
&c. chap. Arnobius.   10. Cave and Lardner place this work at A.
D. 306; and the latter assigns his reasons against the former critics,
who had, for the most part, brought it down to about A. D. 321.

"shall then be judged. For since those who never "confessed God, cannot possibly be absolved, they "have been already judged and condemned: as the "holy Scriptures testify, that the impious are not to "rise in the judgement. (Ps. i. 5.) Accordingly those "only will be judged who believed in God ; and their "deeds shall be weighed, the evil against the good, "that if their righteous works are more in number and "weight, they may be admitted to happiness ; but if "their wicked acts exceed, they may be condemned "to punishment."[11] He proceeds, afterwards, to describe more particularly the future conditions of these several classes : the impious who have never acknowledged the true God, shall be consigned to endless torment, in devouring yet unconsuming flame ; but the professors, whose sins exceed their righteousness, shall be more slightly touched and scorched by the fire ; while they who are fully matured in holiness, shall pass through it without any sensation of pain.[12]

Neither the sentiment of Arnobius, nor that of Lactantius, on this subject, though different from each other, appears to have occasioned any complaint or dissatisfaction. Both of these authors acquired considerable fame. The latter was the most elegant and classical writer of all the Latin fathers ; and the fond partiality of his admirers, has ventured to compare his style, for excellence, with that of Cicero.

V. Resuming the history of Origen's doctrine, we discover that, in addition to the particulars on which Methodius had inveighed against him, he began now

---

[11] Lactantii Institut. Lib. vii. cap. 20. [12] Ditto. Lib. vii. cap. 21. Du Pin has not exactly stated Lactantius's meaning, here.

to be accused of error concerning the Trinity and Incarnation. To the former of these points the public attention had been awakened, more than half a century before, by Origen's own controversy with Beryllus; and afterwards, by those that the church carried on against Noetus, Sabellius and Paul of Samosata. And if, as is thought, Lucian, a learned presbyter of Antioch, had still more lately advanced notions contrary to trinitarianism, the circumstance would naturally add fresh excitement to feelings already on the alarm. The jealousy, thus roused and cherished, was now scrutinizing every form of expression in order to detect heresy on this subject; though the self-constituted censors were by no means clear nor unanimous as to the precise point they themselves would regard as truth. Many began to discover, in the writings of the venerated Origen, expressions inconsistent with their favorite tenet; and consequently the enmity against him, which had hitherto been confined to a few individuals, instantly spread to a considerable extent. Some became satisfied, perhaps from candid examination, that if he were not really heretical, he had given too much occasion to error; but others, having gathered up some of his more adventurous speculations concerning the Godhead, broke out into clamor, and pronounced him, at once, a heretic. And there were others again, unable to read the Greek, who took up against him on mere report; of which, as usual in such cases, the loud tone of hatred and abuse, was much sooner heard, than the still, small voice of truth and commendation. They accused him of various

and opposite errors; but so manifest was the falsehood of most of their charges, that nothing could
more conclusively demonstrate the unreasonable motives of the attack. So high did the indignation rise,
that even those who only read his writings or cherished his reputation, were severely censured.[13]

This angry commotion, though we cannot now
ascertain its authors, was then regarded as sufficiently
formidable to require a public defence of Origen;
and two distinguished admirers of his writings, who
held offices in the church where he himself had flourished sixty or seventy years before, undertook the
work. Pamphilus, a learned presbyter of Cesarea in
Palestine, and Eusebius, his fellow presbyter, the
renowned father of ecclesiastical history.
A. D. 307, wrote a large and labored *Apology for*
to 310. *Origen*; in part of which they stated,
and thoroughly canvassed, the accusations brought against his doctrine. Happily for us,
this part, which was the first book of the work, is still
extant, in the Latin translation of Rufinus. The
authors formally arrange the charges of his enemies
against him, in the following order: " 1. They [*his*
" *accusers*] say he asserted that the Son of God is
" unbegotten; 2. they accuse him of teaching, like
" the Valentinians, that the Son of God came into
" existence by *emanation*; 3. they charge him, con-
" trary to the former accusations, of holding with
" Artemas and Paul of Samosata, that Christ, the
" Son of God, was a mere man, and not God; 4.

[13.] Pamphili Præfat. ad Apolog. pro Orogene, compared with
Apolog. cap. v. &c. inter Origenis Opera, Edit. Delarue, Tom. iv

"next, they contradict all these charges by saying
"(so blind is malice,) that he taught that it was only
"in appearance the Saviour performed the deeds
"ascribed to him, and that the history of him is but
"an allegory, not a reality; 5. another charge they
"bring, is, that he taught there were two Christs; 6.
"they add that he wholly denied the literal accounts
"which the Scriptures give of the lives of the saints;
"7. they calumniously attack him on the resurrec-
"tion of the dead, and the punishment of the impi-
"ous; accusing him of denying that torments are to
"be inflicted on sinners; 8. they censure some of his
"arguments or opinions concerning the soul, [*i. e. its*
"*pre-existence;*] 9. the last charge of all, which is
"circulated in every shape of infamy, is, that he
"asserted that human souls will, after death, be
"changed into dumb animals, either reptiles or quad-
"rupeds; and also that brutes have rational souls:
"which charge we have placed last, that we may
"collect the more testimonies from his books, to
"render the falsehood of it the plainer. Now," continue they, "observing the order of the charges
"above stated, we will begin with the first."[14] They
accordingly proceed with them in course; and, by
adducing copious extracts from Origen's own writings,
successfully defend him from each of the accusations,
except the eighth, which relates to the pre-existence
of human souls. This, they admit, was truly his
sentiment; but they excuse it, as being probably
correct, or at least of no consequence even if erroneous.

14. Apolog. pro Origene, cap. v.

13

VI. We cannot discover, in all this affair, that his doctrine of Universal Salvation was regarded as censurable; and an incidental circumstance shows that his learned Apologists neither knew that he had ever been reproached for that tenet, nor suspected that it could occasion any odium whatever. For, when they come to defend him against the latter item in the seventh charge, that is, against the charge of having denied all future punishment, they select, among several other testimonies from his works, two distinct paragraphs, in which he had, as usual, spoken of torments to be hereafter inflicted by fire; but in which he, at the same time, represented them as altogether remedial: "we are to understand," said he, "that God, our physician, in order to remove "those disorders which our souls contract from vari- "ous sins and abominations, uses that painful mode "of cure, and brings those torments of fire upon such "as have lost the health of the soul, just as an "earthly physician, in extreme cases, subjects his "patients to cautery." "And Isaiah teaches that "the punishment said to be inflicted by fire, is very "needful; saying of Israel, *the Lord shall wash away* "*the filth of the sons and daughters of Zion, and* "*purge the blood from their midst, by the spirit of* "*judgement, and the spirit of burning.* (Isa. iv. "4.)" &c.[15]

This testimony from Origen, like a thousand other passages which might have been selected from his writings, was, indeed, an effectual refutation of the particular charge brought against him; but it was, at

[15.] Apol. pro Origene, cap. viii.

the same time, a proof that he regarded future punishment as purifying and salutary. Had this sentiment been obnoxious at that day, Pamphilus and Eusebius would rather have avoided such passages, than have obtruded them, [thus unnecessarily, upon the attention of his captious enemies; lest, in defending him from an accusation so easily refuted, they should bring upon him one that could never be removed. And we may add, that their introducing such passages, without remark, while maintaining that Origen was sound in the faith, gives, at least, some color of probability to the charge, which was nearly a century afterwards brought [16] against them, of holding with him the doctrine of Universal Restitution, as well as that of Pre-existence. Of Pamphilus there is nothing else extant; so that, in his case, this appearance can neither be confirmed nor removed. And it would probably be difficult, if not impossible, to determine, from the numerous works which Eusebius afterwards published, what was his opinion on this subject.[17] Both, however, were ardent admirers of Origen's writings; a large part of which, the former had laboriously transcribed, with his own hand, for a famous ecclesiastical library, which he established at Cesarea. The two friends had likewise published corrected copies of the Septuagint, taken

[16] By Jerome, Lib. ii. Adversus Rufinum, p. 407. Tom. iv. Part. ii. Edit. Martianay; and afterwards by an anonymous writer of the sixth century, published by R. P. Lupo. See Delarue's Admonitio in Apolog. S. Pamphili pro Origene. Both of these authors, however, seem to have grossly misrepresented, at least, the circumstances of the case. [17] I have not access to all the works of Eusebius; but judge this statement correct, from the general character of his writings, and from the silence of all the ancient fathers and modern critics.

from the Hexapla.   We may add, that Eusebius has
been accused of holding Origen's peculiar notion, that
human bodies, at the resurrection, will be of an aerial
substance.[18]

VII. Pamphilus was thrown into prison at Cesarea, in the year 307, by the heathen persecutors; and
Eusebius either underwent the same sentence, or vol-
untarily shared his confinement.   It was here, that
the two friends began the *Apology*.   When they had
proceeded to the end of the fifth book, Pamphilus
was led forth from prison to martyrdom.   This was in
the year 309.   Eusebius then added the sixth, or
last, book to the common work, and dedicated the
whole to those Christians who were condemned to
labor, as slaves, in the mines of Palestine.[19]

Eusebius survived to witness the most eventful and
momentous change which the church has ever experienced.   He was elevated to the bishopric of Cesarea,
about A. D. 313, when Christianity first received a
full and effectual toleration; and, in succeeding years,
he beheld it continually rising in the favor of Constantine, till it was, at length, declared
A. D. 324.   the established religion of the empire.

Amidst the scenes of security and worldly splendor, which now succeeded the long and tem-
pestuous reign of persecution, the bishop of Cesarea,
high in the imperial favor, often looked back, in
tender remembrance, to his early associate and martyred friend; and as a testimonial of an affection
which neither time nor honors could extinguish, he

[18.] Photii Epist. 144.   [19.] Delarue Admonit. in Apolog. pro
Origene.

wrote his life, and took upon himself the surname of *Pamphilus*. That his admiration also of Origen did not diminish with increasing years, we find ample proof in his *Ecclesiastical History*, and in his succeeding works. He was by far the most learned bishop of his time; and, what is greater praise, he was moderate and unaspiring, in an age of clerical violence and ambition. Though the favorite of Constantine, he never abused his influence either for personal or party purposes; and when the great bishopric of Antioch was offered him, on the deposition of Eustathius, he declined exchanging his own diocess of Cesarea, for that of all the East, the third for dignity in christendom.

The latter part of his life was disturbed by the unholy and cruel contest which began to rage between the Arians and Trinitarians; in which he often concurred in the measures of the former, though he did not approve their doctrine. They were, in his time, the injured party. Whether his views on the contested question itself, were fully orthodox, is disputed; and it is certain that in the famous council of Nice, he not only urged the petulant bishops to adopt such a Declaration of Faith as both parties could receive, but that he also refused to subscribe their Creed, except with an interpretation of his own.[20]

VIII. The Arian controversy, to which we have just alluded, began, at Alexandria, about A. D. 317, bringing a dark cloud over the church, in the very morning of her political establishment. It spread,

---

20. Jortin (Remarks on Eccl. Hist. Vol. iii.) treats largely and impartially of Eusebius's character.

instantly, like a conflagration, over all Egypt, and soon involved Europe and Asia. The great and imposing synod of all christendom, which assembled, A. D. 325, at Nice, in Asia Minor, was called together, by the Emperor, with the vain hope of determining this dispute ; but, though it managed to decide against Arius, by an almost unanimous decree, that the Son was CONSUBSTANTIAL *with the Father*, it resulted only in dignifying the contention, and enraging the temper of the partisans. These separated into three divisions : the *Consubstantialists*, or patrons of the Nicene Creed ; the *Semi-Arians*, a sort of imperfect trinitarians ; and the *Arians*, who held that Christ was a created being. A most disgraceful scene followed, till toward the close of this century. Council against council assembled, and deliberately opposed falsehood to falsehood, and fraud to fraud ; deposition and excommunication were decreed, as either party gained a momentary ascendancy in the church ; the imperial authority obsequiously enforced the mad decrees alternately of each sect, till it filled the deserts of Egypt, and the remote regions of the empire with exiled bishops ; and the furious rabble, on both sides, resorted at length, to riots and massacres, to gratify their revenge, or to exercise their malicious zeal. The heathens, from whom the power of persecution had been so lately wrested, might have consoled themselves, in prospect of its being more effectually exerted in the self-destroying hands of a divided and factious national church.

Into this scene of contention we must now follow the history of Origen's doctrine. It does not, indeed, appear to have been, at first, so deeply implicated as some writers represent. The virulent attacks from which Pamphilus and Eusebius had defended him, seem to have subsided ; and all the concern that his name, or his writings, had with the grand controversy, till some time past the middle of this century, may be described in a few words. As his great authority would give considerable advantage to any cause in which it was exerted, the several parties gladly availed themselves of it, whenever it could be brought to operate in their favor ; but on the contrary, when it seemed to oppose their views, they would naturally endeavor to depreciate it. The Arians, however, do not appear to have been very confident of securing the patronage of his name, though some of them claimed him for their own. But of the two other parties, the Semi-Arians were generally his professed admirers ; and the Consubstantialists, also, appealed to his testimony, as full and explicit upon their own side. So far as we know, only one of them, Marcellus, bishop of Ancyra in Galatia, incidentally impeached the soundness of his faith concerning the trinity.[21] This was about A. D. 330. But he was an author whose complaint could have little weight, as it was suspected that his zeal against the damnable heresy of Arius, had precipitated him, on the other hand, into the perdition of Sabellianism. We must, here, digress

A. D. 320, to 360.

[21.] Eusebii Contra Marcell. Lib. i. See Du Pin's Biblioth. Patr. Art. Eusebius Pamphilus.

so far as to mention that Marcellus seems also to have held the doctrine of universal salvation, as at least to have used its language.[22]   To return, however, to the Arian controversy : The guardian genius of the Nicene faith, the great and intrepid Athanasius, always quoted Origen as orthodox ; Hilary of Poictiers in France, the ablest and most active defender of the same faith, in the West, became an imitator of his writings ; and so did Eusebius Vercellensis,[23] another Athanasian bishop of distinction, who presided over the churches scattered round the sources of the modern Po, in Italy.   This example of their leaders was followed by most of the party.   Some years afterwards, or about A. D. 370, when Basil the Great, Didymus, and the two Gregories Nazianzen and Nyssen, stood at the head of the Consubstantialists in the East, we find them among Origen's warmest admirers, defending him from the occasional claims of the Arians. This sketch, though brief, is a pretty full account of the treatment his name experienced in the Arian dispute, till A. D. 360, and indeed till several years later.

IX. On certain other subjects, however, not immediately connected with the main controversy, he was once attacked, during this period, with a very angry spirit, by Eustathius, an eminent orthodox bishop of the East.   This prelate had been translated from the bishopric of Berœa, the modern Aleppo, to the great see of Antioch, about the time of the Nicene council ;

[22] Neander Allgem. Geschichte der Christl. Ral. und Kirche, Band ii. s. 609.   He quotes Eusebius contra Marcell. Lib. ii. cap. 2 and 4 ; which I have not seen.

[23] Hieronymi Epist. lxxiv. ad Augustin. Tom. iv. Part. ii. p. 627 ; and Epist. xxxvi. ad Vigilant. p. 276.

but in A. D. 330, he was deposed by an Arian faction, and, as we have observed, his archbishopric was offered, though in vain, to Eusebius Pamphilus, who had concurred with his adversaries. Whether it was after this deposition, that Eustathius made his attack upon Origen, cannot be determined ; nor whether it was his motive to mortify his hated rival of Cesarea, by bringing a general odium on the favorite father, whom that learned historian had so highly extolled. But he published, at what time is unknown,[24] a treatise against Origen, in which he assailed him with much asperity, and foolishly charged him with lying against the Scriptures, and with endeavoring to introduce idolatry and magic into the church. The professed object of his book was, like that of the *Pythoness* of Methodius, to prove that it was not the soul of the prophet Samuel, that the Witch of Endor raised, as Origen had somewhere asserted, but only a phantom, produced by the imposture of the devil. He frequently takes occasion, however, to rail against several other notions of Origen, particularly against his views of the resurrection, and his extravagant allegories. Of the latter he recites and misrepresents numerous instances, with the manifest design to expose his doctrine in the worst possible light ; but in all this learned bishop's reproaches, which fell even upon Origen's style of writing, Universalism, it seems, escaped with impunity.[25] And what is equally re-

[24.] There is much uncertainty in the history of Eustathius. Some think he died about A. D. 337 ; others, that he lived till about A. D. 360. See Cave, Hist. Literaria, and Du Pin's Bibliotheca Patr. Art. Eustathius.

[25.] Eustath. de Engrastrimytho, adverses Origenem. I have not

markable, this was likewise the case amidst all the clamor of the Arian controversy, so far as we have just surveyed it.

The next attack upon him was that of Apollinarius the Younger, a learned bishop and distinguished writer of Laodicea in Phrygia, who was afterwards condemned for Sabellianism. He is said to have written against Origen, not far, probably, from A. D. 360 ; but on what points is unknown, except that it was not on the doctrine of the trinity.[26] This completes[27] the account of censures on his sentiments, till we arrive at the year 376, when the attack of Epiphanius will come under our notice.

X. Such was the general character of the proceedings relative to Origen and his sentiments, and such the peculiar circumstances and facts we have narrated, as to show, satisfactorily, that the doctrine of Universal Restoration was regarded, in the church, as neither heretical nor even unpopular ; and that the standard of orthodoxy, so far as it concerned that particular

been able to find this book, and have therefore drawn my account from the notices of it scattered through Huetii Origeniana, and from Du Pin's abstract, Biblioth. Patr. Art. Eustathius.

[26.] Theophili Alexandrini Paschal. Lib. i. inter Hieronymi Opera, Tom. iv. p. 694, Edit. Martianay. And Socratis Hist. Eccl. Lib. vi. cap. 13. [27.] Cave mistakes when he says, in his Life of Origen, § 29, (Lives of the Fathers) that Athanasius indirectly condemned his notion of the end of hell-torments ; for the piece to which he refers (Testimonia ex Sac. Script. de Nat. Commun. simil. Essent. inter Pat. et Fil. et Spirit. Sanct.) is not Athanasius's, but a much later author's. See Cave, Hist. Literaria, and Du Pin's Biblioth. Pat. Art. Athanasius, and the Benedictine Editors' Preface to that piece in Athanasii Opera, Tom. ii. p. 3.

If Huet (Origeniana, Lib. ii. cap. 4, Sect. i. § 5,) alluded, as I think he did, to Vitæ Sancti Antonii cap. 75, for Athanasius's covert censure of Origen's notion of the lapse of souls, he also mistook ; for the passage regards only the notions of heathens on that point, not Origen's.

point, was then supposed to require only a belief in future punishment. Still, we must not thence conclude that the fathers of this age were, in general, decided Universalists. Many of them had, probably, no definite opinion at all upon a subject which had never undergone the ordeal of controversy ; and several would seem to have believed in endless misery. This will be sufficiently apparent, if we select some of the strongest expressions which the more distinguished of them used respecting the fate of the damned. Every body knows that the first, in influence, A. D. 347, among the orthodox at this time, was to 370. Athanasius : " Repent," says he, " lest " at any time your soul should be snatch- " ed away by death ; for none can deliver those who, " on account of their sins, are confined in hell. "[28] Yet the same author held that Christ descended to hell, or the place of the dead, after his crucifixion, and released the saints of the old dispensation, and likewise the souls of such Gentiles as had, before his coming, lived virtuously according to the light of nature.[29] This, too, was the opinion of Cyrill,[30] bishop of Jerusalem ; whom we might also pronounce a believer in endless misery, if his frequent application of the word *everlasting* to punishment, were proof. At the future coming of Christ to the general Judgement, then just at hand, and which is described, he thinks, in the last chapter of Daniel, and in the twenty fourth and twenty fifth of St. Matthew, the just were to be admitted to

28. Athanasii Exposit. in Psalm. xlix. Tom. i. p. 1086. Edit. Paris. 1698.   29. Du Pin's Biblioth. Pat. Art. Athanasius.   30. Cyrilli Hierosolymit. Catechesis iv. cap. 8 ; and Catechesis Mystagogica v.

eternal life, and the wicked consigned to everlasting fire.[31] We may venture, nevertheless, to assert that neither of those two bishops regarded Universalism with any antipathy. Ephraim the Syrian, a gloomy, rigid, and somewhat fanatical monk of Mesopotamia, but still a very eminent writer, asserted that " there is " no confession in hell ; no tears, no groans, can there " avert the sentence of the Judge. There will, no " longer, be any time to repent. There is no return " after death ; but every thing terrible and severe falls " on those who have lost the opportunity for repen- " tance. "[32] In the western church, the celebrated Hilary, bishop of Poictiers, taught, with a slight variation from what Lactantius had advanced, that in the general judgement, neither the pious nor the infidels are to be arraigned ; because Christ had said, *He that believeth on me shall not be judged*, and, *He that believeth not, is condemned already.* The judgement, accordingly, shall be for those only who hold a middle grade between these two characters.[33] And such, he probably held, would be saved, after suffering the arrears due them from justice ; while the case of the obstinate infidels would be utterly hopeless. But still it was his opinion that all mankind, even the very holiest, must pass through the intense and painful fire of the general conflagration : the Virgin Mary herself cannot be exempted from this terrible purification ; for Simeon had forewarned her, that *a sword should pierce her own soul also.* (Luke ii. 35.)[34] As Hilary

---

[31] Catechesis, xv.   [32] Ephræm Syri Lib. De Extremo Judicio cap. 4.   [33] Hilarii Enarratio in Psalm. i.   [34] Enarratio in Psalm. cxviii. liter, Gimel.

had been an exile in Phrygia, he may have obtained some of these notions among the eastern Christians ; and perhaps from Origen's works in particular, which he certainly admired and imitated.

XI. Another writer among the ortho-
A. D. 350, dox of the West, Fabius Marius Vic-
to 370. torinus, uses language which seems to express the ultimate purification and holiness of all intelligent natures ; yet, as he introduces it but incidentally, and in a very blind illustration of the divinity of Christ, we ought not, perhaps, to rely on it as absolute proof of his views on the former point. We despair of giving any intelligible translation of his argument, in its relation to the trinity. In it, however, he contends that Christ, or the Logos, who is the active power of God, created all things, and will regenerate all things. By the life that is in him, and which is universally diffused, all things will be purged, and return into eternal life. He is to subject all things to himself, whether men, or principalities, or powers, in order that God may become all in all. When this shall have been accomplished, God will be all things ; because all things will be full of God. All things, adds he, will still exist ; but God will exist in them.[35] Such is the tenor of his representations on this subject. It is worthy of remark that, in a poem, he applies the epithet *œternus*, or *everlasting*, to the fire of future punishment.[36]

---

[35] F. Marii Victorini Afri Adv. Arium, Lib. i. et iii. I find the work in a collection of tracts of the ancient fathers, entitled Antidotum contra diversas omnium fere Saculorum Hœreses. Basil 1528. see pp. 52, 63, 64. [36] Ut Supra, De Machabœis, p. 81, &c.

Victorinus was an African by birth, but became a distinguished pagan rhetorician at Rome, where he was so much admired, that a statue was erected to him in one of the public places of the city. After he had taught, there, many years, and had grown old, he was converted to Christianity, about A. D. 350. He wrote several works, chiefly in defence of trinitarianism, and against the Manicheans ; and died about the year 370.[37]

XII. There were, at this time, some decided Universalists among the orthodox bishops and writers, especially of the

A. D. 360, to 370.

East. About forty miles east of the river Jordan, beyond the hilly tract of the ancient Perea, the traveller descends upon a spacious, barren plain, where. vestiges of forgotten towns appear, here and there, and a few sunken reservoirs still supply the wandering hordes, and the regular caravans, with water preserved from the winter torrents. Traversing this neglected waste to the distance of a dozen or fifteen miles still eastward, he arrives at the ruins of an ancient city, near the borders of the Desert Arabia. Fragments of the old walls, remains of a splendid temple, of triumphal arches, of a church and monastery, and of a great mosque, together with numberless pillars broken and lying among rose-trees in bloom, indicate the site of the ancient Bostra.[38] In the fourth century it was a populous city, the capital of a small province to which the vanity of the Roman conquer-

[37.] For the account of his life, see Du Pin's Bib: Pat. Art. Victorinus of Africk. Murdock's Mosheim, vol. i. p. 309. [38.] D'Anville's Ancient Geography, vol. i. p. 425 ; and Burckhardt's Travels in Syria and the Holy Land, pp. 226—236. London 1822.

ors had arrogantly appropriated the name of Arabia. At the period of which we write, Titus, a bishop of considerable eminence, presided here, over the churches in this district, and numbered, among his own Christian flock, half of the inhabitants of the city. Though he appears to have published several works, none remains, except part of his books *Against the Manicheans*, written, it is thought, about A. D. 364. He says that the "abyss of hell is, indeed, the place "of torment ; but it is not eternal, nor did it exist in "the original constitution of nature. It was made "afterwards, as a remedy for sinners, that it might "cure them. And the punishments are holy, as they "are remedial and salutary in their effect on trans- "gressors ; for they are inflicted, not to preserve them "in their wickedness, but to make them cease from "their wickedness. The anguish of their suffering "compels them to break off their vices."[39] His treatment of this point, after passing unreproached through all the contests of antiquity, has, in modern ages, attracted the notice of our ecclesiastical critics, and engaged them in the contrary attempts of expos- ing, and of exculpating, the author,[40] It is remarka- ble that he contended that death, as well as every

---

[39] Titi Bostriensis Contra Manichæos Lib. i. p. 85. N. B. This work is published only in Canisii Lector, and in the great Biblio- theca Patrum, to neither of which I have access. I therefore quote from Ceilleir's Histoire des Auteurs Sacres et Ecclesias- tiques, Tom. vi. chap. 6, p. 54.

[40] Tillemont, though a most strenuous defender of the fathers, is candid enough to acknowledge (Memoires Eccl. Tom. vi. p. 671,) that " Titus seems to have followed the dangerous error as- " cribed to Origen, that the pains of the damned, and even those " of the demons themselves, will not be eternal." But Ceilleir has the hardihood to plead that the passage is not clear, &c.

other dispensation of providence, was designed for the benefit both of the just, and of the unjust ;[41] and that he maintained, against the Manicheans, that, even in this world, mankind are happy or miserable, according to their virtue or vice. With the doctrine of original sin, he seems to have been utterly unacquainted ; and he supposed that human agency was fully adequate, without any supernatural control, to do good as well as evil.[42]

Of the events of his life, we know little more than that, like most of the distinguished orthodox bishops of this time, he was honored with the notice and the persecution of the emperor Julian. In the year 362, this zealous apostate endeavored to excite the people of Bostra to expel their bishop ; but the influence of the prelate seems to have prevailed over the exhortation of the sovereign, and the malicious attempt proved ineffectual. On the accession of Jovian to the empire, A. D. 363, Titus attended the council of Antioch under Meletius ; and, though his name appears, with those of some other orthodox bishops, among the subscriptions to a Semi-Arian explanation of the Nicene Creed,[43] he nevertheless seems to have been considered one of the Athanasian party. He died, it is thought, about A. D. 370.

XIII. More learned and classical than A. D. 370. Athanasius, and next to him in weight of authority among the orthodox of the East, was Basil the Great, bishop of Cesarea in Cappadocia.

[41.] Contra Manich. Lib. ii. p. 107, 112. See the quotations in Ceilleir, p. 51.   [42.] Du Pin's Bibliotheca Pat. Art. Titus of Bostra.
[43.] Socratis Hist. Eccl. Lib. iii. cap. 21.

With a constitution naturally feeble, and broken more-over by monkish austerities, he possessed a strong mind, a courageous resolution, a temper active, but too ambitious, and an eloquence of a manly and noble kind. Of his views respecting the doctrine under consideration, we cannot pronounce with confidence, as his language is not uniform, nor always reconcileable. He repeatedly states, at considerable length, that those who, after baptism, indulge in sins, however heinous, and die under the guilt of them, are to be purified in the fire of the general judgement ;[44] distinguishing them, however, from such as have never professed Christianity. Yet, at another time, while admonishing one of those very characters, he conceals that notion, and for the sake, perhaps, of striking the greater terror, asserts that their future torments " will have no end, " and that " there is no release, no way to flee from " them, after death. Now is the time in which we " are allowed to escape them. "[45] On the contrary, again, he sometimes represents the purifying and salutary operation of future fire or punishment as extending, without distinction, to guilty souls in general : Commenting on these words of Isaiah, (ix. 19, Septuagint version) *because of the wrath of the Lord, the whole earth is kindled into flame, and the people shall be as though they were burnt up with fire*, Basil says, " the prophet declares that, for the benefit of the soul, " the earthly things are to be consumed by penal fire ; " even as Christ himself intimates, saying, *I have come*

---

[44] Basilii Comment. in Cap. iv. 4, Esaiæ, and cap. xi. 16, &c. Edit. Paris. 1637.   [45] Basilii Epist. ad Virginem lapsam, Tom. iii. p. 18.

14*

" *to send fire upon the earth ; what would I, except* " *that it be kindled ?* " (Luke xii. 49.) And the prophet adds, " *the people shall be as though they* " *were burnt up with fire :* he does not threaten an " absolute extermination, but intimates a purification, " according to the sentiment of the apostle, that *if* " *any one's work be burned, he shall suffer loss, but* " *he himself shall be saved, yet so as by fire.* " (1 Cor. iii. 15.)[46] From this solitary passage we can only suspect that our author was, at times, inclined to Universalism.

His own brother, the bishop of Nyssa, was a Universalist ; and his most intimate friend, Gregory Nazianzen, may in some degree merit that appellation. Like them, Basil was also a professed admirer of Origen's writings ; and with the assistance of the latter, he selected from them and published a volume of choice extracts, consisting of such passages as the two friends most highly valued. It is a gratification to light on circumstances that seem to connect the writers of this age with earlier fathers, to whose acquaintance we have been introduced at a former period. Basil was brought up in the metropolis of Cappadocia, and perhaps in the very church where Firmilian presided, a century before. His grandmother, Macrina, under whom he received his juve-

---

[46.] Basilii Comment. in Cap. ix. 19, Esaiæ. If the Regulæ Breviores be Basil's, he there (Interrog. 267,) labored to reconcile the absolute eternity of punishment with the fact that some shall be beaten with many stripes, and others with few. But this piece has been ascribed to Eustathius of Sebastea, (See Du Pin's Bibliotheca Pat. Art. Basil,) a cotemporary with Basil. Whoever the author was, he certainly meant to be considered a believer in strictly endless misery.

nile education and his first impressions of piety, had been, in her youth, a hearer of Gregory Thaumaturgus, in Pontus ; for whom she inspired her young scholar with a profound and lasting veneration. He himself, in middle life, spent some time, as a monk, in the solitudes adjacent to the ancient residence of the famous Wonderworker ; and soon afterwards, on his return to Cappadocia in the year 370, he was ordained over the same bishopric which Firmilian had once governed.

In his general system of doctrine, there was nothing that can have struck his cotemporaries as very peculiar. Though addicted to the allegorical mode of interpreting the Scriptures, he was quite moderate in this respect, compared with some others of that age. It is worthy of remark, that he approached nearer to the notion of original and total depravity, than had any of the earlier fathers ; though he still fell short of the modern standard, and was what we should now call an Arminian.

In early life he travelled extensively, studying at Cesarea in Palestine, at Constantinople, at Athens, and finally in the monasteries of Egypt. Here he was initiated into the monastic life ; for which, like most of his cotemporaries, he always maintained a zealous attachment. Like them, too, he formed his views of practical religion, by the false standard of that perverse and fanatical discipline.

XIV. That class of devotees, to which A. D. 370, we have once or twice alluded, the monks, to 376. had now become numerous in many parts of the East, where their unnatural mode life began to be held in general veneration, and to be patronised by nearly all the bishops and doctors. Athanasius, Basil, Ephraim the Syrian, the two Gregories, Epiphanius, and others, were its strenuous advocates. It had been very lately introduced, with great success, into the desert parts of Palestine, Syria, Pontus, and Mespotamia ; but to Egypt belonged the glory, or more truly the dishonor, both of its origin, and of its rapid growth to maturity. A century before the present period, one or two individuals fled from the heathen persecutions into the frightful wastes that border the long, narrow tract of vegetation watered by the Nile. Habit and a mistaken devotion gave them a relish, at length, for what necessity had thus forced upon them ; and they continued to follow, from choice, a kind of life more suited to the reptiles, their associates, than to human beings. Their example, so congenial with the absurd notions of the times, drew many after them. Multitudes succeeded multitudes ; till the number of monks, in that country alone, had now increased to tens of thousands, all governed by established rules, and forming an institution which was thought the brightest ornament of the church.

Among them we discover that, about this time, a considerable body had become distinguished by an appellation which seems to have been but newly introduced ; that of *Origenists*.[47] These were, of course, certain followers of Origen. The name, however, of every indefinite application probably at first, did by no means extend to all his admirers, nor

---

[47.] Epiphanii Panarium, Hæres. lxiv. § 3. This is the earliest passage in which I have found that appellation.

even to all his imitators; for though the celebrated fathers, Gregory Nyssen, Didymus and Jerome, were known to be of the latter class, it does not appear that they were considered, till after many years, as belonging to the particular party under consideration.[48] What distinguished the Origenists properly so called, from other avowed disciples of their master, cannot be ascertained, perhaps it was some special combination among themselves for party purposes, or a more clamorous zeal in urging their designations. That they were, in some sense, a specific party, appears from the circumstance of their sectarian denomination; but it should be remarked, that they were as yet in the full fellowship of the orthodox communion, and that they seem to have been scattered among the churches, as well as monasteries, in various parts of Egypt.

There was one celebrated retreat, however, where they particularly abounded. About fifty miles south of Alexandria, beyond the lake Mareotis and a long extent of burning sands succeeded by plains heaped with pebbles, rose the bare and sun-burnt hills of Nitria, amidst a boundless prospect of desolation.[49] It was in the borders of the great Lybian Desert. Around these hills the monks had gathered into a vast community, the most famous, perhaps, and with the exception of that at Oxyrinchus, the most numerous,

[48] In proof of this, among many other facts, is that of Jerome's contention with some Origenists at Rome, about A. D. 382, and his forsaking Nitria, in A. D. 386, out of dislike to them; though he himself was, at this time, a devout admirer of Origen's works.

[49] Sonnini's Travels in Egypt, chap. 26 and 27. The desert of Nitria is about 35 miles west of Terane, a village on the Nile.

of all they had yet formed. This was the principal seat of the Origenists. They appear to have constituted the smaller part of five or six thousand recluses.[50] As strangers resorted hither, even from distant countries, in order to acquire the monastic discipline and precepts in their perfection, many attached themselves to the new sect; and travelling afterwards through different parts of christendom, they propagated their views and partialities wherever they went. Few years later, we shall find some, though perhaps not all, of them to have been Universalists.

XV. The Origenists, as a party, were A. D. 376. attacked by Epiphanius, bishop of Salamis on the island of Cyprus. He was a man of much reading, but very careless, inaccurate, and notoriously disposed to adopt every slanderous report against those whom he disliked. In a large work, designed to confute all the heresies that had ever appeared, he devotes one of the longest articles, of thirty or forty folio pages, to the errors of Origen Adamantius and his party.[51] Having given an account of his life, in some points false and injurious, he says, "As to the heresy of Origen, it was first "propagated in Egypt; and at this day it flourishes "chiefly among those who profess the monastic life. "It is a pestiferous heresy, exceeding in wickedness "all former ones, the errors of which it indeed em- "braces. For though it is attended with no appear-

[50.] For the number of monks at Nitria, see Fleury's Eccl. Hist. Book xvi. chap. 36.   [51.] The Origeniani, whom Epiphanius describes in Hæres. lxiii. are suspected to have been creatures of his imagination. See Lardner's Credibility, &c. chap. *Noetus, and others called Heretics, &c.*

"ance of vice among its votaries, it teaches the
"most absurd notion concerning God. From this
"fountain it was, that Arius and his sectaries derived
"their errors. Origen proceeded to such an extent
"of temerity, as to assert that the only begotten Son
"cannot behold the Father, nor the Holy Ghost see
"the Son, nor angels the Holy Ghost, nor man the
"Angels. This was his first error: For he held the
"Son to be of the substance of the Father in such a
"way as that he was nevertheless created. He held
"still more heinous errors; for he taught that the
"souls of men existed before their bodies, and were
"angels or superior powers, who have been consigned,
"on account of their sins, to these mortal frames, for
"the purpose of punishment. We could mention
"ever so many of his notions: that, for instance,
"which he entertained, that Adam lost the divine
"image by transgression. Hence it is, says Origen,
"that the Scripture mentions the coats of skins with
"which God clothed our first parents: which coats
"he takes to be their bodies. There are, indeed, an
"infinite number of dogmas advanced by him, worthy
"of ridicule and laughter. He even represented the
"resurrection in an imperfect and defective manner,
"partly asserting it in appearance, and partly deny-
"ing it in reality. In other words, he supposed that
"only a part of man is to be raised. And finally, he
"turned whatever he could into allegories: such as
"Eden or Paradise, and its waters; and the waters
"which are above the firmament, and those which are
"under the earth," &c.[52] Epiphanius then proceeds

[52.] Epiphanii Panarium, Hæres. lxiv. § 4. This passage, which

to treat, at considerable length, on his views of the trinity and the resurrection, inserting nearly all the treatise of Methodius on the latter subject ; after which, he returns to inveigh once more against his notions of the coats of skins, of pre-existence, and of the resurrection, calling him "an infidel, and worse than an infidel." It is remarkable that, like all the former opposers of Origen, he too passes over the doctrine of Universalism in silence ; though we discover that he, himself, at the same time, believed that there is no change of condition, nor room for repentance, after death.[53] This attack, though professedly against the Origenists, was directed more particularly against their master himself. It seems to have been the last he suffered, till the famous contest that arose at the end of this century, in which Epiphanius will again appear, as a principal actor.

XVI. We have already advanced into A. D. 370, a period that forms a distinguished era in to 383. our history. Universalism appears to have been, for awhile, the sentiment of a majority of the most eminent orthodox fathers in the East. Gregory Nyssen, Didymus, Jerome and Diodorus of Tarsus, were its advocates; and the celebrated Gregory Nazianzen, who was elevated, at length, to the bishopric of Constantinople, hesitated between this doctrine and that of endless misery. His readiness in expounding the Nicene faith, acquired for him the appellation of *The Theologian;* and of

I have compressed a little, contains about every point that Epiphanius censures throughout the whole article. This part of his work is supposed to have been written in A. D. 376. See Lardner's Credibility, &c. chap. Epiphanius.   53. Ditto. Hæres, lix.

all the fathers, except Chrysostom, he is the most renowned for a brilliant and glowing eloquence. His works are, of course, declamatory and exhortative, rather than doctrinal; but he has still left sufficient proofs of the unsettled state of his opinion. Sometimes he represented future misery as a dispensation of mere torment, opposed to all corrective suffering; and asserted that in hell, or the place of the dead, there can be no confession nor reformation.[54] But, at other times, he thought it probable that those torments would be directed to the salvation of the sufferers; "I have mentioned," says he, "the purifying fire "which Christ came to kindle upon earth; who is "himself figuratively called *fire*. It is the nature of "this fire to consume the grosser matter, or vicious "character, of the mind. But there is also another "sort of fire, not of purgation, but intended for a "vindictive punishment of wickedness: whether it be "that of Sodom, which, mixed with sulphur and "storm, God pours upon all sinners; or that which is "prepared for the devil and his angels; or even that "which proceeds before the face of the Lord; or "lastly, that more formidable than all, which is con- "nected with the unsleeping worm, and is never extin- "guished, but is continual and everlasting, for the "punishment of wicked men. It is the nature of all "these to ruin, to destroy; unless, however, one may "suppose that the fire, in this case also, is to be "understood more moderately, and as is worthy, "indeed, of the God who punishes."[55] In another

[54.] Gregorii Nazianzeni Oratio Decimaquinta, p. 229, Tom. i. Edit. Paris. 1630. [55.] Greg. Nazianz. Oratio xl. pp. 664, 665. Tom. i.

15

passage, speaking of the Novatians, an heretical sect, he says, "perhaps they will be baptized, in the next "world, with fire, which is the last baptism, and is "not only keen, but of great duration, and which "shall feed on the dull matter, as on hay, till it shall "have consumed all their sins." [56]   Such is the indecision of Gregory upon this subject, that it is of little consequence to mention his repeated application of the word *everlasting* to future punishment.

XVII. It has been said, by one of the best critics[57] on ecclesiastical history, that of all the fathers of the fourth century, there was not a more moderate nor worthier man, than Gregory Nazianzen. Uniting a quick and deep sensibility with a lofty imagination, he was too contemplative, too fond of retirement, to engage willingly in the perpetual contentions of his age, or even to relish the tumults of a public life. He condemned the captiousness of the zealous bigots upon doctrinal points ; though one would suppose that he himself was, in this respect, fastidious enough. The clergy of that day, he boldly, and it appears justly, represented as a body of men avaricious, quarrelsome, licentious, and, in one word, unprincipled ; and of the frequent councils, which then disturbed the peace of the church, he declared that he was afraid of them, because he had never seen the end of one that was happy and pleasant, or that did not rather increase than diminish the evil.[58]   Nothing can more strikingly evince the universal intolerance of

---

[56]. Ditto, Oratio xxxix. p. 636, Tom. i.   [57]. Le Clerc. See Jortin's Remarks on Eccl. Hist. vol. iv. p. 95. London, 1773.
[58]. Greg. Nazianz. Epist. lv.

the age, than that one of its most pacific men approved, and sometimes urged, the persecution of heretics, and openly lamented that the apostate emperor Julian had not been put to death by his predecessor.

His intimacy with Basil the Great, began in early life, amidst the schools of Athens. Having already studied both in Palestine, and at Alexandria, Gregory repaired to this seat of Grecian literature about the year 344; and was, not long afterwards, joined by his young companion. Here they became acquainted with Julian, the future emperor, then a youth like themselves. Gregory at length returned home to Nazianzum, a small city in the south-western part of Cappadocia, of which his father was bishop. But when Basil, on his return from the monasteries of Egypt, retired to a ·solitude in Pontus, he followed him to that retreat, assisted him in establishing the monastic institutions there, and, as it seems, remained awhile after his friend had engaged in a more public and distinguished sphere. The latter was ordained bishop of Cappadocia, in A. D. 370; and wishing to pre-occupy, against the attempts of a rival, the small and obscure village of Sasima, on the confines of his jurisdiction, he recalled Gregory from his retirement, and appointed him bishop of the contested place. Gregory resented this heartless conduct in his friend; and, refusing to accept the unworthy appointment, took up his residence again at Nazianzum, assisting his aged father in the care of the church. After the death of his venerable parent, he went to Seleucia, and thence, at the urgent request of the bishops, to Constantinople, where he arrived about A. D. 378.

He found the city full of Arians, who occupied all the churches; the orthodox few, dispirited, and destitute of a place for public worship. After preaching awhile in private houses, his eloquence and austere life drew into his flock a number sufficiently large to erect a spacious church, which they called *The Anastasia*, or Resurrection, to intimate the revival of the Consubstantial faith. The attention of the whole city was roused: the triumphant orthodox, the heretics of all kinds, and even the heathens, crowded in a mingled mass to the Anastasia, to feast on his doctrine, or to admire the enchantment of his eloquence; and such was the pressure of the throng, as sometimes to crush down the railing which enclosed the pulpit.

In the midst of his success, however, he was deeply wounded by the ingratitude of an unprincipled but sanctimonious wretch, whom he had cherished. This impostor, named Maximus, formed a faction among the orthodox themselves, at Alexandria and other places, to usurp the bishopric of Constantinople; came with his partisans, and forcibly entered Gregory's own church; and, when driven out by the alarmed multitude, appealed, though in vain, to the emperor Theodosius. He finally succeeded, however, in prevailing on the Italian bishops to countenance his project; and he found too many among the eastern clergy, who, out of envy, favored his cause. Few men, perhaps, were less fitted than Gregory, to act amidst such circumstances. Though bold, vehement and resolute when surrounded by avowed enemies to his faith, opposition from his own party withered his heart, and sickened him of life. He sought to retire from Constantinople to solitude. But the anxious entreaties of his people so far prevailed that he deferred his resolution ; and the new emperor Theodosius, making his first entry into Constantinople towards the end of the year 380, drove the Arians from all the churches in the city, banished their bishop, and introduced Gregory to the possession, and to the revenues, of their great or cathedral church.[59] This new state of things seemed to afford him a space of quiet; and in the General council which assembled the next year, at Constantinople, he was confirmed in his bishopric. Before the close of the session, however, or perhaps in another session held at the same place in A. D. 382, new difficulties broke out : Gregory's stern integrity gave offence to some, as it thwarted their intrigues ; and his popularity aroused the jealousy of others. Sinking under premature old age, wearied with contention, and disgusted with the vices of the bishops, he resolved, notwithstanding the bitter lamentations of his friends, to resign a post that continually exposed him to the abuse of clerical envy and ambition. In the great church of Constantinople, so lately wrested from the Arians, he ascended the pulpit for the last time, surrounded by the members of the General council, by his own beloved people, and by the wonted crowd. He repeated the history of his success in that city, described the doctrine he had preached, besought the bishops by forsaking their contentious practices, to

[59.] It stood on the spot now occupied by the great mosque of St. Sophia.

15*

heal the divisions of the church, and concluded by taking leave of public life and of the scenes of his labors.[60]   He retired immediately to Nazianzum, where he lived in obscurity and quiet, employing himself in devout exercises, and in poetic composition. He died about A. D. 389, aged not far from seventy years.   His plain determined integrity is worthy of all praise ; and the unblemished purity of his life and manners, though veiled under the shade of monastic gloom, commands our highest respect.   His eloquence, which has been absurdly compared to that of Demos-

[60.] "Farewell, Anastasia !" said he ; " thou that sawest our " doctrine raised up from its low despised estate ; dear seats of " our common victory, our new Siloam, where first the ark of our " God rested, after its hopeless wanderings in the desert.   Fare- " well, too, this great and august temple, where we meet ! our " new heritage ; thou that wast a Jebus before, now converted to " a Jerusalem.   And ye other sacred edifices also scattered over " the whole city and its suburbs, farewell ! the grace of God, and " not our feeble exertions, hath now filled you with the faithful. " Thou envied and dangerous pre-eminence, episcopal throne, " farewell.   Farewell, pontifical palace, venerable for thine age " and the majesty of the priesthood.   Farewell ye choirs of " Nazareans ! whose strains of psalmody I shall no more hear, " whose nocturnal celebrations of our Lord's resurrection, I shall " no more attend.   Ye holy virgins, ye widows and orphans, ye " eyes of the poor, turned alternately to heaven and towards the " preacher, farewell.   Farewell, ye hospitable domes, devoted to " Christ, which have so often assisted my infirmity.   Ye min- " gling throngs that crowded to my sermons, ye swift-handed " notaries, ye rails pressed by my greedy auditors, farewell. " Farewell, emperors and courts.   Farewell thou imperial city, " whose zeal, though not perhaps according to knowledge, I yet " will frankly testify.   May thy service of God be more sincere, " and thy fruits of righteousness more abundant.   Ye bishops of " the East and West, farewell ! why will not some of you imitate " this my resignation, and restore peace to the divided and con- " tentious church ?   I call you but to relinquish dignities upon " earth, for heavenly thrones, far safer, and more exalted.   Ye " angels, the guardians of this church, and of my presence and " wanderings, farewell.   Thou sacred Trinity ! my meditation " and my glory, O may I hear of the daily increase of this my " people, their growth in knowledge and grace.   And ye, my " people, for mine ye are, though another shall govern you,—my

thenes, was formed on the turgid style of the Asiatics, rather than on the severe simplicity of the Grecian; and it was therefore the better adapted to discourse on mysteries, and to excite the wonder of an ignorant populace.

The feebleness of a body, subdued by rigorous austerities, must have increased the sensibility of his temperament; and this, united with the generous and confiding character of his affections, exposed him to perpetual afflictions from the baseness and ingratitude of mankind. It is no wonder that to such a man, the difficult station, which he prudently resigned, was attended with a weight of cares insupportable. The church, however, has always held his memory dear; and his name still occupies a respectable place on the pages of ecclesiastical history.

Like Basil, he was moderately given to the allegorical method of exposition. We have already mentioned their mutual admiration of Origen's writings.

XVIII. But in this, he was perhaps surpassed by his friend, Gregory Nyssen, the brother of Basil the Great. This eminent father and bishop followed Origen's system in allegorizing the Scriptures, farther than most of his cotemporaries; though he, still avoided many of his extravagances, and rejected some of his notions.[61] The doctrine of Universal Salvation, however, he adopted and taught more frequently[62] than,

---

"little children, keep the faith I have delivered you, remember-"ing my labors and my sufferings." Greg. Nazianz. Oratio xxxii. fin. Tom. i. pp. 527, 528.

[61.] See Gregorii Nysseni Disputat. de Anima et Resurrect. pp. 264, 265, 269.—Lib. de Creatione Hominis cap. 29, p. 459, and cap. 30, p. 462.—De Hist. Sex Dierum, pp. 293, 294. Edit. Basil. 1562.

perhaps, any other early writer, whose works are extant.

Endeavoring to wrest from the Arians that expression of St. Paul, *Then shall the Son also be subject unto him who put all things under him,* (1 Cor. xv. 28,) and to make it appear consistent with trinitarianism, he takes occasion to explain the connexion at large, in order to point out what he supposes to be the Apostle's argument: " What therefore, " says he, " is " the scope of St. Paul's argument in this place ? " That the nature of evil shall, at length, be wholly

[62.] A plea, first advanced more than three hundred years after Gregory Nyssen's death to defend him from the imputation of Universalism, is sometimes repeated, though in a faltering manner, by modern critics. Germanus, bishop of Constantinople, who flourished about A. D. 730, contended, that in Gregory Nyssen's *Dialogue on the Soul*, in his great *Catechetical Oration*, and in his *Tract on the Perfect Life of a Christian*, all such passages as taught the restoration of the devils and of the damned, had either been corrupted or added by the Origenists; and for proof he referred to the connexions of the passages in question, and to the alleged fact that in other places Gregory had contradicted that sentiment. (See Photii Biblioth. Cod. 233.) Du Pin, who by the way misrepresents Germanus, manifestly desires to avail himself of this plea; but at the same time, betrays his want of confidence in it. (Bibliotheca Patrum, Art. Gregory Nyssen.) The truth is, it would be impossible to take Universalism out of Gregory Nyssen's works, without destroying some of his pieces, and rendering others unintelligible; and there is no reason to suspect that it was wrongfully inserted in the three books which Germanus names. That Gregory ever denies the doctrine in question, I have not discovered. The independent Daille (De Usu Patrum Lib. ii. cap. 4, *Latin edition*, for the English, and probably the French are incomplete) treats Germanus's supposition with merited contempt: " it is the last resort," says he, " of " those who with a stupid and absurd pertinacity, will have it, " that the ancients wrote nothing different from the faith at pres- " ent received; for the whole of Gregory Nyssen's Orations are " so deeply imbued with the pestiferous doctrine in question, that " it can have been inserted by none other than the author him- " self." Dr. T. Burnet also (De Statu Mort. et Resurg. p. 138. London, 1733,) pronounces the plea of Germanus vain. *See note 66 following.*

" exterminated, and divine, immortal goodness em-
" brace within itself every rational creature ; so that
" of all who were made by God, not one shall be ex-
" cluded from his kingdom.   All the viciousness, that
" like a corrupt matter is mingled in things, shall be
" dissolved and consumed in the furnace of purgatorial
" fire ; and every thing that had its origin from God,
" shall be restored to its pristine state of purity. "
The author proceeds to contend, in his abstruse and
mystical way, that the human nature which Christ
assumed, being so intimately connected with the common nature of man, that the Apostle here calls it " the
first fruits " of the human race ; the subjection of all
mankind to God may, by a figure, be called the subjection of Christ himself, the first fruits.   " When
" therefore the dominion of sin within us, shall be en-
" tirely overthrown, every thing must, of course, be
" subject to him who rules over all ; because there
" can be no opposing inclination in the universe.
" Now, subjection to God is perfect and absolute
" alienation from evil.   Wherefore, when we all shall
" be freed from sin, and perfectly assimilated to Christ,
" our first fruits, and made one uniform body with him,
" then what is called the subjection of Christ, is, in
" reality, accomplished in us ; and because we are his
" body, our subjection is attributed to him who effect-
" ed it in ourselves.   Such we think is the meaning of
" St. Paul in this passage : *For as in Adam all die,*
" *so also through Christ shall all be made alive ; but*
" *every one in his own order : Christ, the first fruits ;*
" *then they who are Christ's at his coming ; then*
" *cometh the end, when he shall have delivered up the*

" *kingdom to God even the Father, when he shall*
" *have abolished all dominion, and authority, and*
" *power. For he must reign till he hath put all ene-*
" *mies under his feet. The last enemy, death, shall*
" *be destroyed. For he hath put all things under his*
" *feet. But when he saith, All things are put under*
" *him, it is manifest that he is excepted who did put*
" *all things under him. And when all things shall*
" *be subjected to him, then shall the Son also himself*
" *be subjected to him who put all things under him ;*
" *that God may be all in all.* (1 Cor. xv. 22—28.)
" It is manifest that here the apostle declares the ex-
" tinction of all sin, saying, that God will be all in all.
" For God will be truly all in all only when no evil
" shall remain in the nature of things, as he is never
" engaged in evil, " &c.[63]

Gregory held different degrees of happiness in heav-
en, apportioned to the different merits which the blessed
had acquired upon earth ;[64] and different degrees of
future punishment, according to the various characters
of the sufferers : " I believe," said he, " that punishment
" will be administered in proportion to each one's cor-
" ruptness. For it would be unequal to torment with
" the same purgatorial pains, him who has long in-
" dulged in transgression, and him who has only fallen
" into a few common sins. But that grievous flame
" shall burn for a longer or shorter period, according
" to the kind and quantity of the matter that supports
" it. Therefore, to whom there is much corruption

[63] Tract. in Dictum Apostoli, *Tunc etiam ipse Filius subjicietur*,
&c. p. 137, and seqq. [64] Lib. De Infantibus quæ præmature abripiuntur.

" attached, with him it is necessary that the flame,
" which is to consume it, should be great, and of long
" duration ; but to him in whom the wicked disposi-
" tion has been already in part subjected, a propor-
" tional degree of that sharper and more vehement
" punishment shall be remitted. All evil, however,
" must, at length, be entirely removed from every
" thing, so that it shall no more exist. For such be-
" ing the nature of sin, that it cannot exist without a
" corrupt motive, it must, of course, be perfectly dis-
" solved and wholly destroyed, so that nothing can
" remain a receptacle of it, when all motive and influ-
" ence shall spring from God alone. " &c.[65]

In another place he asserts that as the devil ' as-
' sumed a fleshly shape in order to ruin human nature,
' so the Lord took flesh for the salvation of man ; and
' thus he blesses not only him who was ruined, but him
' also who led him into perdition ; so that he both de-
' livers man from sin, and heals the author of sin him-
' self. "[66]

Like the earlier Universalists, Gregory freely applied
the word *everlasting* to future punishment ; a circumstance which, probably, has betrayed some critics into
the hasty conclusion, that he sometimes denied the
doctrine of Universal Restotation, and asserted that of
endless misery. A remarkable use of that phrase occurs in a passage where he alludes to the ultimate fate

[65] Disputatio de Anima et Resurrectione, p. 260. [66] Oratio
Catechetica, cap. 26. I here subjoin the titles of those works in
which Gregory Nyssen teaches Universalism : De Anima et Resurrectione.—Oratio Catechetica.—De Infantibus qui præmature
abripiuntur.—Oratio de Mortuis.—In dictum Apostoli, *Tunc ipse
Filius subjicietur Patri.*—De Perfectione Christiani.

of such as have become confirmed in debauchery :
" whoever, " says he, " considers the divine power,
" will plainly perceive that it is able, at length, to re-
" store, by means of the *everlasting* purgation and ex-
" piatory sufferings, those who have gone even to this
" extremity of wickedness. "[67]

XIX. His general system of doctrine, it is unnecessary to state at large, since it was the same that distinguished the orthodox of his age. A few particulars,
however, may be specified : The opinion, universally
received by the Christians of this century, that regeneration was experienced only in the rite of water baptism, was, of course, entertained by Gregory ; and
with them he agreed, that it was effected by the exertions of the human will, aided by the proffered assistance of the divine spirit. Predestination and irresistible grace, in their modern sense, were as yet unknown
in the church. In one or two respects, our author
was an honorable exception to the prevalent superstition of his cotemporaries : he dissuaded from the growing practice of pilgrimages to shrines and holy places ;
and, though a patron of the monastic life, he defended
the excellence of matrimony, both by precept and example ; being himself one of the few married bishops
of that age.

He has left one production, his *Life of Gregory
Thaumaturgus*, which involves him, as an author, in
the charge, either of unbounded credulity, or of total
disregard of historical truth. It is a worthless legend,
enlivened only with fictitious miracles the most foolish,

[67.] De Infantibus qui præmature abripiunter, p. 178.

and with disgusting tales the most incredible. That he even presumed to lay it before the world, is a sufficient indication of the universal stupidity, and of the thorough corruption of the public taste. Could illustrious precedent, however, exonerate from the criminality of falsehood or disingenuous fiction, he might justly plead that of the great Athanasius, who appears to have set the first example of these monkish romances, by his *Life of Anthony;* and three or four productions, of the same character, which soon afterwards appeared under the honored names of Jerome and Sulpitius Severus, have contributed much to relieve Gregory from the disgrace of solitary folly. The rest of our author's works are composed in a style dry, involved and obscure ; and they abound in absurd allegories and abstruse mysticism. In learning, he was second to few of his day ; in influence, he stood among the first in the orthodox party. It is remarkable that he has never been condemned for his Universalism ; and that he was never even censured for it, till two or three centuries after his death.

In his youth he was so strongly inclined to a literary life, that it was with much difficulty he was persuaded to abandon his favorite study of rhetoric, in order to take upon himself the duties of the ministry. About A. D. 371, when not far from thirty-two years old, he was ordained bishop of Nyssa, a small city in the western part of Cappadocia. Valens, the Arian emperor, being then on the throne of Constantinople, drove several orthodox bishops into exile ; and in the year 374, procured, by the means of his lieutenant Demosthenes, the expulsion of Gregory from his

16

church. But, after four years of absence, he was recalled, with the rest of the banished bishops, on the accession of Theodosius the Great, and permanently established in his office. Soon afterwards, either the council of Antioch, or that of Constantinople appointed him to visit, with other delegates, the churches of Pontus and those of Arabia, in order to revive among them the orthodox faith and discipline ; and the new emperor honored him, in the prosecution of this duty, with a public conveyance. It appears that some time after his return, he was called to Constantinople, on the death of the empress Placilla, in A. D. 385, to pronounce her funeral oration. He died at Nyssa, about the year 394, aged nearly sixty.

XX. We have somewhat delayed the introduction of an eminent Universalist who flourished, at this period, among the orthodox in Egypt, and whose renown for profane and sacred learning filled all the East. Didymus, *the blind*, of Alexandria, though much older than Basil or either of the Gregories, seems not to have acquired his extensive reputation, till their fame also had spread through the church. Deprived forever of his eye-sight when only five years old, he nevertheless succeeded in making himself master of grammar, rhetoric, logic, music, arithmetic, and even the most difficult parts of the mathematics ; and his knowledge of divinity was so highly esteemed, that he was elected President of the great Catechetical School in his native city. He was a professed admirer of Origen, whom he considered as his master, and whose books *Of Principles* he illustrated with brief *Commentaries*, defending them against the misconstructions of the Arians.

That he was a Universalist, the uncontradicted testimony of cotemporary and succeeding writers,[68] is, perhaps, sufficient evidence; but his condemnation, as such, by the General council of Constantinople, more than a century and a half after his death, confirms the fact, and at the same time proves that, with the doctrine of the Restoration, he also held that of the Preexistence of souls.[69] That posthumous sentence of excommunication, however, by consigning his heretical works to destruction, has denied us the satisfaction of adducing his own language; but even in the few of his writings that still remain, we find some traces of the obnoxious doctrine, which were probably overlooked by the ancient censors. He says that " as man-" kind, by being reclaimed from their sins, are to be " subjected to Christ in the fulness of the dispensation " instituted for the salvation of all, so the superior ra-" tional intelligences, the angels, will be reduced to " obedience by the correction of their vices. "[70] It is said that he also disapproves of all servile fear.[71]

Though not reckoned among the Origenists of his time, Didymus was undoubtedly regarded by them, and justly too, as their chief patron. We can hardly

---

[68] Jerome and Rufinus allude to it, as a well known fact. Cyrillus Scythopolitanus, (Vitæ S. P. Sabæ cap. 90. inter Cotelerii Mon. Eccl. Græcæ Tom. iii.) a writer of the sixth century, is the next whom I recollect. [69] Cyrill. Scythopolit. Vit. S. P. Sabæ cap. 90. [70] Didymi Comment. in 1 Pet. iii. I have not access to this work, which is to be found only in the great Bibliotheca Patrum; and I therefore quote from Huetii Origenian. Lib. ii. cap. 2. Quæst. iii. § 26. [71] Du Pin's Biblioth. Pat. Art. Didymus. He refers to the above-named work.

suppose that their own character was so perverse as it was afterwards represented, when we consider the favor manifestly shown them by a Christian scholar of his apparent good sense, and, what was yet more rare, invariable candor.   He was a voluminous writer ; but only two or three of his works, his treatise *On the Holy Ghost,* his *Commentaries on the Canonical Epistles,* and a fragment of his book *Against the Manicheans,*[72] have survived the waste of time, and the exterminating decrees of later ages.   During his life, however, he was accounted a distinguished champion of the orthodoxy of that period ; and he died peacefully in the general communion, honored and esteemed by the church.   Like most of his cotemporaries, he engaged heartily in support of the monastic institution ; and his renown, and his influential station as president of the first school in christendom, enabled him to exert his zeal with much effect.   In the list of scholars, who, at various times, studied under him, appear the names of Jerome, Rufinus, Palladius and Isidorus.   He died probably in the year 394, aged about ninety.[73]

XXI. Could learning, talents, and immortal renown, when dissociated from sound integrity and the mild spirit of the gospel, confer honor on any doctrine, Universalism might exult in pronouncing the famous

A. D. 380, to 390.

[72.] There are some fragments of *Commentaries on the Psalms,* bearing his name, in the " Aurea Catena, interprete Daniele Barbaro." Venetiis, 1569. But I suppose that we have no good authority for attributing these to Didymus.   [73.] Hieronymi Catalog. Art. Didymus Alexandrinus. Tom. iv.   Du Pin mistakes his age, if indeed the figures in his account, be not an error of the press.

Jerome one of her advocates. About the middle of this century,[74] he was sent, while yet a boy, from his native Pannonia beyond the Adriatic, to pursue his studies at Rome. Having at length completed his education there, and received baptism, he travelled, with an insatiable thirst for knowledge, first into the West, and visited the learned men in Gaul ; whence he returned, and, after a short stay in Italy, continued his journey, around the head of the Adriatic, into the East. Here he spent many years in Syria, Palestine and Egypt, studying with the eminent fathers and doctors, attending the councils, and practising the monastic discipline in all its rigors. In the course of these various pursuits, he studied awhile (about A. D. 380,) under Gregory Nazianzen at Constantinople ; and after making a visit, of some length, at Rome, he sailed to Egypt, and entered the monasteries of Nitria, in the year 386. He soon came down to Alexandria, however, and there spent about a month under the instructions of Didymus. But disliking the Origenists, though himself a professed admirer of their master, he left Egypt and retired to Palestine. Secluded in a little cell at Bethlehem, amid the scenes of our Saviour's nativity, he devoted his time to monkish austerities, and to writing *Commentaries*, in imitation of Origen, *on the New Testament.* These appeared about A. D. 388.

In that upon *Ephesians*, he represents the Apostle as teaching that all mankind shall eventually come, in

[74.] The year of Jerome's birth is uncertain. Du Pin whom I follow, has attempted a chronology of the principal events of his life, according to which he must have been born about A. D. 340, or 342, Biblioth. Pat. Art. Jerome, Note (b.)

16*

the unity of the faith, and in the knowledge of the Son
of God, into a perfect man in Christ Jesus ;[75] and that
" in the end, or consummation of things, all shall be
" restored to their original state, and be again united
" in one body. "[76]   He says " we cannot be ignorant
" that Christ's blood benefitted the angels and those
" who are in hell ; though we know not the manner
" in which it produced such effects. "[77]   In another
passage, he represents " the whole intelligent creation
by the simile of an animal body, " of which the flesh,
arteries, veins, nerves and bones, having been dissect-
ed and scattered around, are all to be united again,
by a skilful hand, and reanimated.   " Now, " continues he, " in the restitution of all things, when Christ,
" the true Physician, shall come to heal the body of
" the universal church, torn at present and dislocated
" in its members, then shall every one, according to
" the measure of his own faith and knowledge of the
" Son of God, assume his proper office, and return to
" his original state ; not, however, as some heretics
" represent, that all will be changed into angels, or
" made into creatures of one uniform rank.   But each
" member shall be made perfect according to his pe-
" culiar office and capacity.   For instance, the apos-
" tate angel shall become such as he was created ;
" and man, who has been cast out of paradise, shall
" be restored thither again.   And this shall be accom-
" plished in such a way, as that all shall be united to-
" gether by mutual charity, so that the members will

[75] Hieronymi Comment. Lib. ii. in Epist. ad Ephes. cap. iv. 13.
Tom. iv. Part. i. Edit. Martianay.   [76] Ditto. ad Ephes, cap. iv.
4.   [77] Ditto. ad Ephes. cap. iv. 10.

" delight in each other, and rejoice in each other's
" promotion. Then shall the whole body of Christ,
" the universal church, such as it was originally, dwell
" in the celestial Jerusalem, which, in another pas-
" sage, the Apostle calls the mother of saints. "[78]
Again, Jerome says, " the apostate angels, and the
" prince of this world, and Lucifer the morning star,
" though now ungovernable, licentiously wandering
" about, and plunging themselves into the depths of
" sin, shall, in the end, embrace the happy dominion
" of Christ and his saints. "[79]

At the time of writing these *Commentaries*, Jerome
was towards the age of fifty. His influence among
the orthodox, we shall have abundant occasion to exemplify. At present, however, we may only trace
a particular friendship, the unhappy termination of
which, we shall be obliged hereafter to describe as
agitating the church, and, in some measure, affecting
the cause of Universalism. Nearly twenty years
since, during his first journey into the East, he happened to stop awhile in the city of Aquileia, at the
northern extremity of the Adriatic, and there formed
an acquaintance with Rufinus, a young and promising
scholar of the place. Their friendship continued undisturbed down to the present period, and even somewhat later. Rufinus had early followed him into the
East : in company with Melania, a noble lady of
Rome, he had sailed to Egypt in A. D. 372, visited

78. Ditto. ad Ephes. cap. iv. 16.   79. Ditto. Lib. i. in Epist. ad
Ephes. cap. ii. 7. In two other works, also, written about this
time, Jerome asserted Universalism : Hieronymi Comment. Lib.
ii. in Epist. ad Galatas, cap. iv. 1.—and Comment. in Amos cap.
iv. The latter was not composed till about A. D. 390.

the monks of Nitria, spent some time with Didymus at Alexandria, and then retired, probably the next year, with his patroness, to Jerusalem. Here, Melania employed her abundant wealth in religious and charitable donations, in advancing the monastic cause, and in supporting the numerous pilgrims who resorted to the holy places. With her, Rufinus among others enjoyed a quiet retreat, and devoted himself to study and pious services, surrounded by the venerable objects which the Holy City presented to awaken his devotion. He still remained here, when Jerome took up his permanent abode at Bethlehem, only six miles distant. Both had already entered freely into the sentiments of Origen ; and their present intimacy was well calculated to cherish those notions. There is no reason, however, to suppose that Rufinus was, at any time, a Universalist ;[80] unless we may derive a faint, and it seems unwarrantable, suspicion, from his having preserved, in his numerous translations from Origen, those passages entire which taught Universalism, while he altered or omitted such as disagreed with the orthodox trinitarianism. This circumstance does, indeed, show that if he did not believe the former doctrine, he nevertheless regarded it, like his cotemporaries, as no reprehensible error ; and his faithful attachment to John, the bishop of Jerusalem, confirms this conclusion.

Before we pass, it should be remarked, that both

[80.] Huet (Origenian. Lib. ii. cap. 2. Quæst. xi, § 25,) thinks Rufinus insinuated that though the devil would be endlessly miserable, yet guilty men would suffer only temporary punishment. But to me, the passages to which Huet refers, convey no intimation of the latter opinion, but rather the contrary.

Jerome and Rufinus, though Latin writers, and natives of the West, belonged more properly to the eastern church, where their principal connexions were formed, and where their doctrinal education was matured.

XXII. Evagrius Ponticus, who flour-
A. D. 390. ished among the orthodox of this period, as a scholar and monk of considerable eminence, must be pronounced a Universalist, on the undisputed testimony of the Fifth General council; in which, a century and a half after his death, he was anathematized, with Didymus, for having taught the Restoration of all, and the Pre-existence of souls.[81] But the same sentence that has preserved the memory of his doctrine, destroyed the obnoxious part of his writings, and left nothing but a few works consisting chiefly of ceremonial rules and practical instructions for monks. In these, both their subject and the circumstance of their having been tolerated, render it improbable that any thing is to be found to our purpose. We have, therefore, only to add a brief sketch of his life, and then proceed to some accounts of other individuals.

Having come from his native country of Pontus, to Cappadocia, not far from A. D. 375, he was appointed reader in the church of Cesarea, by Basil the Great; on whose death, Gregory Nyssen ordained him deacon. After awhile, Evagrius went to Constantinople, where he studied the Scriptures under Gregory Nazianzen, and was, by him, promoted to

---

[81]. Cyrilli Scythopolit. Vit. S. P. Sabæ cap. 90.

the archdeaconship.   Here he remained a few years
after his master retired from the city; but, being at
length obliged to flee from the matrimonial jealousy of
a nobleman, he came to Jerusalem, about A. D. 385,
and was received and supported in the charitable
establishment of Melania.   In the society of Rufinus
and others, he was here persuaded to embrace the
monastic life; and, after a residence of five years in
Palestine, he went, in A. D. 390, to the famous
retreat of Nitria, where he took up his permanent
abode among the Origenists.   The remainder of his
life was passed in great austerity, and in close application to study and composition.   He lived in the
orthodox communion, and died, at the age of fifty-
four, with the reputation of much sanctity and considerable learning.[82]

XXIII. Were it allowable to indulge conjecture
on mere appearances, we might conclude that nearly
all the leading Origenists, of this period, were believers in Universalism; for such is the impression
the historian must naturally feel, in contemplating
the peculiar circumstances of their lives, their intimacy with Didymus, and with others who are known
to have held that doctrine, and their respect for the
favorite father whose name they bore. Passing over
the undistinguished multitude, who had, perhaps,
only their wretchedness and austerity to recommend
them to a momentary reputation, and whose names
could now form, at best, but a blank catalogue, there

[82.] We must not confound Evagrius Ponticus with his cotemporary, Evagrius Antiochenus, nor with a later writer, Evagrius
Scholasticus, the ecclesiastical historian.

are still two or three who must here be introduced to notice. Palladius, a native of Galatia, and a disciple of Evagrius Ponticus in Egypt, was one of the ablest and most faithful supporters of the party. He was, now, a monk in the solitude of Nitria ; but ill health soon driving him into the world, he afterwards obtained a bishopric in Asia Minor, became considerably known by the part he took in the public affairs of the church, and preserved his name from oblivion by writing some historical or biographical works, which yet remain. Another influential member of the party was the venerable Isidorus, an aged Presbyter of Alexandria, whom Athanasius had ordained, many years before, and who had spent his early life among the monasteries of the Nitrian desert.

Directing our view to the churches of Palestine, we behold the episcopal chair of the Holy City filled by John of Jerusalem, an Origenist, who with Isidorus, will hereafter appear, bearing an important part in the subject of this history, and affording some evidence that he was a Universalist. He had lately succeeded Cyrill in the bishopric of Jerusalem ; where he enjoyed the friendship and support of Melania, Rufinus, and their associates. Of his earlier life, we only know that he was born about A. D. 356, that his youth was devoted to the monastic discipline, but that, quitting his retirement, he was ordained presbyter before the year 378, and that he was chosen to the see of Jerusalem in A. D. 387.

XXIV. In most of the Universalists, A. D. 378, of this century, the influence of Origen's to 394. writings is abundantly manifest. There were some, however, who had no sympathy with that father's general system of doctrine and turn of thought, and who will not be suspected of having derived their views from him. It is well known, that the Antiochian or Syrian school of divines, so called, differed widely from the Alexandrian, by rejecting the allegorical mode of interpretation and other fantastical speculations. Among them, Diodorus, bishop of Tarsus, is distinguished for the apparent soundness of his judgement, and for the influence which he seems to have exerted in the Syrian churches. By a fragment, preserved from his once numerous writings, we find that he, too, was a Universalist: "a perpetual reward," says he, " is appointed to the good, a recompence of their " works, which is worthy the justice and equity of " the Rewarder. For the wicked, also, there are " punishments, not perpetual, however, lest the im- " mortality, prepared for them, should become a dis- " advantage ; but they are to be tormented for a " certain brief period, proportioned to the desert and " measure of their faults and impiety, according to " the amount of malice in their works. They shall, " therefore, suffer punishment for a brief space ; but " immortal blessedness, having no end, awaits them. " For, if the rewards of the good surpass their works " as much as the duration of the eternity prepared " for them exceeds the duration of their conflicts in " this world ; so, the punishments, to be inflicted for

"heinous and manifold sins, are far more surpassed
"by the magnitude of mercy. The resurrection,
"therefore, is regarded as a blessing, not only to the
"good, but also to the evil. For the grace of God
"copiously and magnificently honors the good ; [i. e.
"*beyond their deserts ;*] and it adjudges punishment
"to the evil, in mercy and kindness." [83]

Diodorus was, in early life, principal of a monastic
school, at Antioch, in which he taught with great
reputation. Here, he was afterwards ordained presbyter ; and, during the banishment of the bishop, by
the Arian emperor Valens, he was honored with the
charge of the church in that metropolis of the East.
About A. D. 378, he was appointed bishop of
Tarsus, in Cilicia, the birth-place of St. Paul ; where
he presided till his death, in the year 393, or 394.
He was a learned and voluminous writer, especially
of Commentaries on the Scriptures ; but his works
have all perished; except fragments quoted by ancient
authors. Amidst the prevalence of allegorical interpretation, he adhered to the natural and simple import
of the sacred text ; and it is supposed that his example contributed to establish this mode of exposition
among the Syrian churches. He was held in high
esteem by the other Greek fathers, of his day, Basil
the Great, Gregory Nazianzen, Epiphanius, and Athanasius ; and, though he was subsequently suspected
of having favored Nestorian views of the trinity, no
fault was ever found with him for his Universalism,
till many centuries after his death. It is worthy of

[83.] Assemani Bibliothec. Orientalis Tom. iii. Part. i. p. 324.

17

distinct remark, that, among the scholars who studied under him, while at Antioch, were John Chrysostom and Theodorus of Mopsuestia, afterwards so cele-brated." [84]

XXV. Having so long confined ourselves to the eastern churches, where alone we can discover the prevalence of Universalism, we may now turn our attention to the West. A multitude of almost for-gotten, and obscure names, and if we except those of Optatus, a Numidian bishop, and Philastrius, an Ital-ian, fill the list of ecclesiastical writers, among the Latins, in the interval between the time of Victo-rinus, and the present. Now, however, they had a very eminent and popular doctor in Ambrose, arch-bishop of Milan in Italy: a man of moderate learn-ing, but of a polite education, of the most vigorous talents, determined courage, and of an influence so powerful as to approach towards absolute authority in the state, as well as in the church. Of the future condition of mankind, his views nearly coincided with those which Hilary and Lactantius had before advanced: All who have attained, in A. D. 384, this life, to the character of perfect to 390. saints, such as the apostles, and some others, will, he supposed, rise from the dead in the first resurrection; and enduring, with little pain, the ordeal of the flaming sword, or the baptism of fire, at the gate of Paradise, they will quickly enter into everlasting joy. But the imper-fect saints will undergo a trial severer in proportion

[84] For notices of his life, see Du Pin's Bib. Pat. Art. Diodorus bishop of Tarsus. Murdock's Mosheim, vol. i. p. 295.

to their vices; and such as have only been believers, without the virtues of the gospel, whom he denominates *the sinners,* will remain in the torments of fire till the second resurrection, and perhaps still longer, that they may be purified from their wickedness. These three classes, the perfect saints, the imperfect, and the sinners, shall each be arraigned, except perhaps the first, at the great Judgement-day; and, what is remarkable, all who are then tried, shall sooner or later be saved. But there is another, a fourth class, which he distinguishes as the impious or the infidels, who, together with the devil and his angels, shall never be brought to judgement, because they have been already condemned. For these he apparently reserves no chance of restoration, but leaves them to an eternity of hopeless suffering.[85]

The author usually quoted under the name of Ambrosiaster, who is generally supposed to have been one Hilary a deacon of Rome, held that all such believers as embrace erroneous doctrines, while they nevertheless retain the essential principles of Christianity, must be subjected to the purification of fire, in the future world, before they can be saved.[86] He likewise taught that our Saviour descended, after his crucifixion, to the invisible regions of the dead, and there converted all, whether impious or ordinary sinners, who willingly sought his aid.[87] Indeed,

85. Ambrosii Mediolanensis in Psalm. 1. Enarrat. § 51, 52, 53, 54, 56; in Ps. cxviii. Exposit. Serm. iii. § 14—17. & Serm. xx. § 12, 13, 14, 23, 24. The dates of these works are placed from A. D. 386 to A. D. 390.   86. Comment. ad Epist. 1 Corinth. cap. iii. 15. in Append. ad Ambrosii Mediolanensis Oper. Tom. ii. 87. Comment. in Epist. ad Ephes. cap. iv. 8, 9.

Christ's mission, according to him, enabled even the erring and apostatized powers of heaven to cast off the yoke of the devil, and to return to God;[88] still, it appears to have been his decided belief that there were cases of such obstinate rebellion, among wicked souls as well as angels, as to be past all recovery.

With the notice of this writer, we close, for the present, our account of the orthodox Christians.

XXVI. During more than half of this century, the Arians were numerous enough to dispute the superiority in the church, especially in the East ; and it is natural to enquire, What were their sentiments with regard to the ultimate salvation of the world ? But we shall seek in vain for their own testimony in answer. Though supported, in their day, by the influence of eminent bishops, and defended by the labors of learned doctors, the victorious fortune of their adversaries has obliterated almost every fragment of their writings, and left a wide erasure which no learning nor art can restore. We only know that, except in what related to the trinity, their doctrine was considered the same with that of the Consubstantialists ; and it seems that, in all the passion of controversial warfare, they never reproached their unsparing opponents for their frequent avowal of Universalism.[89] These circumstances may strengthen

---

[88.] Ditto. ad Ephes. cap. iii. 10. N. B. These Commentaries are supposed to have been written about A. D. 384.   [89.] Eunomius, one of the most celebrated Arians, who flourished from A. D. 360 to A. D. 394, is charged by three Greek writers of the 12th century, with having held that all the threatenings of eternal torments were intended only to terrify mankind, and were never meant to be executed. (See Balsamon ad Canon. i. Constantinopol. And Harmenopulus, De Sect. 13. And J. Zonaras

a conjecture, which is not in itself improbable, that the doctrine received about the same degree of patronage among both parties; so that neither was under temptation to accuse the other. From similar considerations, the suspicion of ambiguity naturally rests, likewise, upon the few Sabellians of this period. And we may extend the remark to the small schismatical sects of Novatians, Donatists, and Meletians; who were separated from the orthodox church only by some trivial distinctions of discipline and ecclesiastical government, or by the irregular succession of their bishops.

The uncertain, or perhaps divided, opinions of the Manicheans, on the subject of Universal Salvation, have been already mentioned. At present, however, it seems to have become the general belief, at least of those in Africa,[90] that many human souls would prove utterly irreclaimable, and be therefore stationed forever, as a guard, upon the frontiers of the world of darkness. The sect had now increased to a vast number, although abhorred by every other party, and indefatigably opposed by a large proportion of the orthodox writers, from Eusebius Pamphilus downwards; and it lurked in all parts of christendom,

ad Canon. in Deiparam.) The authority of these modern Greeks, however, is but small; and in this case it is not sustained by any testimony more ancient, nor by the fragments of Eunomius yet extant. On the contrary, in the formal Declaration of Faith, which he sent to the emperor Theodosius, A. D. 383, he says, " they who persevere in impiety or sin till the close of life, shall " be delivered to everlasting punishment." (Fabricii Biblioth. Græc. Tom. viii. p. 260.) At the end of his Epilog. ad Apologiam, he remarks that in the general judgement, Christ will consign such as make light of sin, to remediless suffering. (Cavei Hist. Literar. Art. Eunomius, p. 222.)   [90.] Lardner's Credibility, &c. Chap. Mani and his Followers. Sect. iv. § 18.

notwithstanding it had been repeatedly proscribed by the edicts of successive emperors. Already could the alarming and inextinguishable heresy boast of many eminent advocates, and of some respectable authors ; and for several years it was honored with the patronage of the young Augustine, the future bishop of Hippo and renowned orthodox father. The care of a pious mother had trained him up in the principles of the catholic faith ; but, at the age of seventeen, he imbibed the sentiments of Mani ; and, though never a very zealous partizan nor a thoroughly instructed disciple, he continued to cherish the proscribed doctrine, till he entered on his thirty-first year. Residing however at Milan in Italy, in A. D. 385, he was so struck with the arguments and illustrations of the eloquent archbishop Ambrose, that he resolved to forsake the heresy ; and in the course of a year or two, he was fully converted to the orthodox religion, and received, by baptism, into the church.

CHAPTER VII.

[From A. D. 391, to A. D. 404.]

I. The three principal sees of christen-
A. D. 391. dom were now filled by Pope Siricius at
Rome, by the ambitious and unprincipled
Theophilus at Alexandria, and by Evagrius, (not Evagrius Ponticus) at Antioch. Of some inferior, yet distinguished bishoprics, that of Constantinople was held
by old Nectarius, successor of Gregory Nazianzen ;
that of the island Cyprus, by Epiphanius, the aged
and persevering enemy of the Origenists ; and John
the Universalist, presided over that of Jerusalem. In
the West, Ambrose governed the churches of Milan,
and by his astonishing influence, controled the civil as
well as the religious concerns of Italy and Gaul. Of
a multitude of ecclesiastical writers who flourished at
this time, we may here mention only three : the learned Jerome, whose fame had already filled the world ;
young Chrysostom, the prince of Christian orators,
whose renown began to extend beyond the sphere of
his labors in the great city of Antioch ; and the immortal Augustine, who was rising into notice, amidst
his native Numidia in Africa. Of the authors formerly mentioned, Titus of Bostra and Basil the Great
had long been dead ; Gregory Nazianzen expired in
his native village, about two years before ; Didymus
still survived, at Alexandria, but in extreme old age ;

and Gregory Nyssen had approached within three or four years the close of his life. Jerome continued at his cell in Bethlehem ; Evagrius Ponticus and Palladius of Gallatia were among the monasteries of Nitria ; and Isidorus was at Alexandria, under the patronage of the archbishop Theophilus.

The long struggle between the Consubstantialists and the Arians, had now ceased throughout the civilized world. The latter, driven from all their numerous churches in the East, by the vigorous and unsparing persecution of Theodosius the Great, and from those in the West, by the imperial authority of Gratian, had taken refuge among the barbarous nations of Goths and Vandals. The schismatical sects were, in a measure, suppressed ; and, or a moment, the weapons of controversy and violence, which the orthodox had so long wielded, seemed to hang useless in their hands. But an occasion for their use soon occurred, among themselves, in a personal contention, obscure and trifling at first, which swelled and extended by degrees, till it agitated the whole church.

II. Epiphanius, visiting Jerusalem, this year,[1] and preaching there before a large concourse in the cathedral church, made an insidious attack upon John the bishop, by inveighing against Origen, whom the latter was known to admire. He reproached that ancient father, in his wonted strain, as the parent of Arianism

[1] The dates in this contention with the Origenists, down to the year 397, I have endeavored, with some care, to calculate from Martianay's chronological notes prefixed to the 4th. Tom. of his edition of Jerome, and from several expressions found in Epist. xxxiii. and xxxviii. Hieronymi Opp. Tom. iv. Part ii. Some of these dates have manifestly been mistaken by Huet, Du Pin, Fleury, &c.

and other heresies ; till at length John sent his arch-
deacon, in view of the whole assembly, to request him
to forbear. A procession followed, to the place of our
Saviour's crucifixion ; and, on the way, the two prelates betrayed some indications of resentment on the
one hand, and of disregard on the other. After their
return, and while the people still waited, John himself
addressed them ; and, as many opposers of the Origenists actually attributed to Deity a body like our
own, he declaimed vehemently against that gross
error, in order to reflect the suspicion of it upon Epiphanius. But the latter, immediately standing up,
joined his brother in severely reprobating the notion ;
then, turning suddenly, called upon the assembly to
condemn likewise the perverse dogmas of Origen ;
and he even besought and warned John himself to
avoid them. This undisguised attack produced some
sensation among the people, and left, it seems, an indelible impression on the minds of both the bishops.[2]

    A year or two afterwards, Epiphanius
A. D. 393. came again into Palestine, and spent a
    while at a monastery he had founded in
his native village, about twenty miles west of Jerusalem. Though the natural simplicity of the bishop of
Cyprus may, perhaps, forbid the suspicion of inten-
tional wrong, yet his inconsiderate officiousness, and
his childish vanity, which led him sometimes to over-
look the prescribed rights of others, gave just occasion
for the apprehensions of John,[3] that this visit would

   [2.] Hieronymi Epist. xxxviii. vel. 61. Tom. iv. Part. ii. pp. 312,
313, Edit. Martianay. And Epiphanii Epist. ad Johannem Hierosolym. in eodem Tom. p. 824. [3.] Epiphanii Epist. ad Johan.
p. 823.

be marked with some act of intrusion.   No sooner had
Paulinianus, the brother of Jerome, arrived on business from Bethlehem, than Epiphanius, who had long
sought the opportunity, ordered him to be seized,
stopped his mouth to prevent his refusal, and then, by
force, made him deacon,—a mode of procedure not
very unfrequent in that age.   A few days afterward,
he seized him again, during the services of the monastery, and with the same violence, imposed on him the
more sacred ordination of presbyter.   This official act,
performed by Epiphanius out of his own jurisdiction,
and in the neighborhood, if not within the diocess, of
Jerusalem, highly exasperated John ; who complained
angrily of the insult he had suffered in the ordination
of one of his monks of Bethlehem, without his knowledge and permission.   An unfounded report also
reached his ears, that Epiphanius was in the habit of
abusing him in his public prayers.   The pilgrims,
who resorted to the Holy City, heard, and on their
return probably circulated, his complaints and invec-
tives ; and he at length threatened openly to send
letters to the churches of the East and West, and
thus publish his wrongs to the world.[4]

III. The news of the disturbance he
A. D. 394.   had left behind him in Palestine, soon
reached Epiphanius at Cyprus ; and he
at length, wrote to John, endeavoring to excuse his
ordination of Paulinianus, by alleging a practice
among the bishops of his island to officiate, on similar
occasions without regard to each other's jurisdictions.

4. Epiphanii Epist. ad. Johan. p. 823, And Hieronymi Epist.
xxxix. vel. 62, p. 337.

He declared, however, that he well knew that John's
wrath arose, not from this ordination, but from the old
reproof for Origenism ; and, earnestly beseeching him
to save himself from the " untoward generation of heretics," he proceeded to enumerate the several errors of
Origen.　This catalogue, though nearly the same he
had published eighteen years before, is distinguished
for containing the first censure, on record, against
Universalism.　" 1. Who among the catholics, " said
he, " and such as adorn their faith with good works,
" can hear, with an undisturbed mind, the doctrine of
" Origen, or believe that notorious declaration of his,
" *The Son cannot behold the Father, nor the Holy*
" *Ghost the Son!*　2. Who can endure him, when
" he says that souls were originally angels in heaven,
" but cast down into this world, after sinning in the
" celestial state, and imprisoned here in bodies, as in
" sepulchres, in order to punish them for their former
" transgressions ! so that the bodies of believers are
" not the temple of Christ, but the prisons of the
" damned.　3. That also which he strove to estab-
" lish, I know not whether to laugh or grieve at : Ori-
" gen, the renowned doctor, dared to teach that the
" devil is again to become what he originally was, to
" return to his former dignity, and to enter the king-
" dom of heaven !　O wickedness ! who is so mad
" and stupid as to believe that holy John Baptist, and
" Peter, and John the Apostle and Evangelist, and
" that Isaiah also, and Jeremiah, and the rest of the
" prophets, are to become fellow-heirs with the devil
" in the kingdom of heaven !　4. I pass over his
" frivolous explanation of the coats of skins : with

" what labor, with how many arguments, he strove
" to make us believe that those coats were human
" bodies!   Among other things, he asks, *Was God a*
" *leather-dresser, that he should take the skins of*
" *animals and fit them into coats for Adam and*
" *Eve?   Therefore it is manifest,* says Origen,
" *that it is spoken of our bodies.* 5. Who can
" patiently bear with him while he denies the res-
" urrection of this flesh? as he manifestly does, in
" his explanations of the first psalm, and in many
" other places.   6. Or who can endure his notion
" that paradise, or the garden of Eden, was in the
" third heaven! thus transferring it from the earth
" to the skies, and, by an allegorical interpretation,
" representing its trees to be angelic powers! 7.
" Who but must instantly reject and condemn his
" delusions, that those waters above the firmament,
" mentioned in Genesis, are not waters, but certain
" celestial spirits ; and that those under the firma-
" ment, are demons!   Why, then, do we read that,
" in the deluge, the windows of heaven were opened,
" and the waters of the flood descended?   O, the
" madness and stupidity of men who have neglected
" what is said in Proverbs, *My son, hear the word of*
" *thy father, and forsake not the law of thy mother.*
" 8. I do not attempt to dispute against all his errors ;
" they are innumerable ; but among other things he
" even dared to say that Adam lost the image of
" God! when there is not one passage of Scripture
" that intimates it.   If, indeed, that were the case,
" then would all things, in the world, never have
" been made subject to Adam's posterity, the human

" race, as James the apostle teaches. "[5] Such are the particulars that Epiphanius selected for special reprehension. He again exhorted John, as his own son, to abstain from the heresy ; and lamented that so many of their brethren had been already made " food for the devil. "

We have said that in this passage occurs the first censure, which is to be found in all antiquity, against the doctrine of Universalism. We must remark, however, that, even here, the censure falls, as the reader may perceive, not on the doctrine of the salvation of all mankind, but on that of the salvation of the devil. This distinction, though it may seem captious, is of some consequence to an accurate understanding of subsequent occurrences.

IV. With the *Letter to John*, Epiphanius sent others, on the same subject, to the bishops of Palestine ;[6] and, as copies of the former as well as of the latter were freely circulated through the province, the matter soon awakened general interest.[7] Many of the people, many of the clergy seem to have adhered to John ; and Rufinus and Melania espoused his cause, as did also Palladius of Galatia,[8] who had lately arrived from Nitria. But others, especially the monks of Bethlehem, took up for Epiphanius, withdrew from

[5] Epiphanii Epist. ad Johannem, inter Hieronymi Opp. Tom. iv. Part. ii. Edit. Martianay. I give a faithful translation of Epiphanius's Catalogue of Origen's errors ; but I have inserted the figures between the several particulars ; omitted three uninteresting, and to most readers, unintelligible arguments which in the original stood between the 2d and 3d, the 4th and 5th, and the 6th and 7th errors ; and passed over the exhortation which occurred between the 7th and 8th. [6] Hieronymi Epist. xxxviii. adv. Johan. Hierosol. p. 334. [7] Hieron. Epist. xxxiii. vel. 101. ad Pammach. p. 248. [8] Epiphani Epist. ad Johan. pp. 827, 829.

the communion of their accused bishop,[9] and in return, suffered from him, it appears, some condemnatory sentence for their refractory procedure.[10]

Jerome, the admirer, and imitator of Origen, we should expect, of course, to discover among his bishop's adherents ; but two or three circumstances conspired to engage him on the opposite side : The strongest affections of nature inclined him to defend the ordination of his own brother ; some personal differences he had formerly had with the professed Origenists, both at Rome and Nitria, were, perhaps, remembered with resentment ; and his pride of learning, his haughty and petulant spirit, must have made him restless under the immediate government of an ecclesiastical superior, who was his junior in age, and whom he might justly regard as far his inferior in talents and acquirements. He joined the party of Epiphanius, or perhaps gathered it, and translated the *Letter to John,* for the private use of such monks as were acquainted only with the Latin language. His translation, though intended for confidential circulation, found its way, the next year,[11] to Jerusalem ; and it was immediately censured, by Rufinus, as unfaithful to the honorable appellations bestowed, in the original, upon his bishop. From this moment, we discover an open breach in the early and long cherished affection of the two friends : Jerome, who could not bear reproof, defended himself, and resented the criticism with his

A. D. 395.

---

9. Hieron. Epist. adv. Johan. xxxviii. p. 308.   10. Ditto. And p. 333. And Epist. xxxix. ad Theophilum, p. 338, &c.   11. Hieron. Epist. xxxiii. p. 248.

accustomed abuse, by calling its author a pseudo-monk.[12]

V. The noise of the quarrel in Palestine had reached Alexandria ; and Isidorus, the aged patron of Origenism, felt himself called upon to encourage his brethren. Relying with a misplaced confidence on the integrity of his former friends, he addressed a letter to one Vincentius, a presbyter and monk at Bethlehem, whom he had probably seen, about ten years before, in company with Jerome in Egypt. He exhorted him to stand firm on the rock of faith, nor be terrified by the threats of the adversaries. " I my-self" added he, " shall soon come to Jerusalem, and " the band of enemies shall be dispersed, who, always " resisting the faith of the church, attempt now to dis-" turb the minds of the simpler sort."[13] But Vincentius, it seems, had already followed the example of his master Jerome, in siding with Epiphanius ; and this letter accordingly proved a providential warning, instead of an encouragement.

The increasing contention, which attracted the notice of foreign Christians, alarmed the friends of tranquillity at home. Archelaus, one of the civil officers of the province, was vainly endeavoring to allay the disturbance. He invited both parties to a mutual conference, in which they should agree upon a common declaration of faith ; but when the day arrived, John was absent on some parochial duty ; and he never appeared, though the council, in reply to his

[12.] Ditto. [13.] Hieron. Epist. xxxviii. p. 330.

excuse, offered to wait his convenience, at least for a few days.[14]

Two months afterwards a deputation arrived, not unexpectedly, from Theophilus, the powerful and aspiring archbishop of Egypt ; who, either on the request of John, or at his own suggestion, gladly embraced this opportunity to extend his influence over the foreign churches of Palestine. Isidorus himself was entrusted with the commission, and as deputy, brought letters from the Alexandrian primate to John and Jerome, the respective heads of the contending parties. But a professed and zealous Origenist was much better qualified to inflame than to compose a difficulty, in which his favorite doctrine was involved ; and on his arrival, his subserviency to the bishop of Jerusalem was so manifest, that Jerome refused, with reason, his partial mediation.[15]

VI. Frustrated in the special object of his mission, Isidorus devoted himself exclusively to the assistance of John. The letter of Epiphanius had A. D. 396. now lain, unanswered, before the public, nearly two years ; and the bishop availed himself of his friend's assistance to produce a *Reply*. It was addressed in the name of John, to Theophilus at Alexandria, to whose decision it appealed. The author, or authors, related the history of the difficulty, complained of the ordination of Paulinianus, inveighed against Jerome, and charged him with inconsistency in reproaching Origen whom he had translated and extolled ; and they finally pro-

[14.] Ditto. pp. 331, 332.   [15.] Ditto. pp. 330, 331.

ceeded to an examination of the errors which Epiphanius had enumerated, and, by implication, charged
against John. Out of the eight, however, the writers answered to three only : to the *first*, concerning
the Trinity ; to the *second*, concerning Pre-existence ;
and to the *fifth*, concerning the Resurrection. On
these three points, they explained themselves favorably,[16] or absolutely rejected the errors alleged ; but, if
we may rely on the minute account, or on the confident judgement, of their prejudiced adversary, Jerome,
they felt unprepared to disclaim the other five particulars in the catalogue. That they cautiously avoided
any notice of them, is indubitable ; and we may adopt
the very natural conclusion, that they really held what
they so warily passed over, the salvation of the devil
as well as the allegorical expositions of Origen.[17]
With this *Reply to Epiphanius*, or *Apology to Theophilus*, Isidorus departed for Alexandria ; and he
probably assisted in spreading copies of it through the
churches.

VII. These copies were extensively dispersed, and
soon reached Italy and Rome, where he *Letter of
Epiphanius* had been already circulated. Here, as
in other places, the people were variously affected,
some inclining to one party, some to the other ; and
one of Jerome's correspondents wrote to him on the

[16.] According to Jerome, (Epist. xxxviii.) they prevaricated on
these points ; but I think it evident from his own account that
they fully denied that of Pre-existence.   [17.] Hieron. Epist. xxxviii.
adv. Johan. Hierosolym. Their rejection of the error concerning
Pre-existence would, however involve a denial of those concerning the coats of skins, and the garden of Eden. John's Apology
to Theophilus is lost ; and we can judge of its contents only from
Jerome's account.

perplexities which the subject had occasioned, re-
questing a full statement of the affair. The commu-
nication of intelligence through a distance of nearly
five hundred leagues, must have been dilatory and
tedious ; and Jerome seems to have taken the earliest
opportunity, on receipt of the request,
A. D. 397. to compose his bitter and sarcastic *Answer to John's Apology.* He addressed
it, for the most part, directly to John himself; but it
was published in the form of a letter to his enquiring
friend at Rome. The origin of the quarrel, the
measures that had been adopted for a reconciliation,
the answers which John had given to the three errors,
and his silence with regard to the rest, were related
and discussed at considerable length ; and Jerome
concluded, by defending his own party from his
bishop's accusations, and by retorting on him the
charge of disturbing the church.[18]

He had just received a letter from Theophilus,
exhorting the monks to peace and reconciliation with
their bishop. It was an object of much importance
to secure the assistance, or at least the neutrality, of
this worldly minded but active and influential prelate,
who had hitherto appeared to favor the cause of John.
Jerome immediately replied to him in a flattering
and insinuating strain ; and declared that, agreeably
to his recommendation, he himself was sincerely for
peace ; for such peace, however, as would, in reality,
be cordial, for the peace of Christ ; intimating, at the
same time, that there never could be hearty concord

18. Hieron. Epist. xxxviii.

between the faithful and the heretics. He embraced this opportunity, likewise, to lay before Theophilus a history of the disturbance, to defend the ordination of his brother, and to exonerate himself from that charge of inconsistency which John had urged against him for having translated the works of Origen that he now condemned.[19]

Perhaps, no man, in that age, possessed means more efficient for diffusing his prejudices, than Jerome. From his narrow and uncouth cell at Bethlehem, he could easily excite disaffection or distrust, in the remotest parts of christendom. He maintained an extensive correspondence ; the fame of his knowledge procured him a welcome introduction wherever he sought assistance ; and his penetrating discernment readily distinguished those who would prove most useful as coadjutors. The celebrated Augustine, now bishop of Hippo in Africa, a hundred and fifty miles west of Carthage, was too eminent for him to over-look ; and he had already addressed him a letter, with the information that Origen's works abounded with errors.[20] But that honest and independent man could never be engaged in his violent measures, though he was, in reality, much farther from Origen's sentiments than Jerome himself.

VIII. Meanwhile, Rufinus had bidden a final adieu to his friends in Palestine, and had sailed, in company with his patroness, for his native Italy. But, before his departure, a seeming reconciliation was effected between him and Jerome ; and in their last interview

19. Hieron. Epist. xxxix. ad Theophilum. 20. Huet. Origenian. Lib. ii. cap. 4, Sect. i. § 14.

they pledged themselves to refrain from their mutual hostilities.[21]

When he arrived with Melania at Rome, intent on diffusing his sentiments and partialities, and urged by Macarius, a civil officer of the city, he translated into Latin the first book of Pamphilus's and Eusebius's *Apology for Origen*, together with Origen's famous books *Of Principles*, and soon published them for the benefit of the western Christians. To these works he affixed *Prefaces* and a *Tract* of his own; in which he apprized the public that, in the books *Of Principles*, he had omitted or amended the many erroneous representations, concerning the trinity, which he supposed had been inserted or corrupted by the heretics. The other notions, he intimates, were preserved unaltered.[22] Unhappily, however, he could not suppress a secret personal resentment, but embraced this opportunity to allude to a certain *accomplished* brother, who had ranked Origen next to the Apostles, and whose commendations of him had excited a general desire to obtain his works: who had already published in Latin above seventy of his Homilies, and who had promised to translate still more. This brother was, of course, Jerome; and the allusion was intended to remind *the few* of his inconstancy, and to imply to *the rest* that he still continued, as he once had been, a follower of Origen. Nor did Rufinus stop here; his smothered enmity broke out in a remark, that there were authors who, having stolen all their works out of Origen, afterwards reproached their master, in order to conceal their own plagiarisms, by deterring the world from reading the original.[23] These sly insinuations, though veiled under the language of respect and esteem, could not escape the notice, nor elude the understanding, of Jerome's western friends ; and it was easily foreseen that the reconciliation, so lately confirmed in Palestine, must soon share the common fate of attempts at renewing old friendships when once violated with insult.

The books *Of Principles*, though they contained, besides Universalism, the doctrine of pre-existence and other novel opinions, were readily
A. D. 397, received by many at Rome, and attached
— 398. a number of priests, monks and common Christians to Origen.[24] Others, however, rose in opposition ; and Marcella, a lady of influence, with whom Jerome maintained a correspondence, appears to have taken the lead in fixing the stigma of heresy on the gathering party of Origenists. Assisted by Vincentius, who had returned from Bethlehem, and seconded by the numerous and powerful friends of Jerome, she soon succeeded in rousing and directing the public indignation.[25] It is probable, however, that even Jerome's own friends did not consider the books *Of Principles* very heretical, as they stood in the translation ;[26] and the more

23. Ditto. And Rufini Lib. De Adulterat. Origenis Librorum.
24. Hieron. Epist. xcvi. vel. 16 ad Principium. p. 782.
25. Ditto.   26. Jerome's friends, Pammachius and Oceanus (Epist. xl. vel. 64.) inter Hieronymi (Opp. Tom. iv.) say they have found in Rufinus's translation of the books Of Principles,

moderate and impartial discovered nothing alarming in the late publications, if we may judge from the conduct of Pope Siricius : It was one of the last acts of his life, to grant letters of recommendation to Rufinus, who was preparing to proceed, after an absence of twenty-five years, to his native city of Aquileia.[27]

IX. Jerome at length received, with
A. D. 398, surprise, an account sent from Italy, of
— 399. the artful procedure of Rufinus ; but, with a moderation unusual for him, he wrote to his false friend in terms of manly and candid expostulation, entreating him, as a brother, to offer no more abuse, and to regard their parting conciliation.[28] As he was, however, accused of inconsistency in his treatment of Origen, not by Rufinus alone, but by many others at Rome, at Alexandria, and indeed throughout christendom, he composed a formal explanation of the praises he had formerly bestowed upon that father, and sent it to his Roman friends. I have, indeed, commended him, said he, as an able interpreter, but not as a correct dogmatist; I have admired his genius, without approving his doctrine. Have I ever adopted his detestable representations concerning the trinity, or concerning the resurrection ? Have I not, on the contrary, carefully omitted them in my translations ? If people would know my sentiments, let them read my *Commentaries on Ephesians*, and on *Ecclesiastes*, where I have uniformly

many things not so very orthodox; still they suspect that Rufinus had omitted whatever would more plainly expose Origen's impiety; and therefore they request Jerome to send them a correct translation. [27.] Huet. Origenian. Lib. ii. cap. 4. Sect. i. § 16. [28.] Hieron. Epist. xlii.

contradicted his opinions. I certainly never followed his notions; or if I have, yet now I repent. And let others imitate this my example; " let us all be " converted to God. Let us not wait the repentance " of the devil; for vain is the presumption that ex- " tends into the abyss of hell. It is in this world, " that life must be sought, or lost." [29] In the conclu- sion, he exposed the absurdity of Rufinus's pretence that Origen's works had been interpolated; and with a daring assurance, denied that the *Apology for Origen* was written by Pamphilus. At the same time, he also sent to Rome, at the request of his friends, an accurate version of the books *Of Princi- ples*, in order, as he said, to expose the mistranslations of his rival.[30]

By the passage just quoted from his *Defence*, we discover that he was now disposed to deny a Restora- tion from hell, which he had formerly asserted. Still, it appears, he did not account that notion one of the heinous, alarming errors in question, as is manifest from his referring to his *Commentaries on Ephesians* in proof that he had uniformly contradicted them; for those *Commentaries*, though they opposed some other tenets ascribed to Origen, abounded, as we have seen, with the fullest declarations of Universalism. What he now treated as the great, detestable errors of his master, may be learned from the following passage in the same *Defence :* " I acknowledge that Origen " erred in certain things: that his opinion was wrong " concerning the Son, and worse concerning the Holy

[29] Hieron. Epist. xli. vel. 65. ad Pammach. et Oceanum, p. 345.
[30] Ditto. p. 348.

" Ghost ; that he impiously supposed that our souls
" fell from heaven ; that he acknowledged the resur-
" rection only in words, denying it in reality ; and
" that he held that in future ages, after one universal
" restitution, Gabriel would at length become what
" the devil now is, Paul what Caiaphas, and virgins
" what prostitutes are.[31]   When you have rejected
" these errors, you may read him with safety." [32]

X. Jerome and Epiphanius now began to discover,
in the disposition of the Alexandrian bishop, a favorable change which they had long sought to procure.
Flattery and exhortation had been spent upon him in
vain : he had still inclined to the side of John.   But,
what no persuasion could effect, self-interest and revenge speedily accomplished.   Theophilus had been,
for some time, involved in a contention with his
Egyptian monks, the smaller, more ignorant, and
therefore the more turbulent part of whom, hated
the name of Origen, because his doctrine was so
directly opposed to their own gross notion, that Deity
possessed a body like man's.*   These Anthropomor-

[31.] " — et post multa sæcula atque unam omnium restitutionem,
" idipsum fore Gabrielem quod Diabolum, Paulum quod Caia-
" pham, virgines quod prostibulas. "   In his Epist. xxxvi. ad
Vigilantium, written about this time, Jerome acknowledges that
Origen " erred concerning the state of the soul. [i. e. Pre-exist-
" ence,] and the repentance of the devil ; and what is of more
" importance than these, that the Son of God and the Holy Ghost,
" he pronounced, in his Commentaries on Isaiah, to be Sera-
" phim." p. 276.   Afterwards, Jerome reproaches Vigilantius for
having misinterpreted the vision of the mountain, in Daniel ii,
and insultingly tells him to repent " if, indeed, this impiety can
" be forgiven you ; and then you may obtain pardon when, ac-
" cording to the error of Origen, the devil shall obtain it ; who
" was never guilty of worse blasphemy than yours." p. 278.
[32.] Hieron. Epist. xli. p. 345.
* Socratis Hist. Eccl. Lib. vi. cap. 7.

phites, so called, were roused to open insurrection by one of their bishop's late addresses, in which he had freely reproached their error ; and, assembling from various parts of Egypt, they crowded to Alexandria with the intention of murdering him. To save his life, Theophilus deceived the fierce assailants into a persuasion that he himself was converted to their belief; and promising, at their instance, to condemn the works of their great adversary, Origen, he dismissed them in peace. Meanwhile, the aged Isidorus, whom he had always honored, and whom he had lately attempted to place in the vacant bishopric of Constantinople, had incurred his dangerous displeasure, by refusing to countenance his unjust and rapacious schemes. Some of the Origenist monks of Nitria, also, where Isidorus sought and obtained refuge, fell under his resentment. Theophilus invaded their quiet retreat, seized and tortured those who refused to deliver up Isidorus, burnt their monasteries, and, bethinking himself of an easier way to satiate his baffled vengeance, denounced them to the fierce Anthropomorphites as Origenists. Sacrificing every thing to his wrath, he now determined to fulfil his late extorted promise ; and, siding with the more dilatory Jerome and Epiphanius, he proceeded to the hazardous measure of engaging the church in his quarrel. Accordingly, he called a synod A. D. 399. of the neighboring bishops at Alexandria, and procured a decree, remarkable for being the first of its kind, condemning Origen, and anathematizing all who should approve his works. He dared not arraign the whole multitude of offend-

19

ers ; but three of them, called *the tall brethren,* were condemned by name, under the pretence of their holding false doctrines, though neither they nor any of their party were present. Theophilus then contrived to obtain, from the governor of Egypt, authority to drive the excommunicated out of the province ; and, taking a band of soldiers, marched again for the famous retreat of the Origenists.[33]

The cells and monasteries of Nitria clustered along two parallel but distant chains of naked hills, and were thinly scattered, perhaps, in the deep and arid waste that lay between. From the summits of the north-eastern ridge, the spectator surveyed, with secret horror, an inanimate world of eternal barrenness and solitude, glowing beneath the scorching firmament. In whatever direction he turned, the great Desert of Lybia stretched away, over uneven plains and precipices, to the verge of the horizon. To the southwest, at the distance of ten or a dozen miles, stood the opposite ridge ; nearer, lay before him the wide valley of sand, furrowed through with deep gorges, and extending far off to the north-west and south-east ; and below him, at the foot of the precipices on which he stood, his eyes rested on the small crusted lakes of natron, surrounded by shrubs and reeds, the only contrast to the universal desolation.[34] All was motionless silence ; except when the beasts and birds of the desert came to allay their burning thirst, or

[33]. In the account of Theophilus, I follow Huet (Origenian. Lib. ii. cap. 4. sect. ii. § 1, 2, 3,) and Fleury (Eccl. Hist. Book xxi. chap. 10, 12.) [34]. Sonnini's Travels in Upper and Lower Egypt, chap. 27, 28, 29.

when the monks swarmed forth from their cells at the appointed hours of social devotion.

Into this abode of mortification and religious musing, Theophilus entered, with his troop, in the dead of night, and drove away the bishop of the mountain ; but unable to discover his intended victims, who had been secreted, he burnt their cells, pillaged the monasteries, and then set out on his retreat. Returned to Alexandria, he encountered a general indignation and horror, which the news of his cruelty and sacrilege soon roused. The Origenists, however, took warning, and fled to other countries. Isidorus and about three hundred of his brethren sought the protection of John in Palestine, and retired, the larger part of them, to the palm-groves around Scythopolis, nearly seventy miles northward from Jerusalem. But Theophilus, with the exterminating zeal of a true foe, wrote immediately to the bishops of that province, forgiving, on the ground of ignorance, their first reception of the condemned, but requiring them, for the future, to exclude the refugees, from every church. It is mortifying to relate, that John of Jerusalem was overcome by this sudden change in the powerful patron to whom he had referred his cause ; and that he appears to have wanted the resolution to defend his guests, and the courage to disobey the Egyptian primate's orders.[35]

Great were the mutual congratulations of Theophilus, Epiphanius and Jerome, on these decisive measures. They informed each other, in their bombastic

[35.] Huetii Origenian. Lib. ii. cap. 4. Sect. ii. § 3. Fleury's Eccl. Hist. Book xxi. chap. 12.

letters, that the snake of Origenism was now severed
and disembowelled by the evangelical sword, that the
host of Amalek was destroyed, and the banner of the
cross erected on the altars of the Alexandrian church.
Theophilus sent letters to Rome, to Cyprus, and to
Constantinople, proclaiming his late measures, and
exhorting the respective bishops to follow his example.   Accordingly, Anastasius, the new Pope, who
had succeeded Siricius at Rome, readily
A. D. 400.   gratified the numerous partisans of Jerome in that city, by issuing a decree
which was received through all the West, condemning the works of Origen; and Epiphanius, soon afterwards, convened a synod of his bishops in Cyprus,
and procured from them a like sentence.   But Chrysostom, who now held the episcopal chair of Constantinople, delayed all notice of the Egyptian prelate's
recommendation,[36] and thereby involved himself in a
scene of troubles that closed only with his life.

XI. We have passed, with barely a hasty notice,
over the decree of the Roman pontiff, and the two
synods of Alexandria and Cyprus, against Origen and
his works.   They constitute, however, an important
event in the history of Universalism, being the first
public acts of the church which at all affected that
sentiment; and it is worth the while to pause and
ascertain the particular points of doctrine which were
then condemned.   All the formal records of those
proceedings have long since perished; but, from
cotemporary authority, we learn that the tenet, which

[36.] Huet. Origenian. Lib. ii. cap. 4. Sect. ii. § 5. et Sect. i. § 19.

gave most offence in the Alexandrian synod, was this: " that as Christ was crucified in our world for " the redemption of mankind, so he would taste " death, in the eternal state, for the salvation of the " devil." [37] This *two-fold* death of Christ, though sometimes intimated by Origen, was by no means one of his fixed opinions; and it can have been only from an ungenerous zeal to take the utmost advantage of his suggestions, that it was inserted in the present charge. It also appears, that in addition to this particular, his doctrine of ' the salvation of the devil and his angels,' was expressly condemned, in some of these public decrees, either at Alexandria, Cyprus or Rome; and likewise another notion, which cannot, with so much justice, be ascribed to him, ' that in the distant ages of eternity, the blessed in heaven will, by degrees, relapse into sin, and descend into the regions of woe, while, on the other hand, the damned will rise to the mansions of purity and joy: thus constituting, by perpetual revolutions, a ceaseless alternation of happiness and misery.' [38] These, we are informed, were the principal errors now condemned; and they were probably alleged to justify the sentence which was passed, forbidding his works to be read, and placing him on the list of heretics. But, what is remarkable, it is certain that his doctrine of *the salvation of all mankind*, was not condemned, and that some of the orthodox continued to avow it with impunity. [39]

37. Sulpitii Severi Dialog. i. cap. 3. I quote from G. Bulli Defens. Fid. Nicænæ cap. ix. § 23.   38. Augustinus De Civ. Dei, Lib. xxi. cap. 17.

39. Augustine De (Civitate Dei Lib. xxi. cap. 17.), about twenty

The prohibition of his writings, and the angry indignity with which his name was treated, were regarded by the more dispassionate throughout all christendom, as unnecessarily severe ; but, as the authoritative acts had been regularly passed, the orthodox generally acquiesced, though with reluctance, reserve, and some exceptions.[40]

XII. When the persecuted Origenists A. D. 400, who had fled to Palestine from the rage to 403. of Theophilus, learned that he had sent a deputation against them to Constantinople, they likewise proceeded thither to defend themselves, and to seek an asylum under the strong protection of the bishop of that city, the celebrated Chrysostom. Fifty aged men, among whom were Isidorus and the three *tall brethren,* came and presented themselves before him ; and such was the wretchedness of their appearance that Chrysostom, it is said, melted into tears at the sight. He gave them the desired protection, till their cause should be heard ; and wrote immediately to Theophilus in their behalf. But his interference was haughtily resented, and drew upon him a long and fierce persecution, the particulars of which have no direct relation to the

years afterwards, reasons with those *merciful brethren* among the orthodox, who held the salvation of *all mankind.* He says they urged the superior benevolence of their doctrine as a proof of its truth ; and he exposes their inconsistency in using this argument, by daring them to extend it, like Origen, to the salvation of the devil and his angels. For this, adds he, the church has condemned him ; and they, of course, dare not go to the same extremity.

[40] Huet. Origenian. Lib. ii. cap. 4. Sect. ii. § 4. 12. Chrysostom, Augustine, Sulpitius Severus, Vincentius Lirinensis, &c. were favorably disposed towards the memory, though not the doctrine, of Origen.

subject of this history. We may only mention, that
the Origenists, having formally disavowed all heretical doctrines, continued to enjoy his countenance, as
well as that of the empress Eudoxia ; and were thus
emboldened to accuse their bishop before the tribunal
of the emperor Arcadius. Upon this, Epiphanius
hastened from Cyprus to Constantinople ; and, awhile
afterwards, the undaunted Theophilus arrived, in obedience to the imperial summons, attended, however,
by a host of bishops, from Egypt. Their vengeance
was directed not so much against the Origenists as
against Chrysostom. That ready engine of mischief,
a synod, was formed ; but when the members were
gathered, they immediately separated in two bodies,
and met in different places : those who hated the
bishop of Constantinople, in the suburbs ; and those
who favored him, in the city. Among his friends,
Palladius of Galatia, now bishop of Helenopolis in
Bithynia, seems to have taken a distinguished part ;
and could a majority have availed against intrigue and
power, Chrysostom had triumphed. But he sunk, at
length, with all his influence, under the combined
assaults of the Alexandrian party, the rage of the
insulted empress Eudoxia, and the obsequious edicts
of the timid Arcadius : and in the year 403, he was
wickedly deposed and banished, together with some
of his adherents. But in the mean time, the relent-
ing Epiphanius had died on his voyage back to Cyprus ; and Isidorus and the three *tall brethren* had
closed their lives, in the city, amidst the cruel storm
which their great and injured patron had brought
upon himself. The objects of his hatred being thus

removed, Theophilus was easily reconciled to the rest of the Origenists, and finally received them into his favor.[41]

XIII. The Alexandrian bishop had A. D. 401, not confined his exertions, all this time, to 404. to the city of Constantinople. While his party was managing his contest there, he himself was often engaged at home, rousing the indignation of the Egyptian Christians against Origen's name and doctrine. It was his practice to publish, annually, a *General* or *Paschal Epistle* to his churches; and in that of the year 401, his newly adopted zeal gave itself full utterance. He inveighed, with much bitterness, against Origen's heresies, which he comprised in the following particulars: that the kingdom of Christ would finally end, and the devil return to his pristine glory, and become subject to the Father; that the blessed in heaven may fall away; that Christ is to be crucified in the invisible world, for the demons and wicked angels; that the bodies of the saints, after the resurrection, will at length decay and become extinct; that the Son is not to be addressed in prayer; that magic is not sinful; and that marriage is dishonorable, being occasioned by our guilty connexion with the body.[42]

In the next year's *Epistle*, Theophilus resumed the unfinished topic, and entered again upon his conflict with the " Hydra of Origenism." The errors he now

---

[41.] Huetii Origenian. Lib. ii. cap. 4. Sect. ii. § 11, 12, 13. And Fleury's Eccl. Hist. Book xxi. chap. 23—32.　[42.] Theophili Paschal. Lib. ii. (properly i.) inter Hieronymi Opp. Tom. iv. Part ii. For the date and order of these books, see Du Pin, Cave, Fleury, &c.

selected as the points of his attack, were, that human souls pre-existed, but for their transgressions were doomed to this world, which was formed for their reception ; that the sun, moon and stars are animated ; that our fleshly bodies are not to rise ; that the dignitaries of the angelic world were not created such, but rose from the original equality of souls to their present elevations, by means of their own self-improvement ; that the Holy Ghost does not operate on irrational animals ; that the immediate providence of God extends only to things in heaven ; that Christ is not the supreme God ; that all souls came from one common and uniform mass of mind ; that the soul which Christ assumed was one with his divine nature, just as he is one with the Father; and that God could govern no more creatures than he has made, so that his power is finite.[43] We have another of his annual *Epistles,* written in the year 404. Here, his zeal had begun to abate ; but amidst a chaos of general and indefinite exhortation, there are some incidental attacks upon Origen's notion of the condemnation of souls to earthly bodies.[44]

These three *Epistles* were afterwards translated by Jerome, for the use of the Latin Christians ; and with them several others, which have since perished.

XIV. While thus Theophilus was pursuing his quarrel in Constantinople, and at the same time, sounding the alarm in Egypt, against the newly denominated heresy, the storm which had arisen in Italy continued

A. D. 400, to 404.

[43.] Theophili Paschal. Lib. i. (properly ii.) [44.] Theophili Paschal. Lib. iii.

without abatement. Soon after the passing of the decree, in **A. D. 400**, against Origen's works, Pope Anastasius cited Rufinus to appear before him, on a charge of heresy. But the latter, instead of leaving his friends at Aquileia, sent to the pontiff a formal *Apology*, or statement of his faith and conduct ; professing his hearty assent to the creeds of the churches at Rome, Alexandria, Jerusalem and Aquileia ; and declaring his belief in the trinity, in the resurrection of this very flesh, in a future judgement, and in the endless punishment of the devil, of all his angels, and of wicked men, *particularly*, says he, " *of those who* " *slander their brethren.* And whoever denies this, " let eternal fire be his portion, that he may feel what " he denies."[45] The same doctrine he also asserted in general terms, but with much explicitness, in his *Treatise on the Apostles' Creed ;*[46] and we have no reason to doubt his sincerity. The Italian bishops, it seems, were generally satisfied ;[47] but Anastasius, either suspecting dissimulation, or determined at all events to crush the obnoxious translator, passed upon him the dread sentence of excommunication. This was in **A. D. 401.** The Pope afterwards refused, peremptorily, to restore him to fellowship, notwithstanding a friendly remonstrance that he received, the next year, with much seeming respect, from John of Jerusalem.[48]

During all these transactions, Rufinus was solacing

---

[45] Rufini ad Anastasium Apologia, inter Hieron. Opp. Tom. v. p. 259.   [46] Rufini Symbolum, inter Hieron. Opp. Tom. v. pp. 127—150.   N. B. See the preceding Chap. Sect. xx. note 80.
[47] Hieron. Apol. adv. Rufin. Lib. iii. p. 453.   [48] Huetii Origenian. Lib. ii. cap. 4, Sect. i. § 20.

himself with secret revenge, by circulating, in private, a work which he had composed to defend his own conduct, to excuse Origen, but especially to expose Jerome. To this production, the partial resentment of the church has since affixed the hostile name of *Invective*, instead of the original and more peaceful title of *Apology*. Paulinianus, then residing in Italy, contrived to obtain sight of it ; and, having secretly transcribed copious extracts, sent them to his brother at Bethlehem. From these, Jerome had the vexation to discover that the *Defence* he had addressed, a few years before, to his friends at Rome, was likely to be turned back, with effect, against himself. He saw that Rufinus had succeeded in exposing much inconsistency, and some prevarication, in the explanations, there given, concerning his former and present treatment of Origen. But, what was more perplexing, a fatal advantage had been taken of his favorite *Comm ntaries on Ephesians and Ecclesiastes.* From these very works, to which Jerome had expressly referred as a clear delineation of his views, Rufinus had now selected ample quotations that taught, in the fullest manner, the several doctrines of the resurrection of aerial instead of fleshly bodies, pre-existence, and the universal restoration, not only of mankind, but also of the devil and his angels. Particular expressions had, moreover, been pointed out, which seemed to intimate a perpetual rotation of happiness and misery, the eventual return of all intellectual creatures into one order or grade of being, and the animation of those glorious bodies, the sun, the moon and stars.

"It is well," said his exulting accuser, "for such as you to condemn Origen."[49]

XV. Disturbed, but not dismayed, by this unexpected attack, Jerome sat down angrily to the composition of his *Apology against Rufinus :* replying haughtily, and sometimes disingenuously, to the numerous charges against his conduct, recriminating on his antagonist for the same acts which he excused in himself, and attempting by the most groundless insinuations to render him suspected of evasion in his late Apology to Anastasius. We have little concern, however, except with what relates to Universalism. To extricate himself from the awkward predicament in which he was placed by the unfortunate reference to his *Commentaries on Ephesians and Ecclesiastes,* he resorted to the desperate plea, that as the passages containing the doctrines of an aerial resurrection, preexistence, and universal restoration, were abridged by him from Origen and other authors, he was not responsible for the sentiments. The truth was, he had incorporated them into his own work, without a mark of censure, and without giving the original writers as his authority.[50]

That he would now be understood to deny the salvation of the devil and of the damned, is certain ; and he even complained that upon this, as well as on other points, Rufinus had not been sufficiently explicit in his *Apology* to the Roman pontiff.[51] But it is remarka-

---

[49.] Hieron. Apolog. adv. Rufinum Lib. i. and ii. Tom. iv. Jerome had not yet seen Rufinus's Invective entire, but only the extracts which Paulinianus had sent him. What these were we can learn only by Jerome's answer. [50.] Ditto. [51.] Ditto. Lib. ii. p. 393.

ble that he still avoided reckoning it among the *impor-tant* errors of Origen, and that he invariably passed it over, when he referred to them ; as in the following catalogue : " I point out to you, in Origen's works," said he to Rufinus, " many evil things, and particu-" larly these heresies : that the Son and Holy Spirit " are subordinate ; that there are innumerable worlds " succeeding each other to all eternity ; that angels " were changed into human souls ; that Christ's hu-" man soul existed before it was born of Mary ; and " that it was this which thought it no robbery to be " equal with God, seeing it was in the form of God, " yet humbled itself, and took the form of a servant ; " that in the resurrection our bodies will be aerial, " without members, and that they will eventually " vanish into nothing ; that in the universal restitu-" tion, the celestial powers and the infernal spirits, " together with the souls of all mankind, will be re-" duced into one order or rank of beings ; and that " from this uniform state of equality they will again " diverge, as formerly, holding various courses, until " at length some, falling into sin, shall be born once " more, into a mortal world, with human bodies. So " that we, who are now men, may fear hereafter to be " women ; and they who are now virgins, to be, then, " prostitutes. These heresies I point out in Origen's " works ; do you now show me in what work of his " you can find the contrary."[52]

This *Apology*, abounding in ridicule and sarcasm, was finished, in two books, and sent to Italy, some

[52]. Ditto. Lib. ii. p. 403. See also Lib. i. pp. 355, 371. and Lib. ii. p. 407. And Lib. iii. p. 441.

time in the year 403,[53] while Rufinus was still flattering himself that the secret of his performance had not
transpired. Stung into madness by the lampoons, the
insults and the misrepresentations of his opponent,
Rufinus immediately sent to Bethlehem the whole of
his *Invective*, accompanied with a letter threatening
prosecution, and perhaps death. Upon this, Jerome
added to his *Apology* a third book, written in a style
which showed that he would not be outdone in rage
nor in vulgar abuse. Though too much engrossed,
by other matters, to pay particular attention to the
old topic of Origen's errors, he nevertheless repeated
his attacks on the notion, that all rational creatures
will eventually return to one common grade of being,
and that they may afterwards relapse, and renew their
present diversity.[54] It is remarkable, that he seemed
almost to concede, notwithstanding his perverse temper, that he had once followed Origen too far.[55]

XVI. With this hot altercation, and
A. D. 404. with the simultaneous triumph of Theophilus, subsided, for the present, the
public contest in the church, concerning Origenism.
Its professors were every where obliged to conceal
their belief ; and their doctrine was generally regarded as heretical, at least as dangerous to the peace of
christendom. Some of its particulars, however, were
still avowed without censure, when no partiality to-

<hr>

[53] Huet, Du Pin, &c. say in A. D. 402 ; but as Jerome mentions Anastasius's Letter to John of Jerusalem (Lib. ii. p. 405,)
which could not have reached Palestine before the close of the
year 402, or beginning of 403, I have given Jerome's Apology
the later date.   [54] Apolog. Lib. iii. p. 441.   [55] Ditto. pp. 445,
447.

wards the sect was suspected. But Universalism, having been condemned in one of its points, received a check from which it never entirely recovered in the catholic church.

We may pronounce it probable that the doctrine of the salvation of the devil and his angels, would, for this time, have escaped condemnation and perhaps reproach, had it not been found in company with other offensive tenets. As to the general character of the violent proceedings now described, it is too manifest that they deserve the brand of personal quarrels, rather than the honorable appellation of a contest for the truth. Of the three chief agents, Epiphanius, an honest but credulous and bigoted man, may indeed be supposed to have acted, in a great measure, from principle, as he had long been distinguished for zeal against Origenism. But Theophilus engaged in the quarrel through policy and grudge, and prosecuted it for private revenge ; and we must pass nearly the same judgement on the motives of Jerome. Both had formerly been admirers of Origen ; and both, after the strife was past, betrayed again, though with caution, their partiality for his works.

CHAPTER VIII.

[From A. D. 404, to A. D. 500.]

I. After two or three centuries of decay, the unwieldy mass of the Roman empire had now fallen into two parts, by a permanent separation of the East from the West. Over these divisions, the innocent but effeminate sons of Theodosius the Great enjoyed the name of sovereignty, while their feeble hands, unable to sway the sceptre, resigned to their favorites and ministers the actual exercise of authority. Arcadius, the eastern emperor, sat on his father's throne in Constantinople ; his younger brother, Honorius, held the western court at Ravenna in Italy. Rome, the eternal city, the boasted mistress of the world, was no longer honored with the empty compliment of the imperial residence. Patriotism, courage, and even bodily strength, had, to a great degree, forsaken a people dispirited by ages of despotism, corrupted by its vices, and enervated by luxury and sloth. Throughout the East, internal disorders agitated the public tranquillity, and open rebellion alarmed the feeble administration. In the West, all hearts were trembling at the portentious movements of the fierce barbarians of the North, who hovered on the frontiers of Greece and Italy, and threatened, not in vain, to pour their forces over the beautiful territories into the ancient seat of empire. Already had they made an alarming incursion, from which they were turned back partly by force of arms, and partly by gold ; and they waited but the preparation of four or five years for their more successful return, when Rome itself was to be taken and sacked by Alaric at the head of his Goths.

In this period of terror and disorder, the church sympathized, of course, in the perils and fears of the state, with which she was so intimately connected ; but her worldly power naturally increased in proportion as the civil establishment grew weaker and more in need of her assistance. The public dangers never made her, for a moment, lose sight of the favorite object of ambition, towards which she advanced with the slow but fatal steadiness of the laws of nature. Nor did she withdraw her attention from her more domestic concerns. Among other employments, her clergy now found a grateful exercise for their zeal and violence, in the overthrow of the last monuments of heathenism, and in the suppression of the rebellious sects among themselves. The affair of the Origenists had been, to all appearance, successfully despatched ; but, in Africa, a very numerous and troublesome party of orthodox believers, the Donatists, stood out, with peculiar obstinacy, against all the invitations and all the threatenings of the church. In the course of three years, as many councils had assembled at Carthage, under the influence of the celebrated Augustine, with the design of compelling them to return to the catholic communion : from which they had separated, in an electioneering quarrel, nearly a century

20*

before. But these measures though seconded by the severe edicts of Honorius, had little success ; the schismatics, for the most part, remained stubborn, and their savage partizans continued to carry sword and fire through the province.

II. The political commotions and ec-
A. D. 405, clesiastical disturbances of the time, ope-
to 412.   rated, undoubtedly, to divert the public attention from the subject of Origenism, and to afford repose to the obnoxious party. The clamour of the late contest seems to have sunk, at once, into silence ; and as the impression was almost universal that the quarrel had been, in a great measure, personal, that it had been marked with unwarrantable violence, and pursued too far,[1] its victims were regarded with less rigor than was usual in cases of adjudged heresy. Rufinus appears to have enjoyed, at Aquileia, the patronage of his own bishop,[2] and the countenance, perhaps, of other dignitaries in the Italian churches.[3] He spent the remainder of his life, unmolested, in composing Commentaries on the Scriptures, and in translating Origen and other Greek writers ; till, in A. D. 409, he fled, at the approach of the northern barbarians, and retired into Sicily, where he died the next year. Melania, his noble and faithful patroness, accompanied him, with a numerous train, to Sicily.

[1] The banishment of Chrysostom roused the grief and indignation of a numerous party in the East, and of all the West. Unremitted efforts were made for his recall, but he died in the mean time ; and though it had been resolved to arraign Theophilus before a General Council, the affair was dropped.   [2] He translated Eusebius's Eccl. History at the request of Chromatius, bishop of Aquileia.   [3] Hieron. Apolog. adv. Rufin. Lib. iii. p. 453.

Proceeding thence to Africa, where she was complimented by Augustine, she pursued her way into Palestine. Her death soon followed, at Jerusalem, the scene of her former munificence; and, notwithstanding her connexion with the Origenists, she was honored with the title of saint, and her name inserted in the public martyrologies.[4] John of Jerusalem was, the meanwhile, strongly suspected of retaining a secret partiality for the proscribed doctrines; but he conducted so warily, as to enjoy his bishopric in quiet; and even his implacable neighbor, Jerome, could find no pretence for renewing the quarrel.[5] Evagrius Ponticus, having been overlooked in the rage of Theophilus, died, probably about this time, in some undisturbed retreat among the Egyptian monasteries; but Palladius of Gallatia, late bishop of Helenopolis, was suffering in banishment, not for his Origenism, but for his adherence to the exiled Chrysostom. He was afterwards recalled, however, and appointed over the church of Aspora, in his native province.[6] Theophilus, himself, now provoked the abhorrence of such as remembered his former violence and solemn prohibitions, by amusing his leisure with the perusal of Origen's works; and he openly asserted, as his justification, that, among some thorns which they contained, he found many beautiful and precious flowers. He had, however, written a large volume against

---

[4] Fleury's Eccl. Hist. Book xxii. chap. 22. And Huetii Origenian. Lib. ii. cap. 4. Sec. 1. § 22. [5] Hieronymi Epist. lxxvii. vel. 81. ad Augustin. Tom. iv. Part ii. p. 642. [6] Du Pin's Bibliotheca Patrum, Art. Palladius. And Cave, Hist. Lit. Art. Palladius. And Fleury's Eccl. Hist. Book xxi. chap. 59, and xxii. 3, 10.

Origen, which, though it has long since perished, survived his death in A. D. 412. It is remarkable, also, that Jerome still continued to quote Origen as an able and authoritative expounder of Scripture,[7] while he, at the same time, maintained his hatred against Rufinus and his party, and never spoke of them but with indecent abuse.[8] *The errors of Origen*, that phrase so indefinite though so often repeated, were also the subject of his occasional reprehension. He continued to dwell on nearly the same particulars as formerly ; still passing over the tenet of Universalism, although it was plainly taught in some of the extracts which he adduced as pernicious on other accounts.[9] His present belief however, at least his professed belief, was, that the devil and his angels,

[7] Hieronymi Epist. lxxiv. vel. 89. ad Augustin. pp. 619, 620.
[8] Hieron. Epist. xcvi. vel. 16. ad Princip. pp. 781, 782, And Epist. xcvii. vel. 8. ad Demetriad. pp. 793, 794.
[9] Hieron. Epist. xciv. vel. 59. ad Avitum. Jerome wrote this letter about a. d. 407, to accompany his translation of Origen's books Of Principles, which he gave to one Avitus, a Spaniard. It was composed for the purpose of pointing out the *errors* which those books contained ; and the following he selects as the principal : 1. That concerning the trinity. 2. The original equality of all intellectual creatures, and their perpetual revolution from bliss to misery, and from misery to bliss, by means of vice and virtue. 3. That all bodies whatever, with which rational beings are clothed, will at length vanish into nothing. 4. That innumerable worlds have preceded, and that innumerable others are to succeed, this present. 5. That the flames and torments of Gehenna, or hell, which the Scriptures threaten to sinners, are nothing but the remorse of their consciences, in the future world. 6. That our present conditions and circumstances are allotted us on account of our merits or demerits in a former state of being. And 7. That as Christ has been crucified for mankind in this world, so he will, perhaps, suffer death in eternity, for the salvation of the devil and his angels. These errors of Origen, Jerome exposes by means of long quotations from the books Of Principles ; and several of these extracts incidentally mention the Restitution of all creatures to purity and bliss ; but on this particular our author makes no direct remarks.

obstinate infidels and open blasphemers, shall suffer endless torments, while such as have embraced Christianity, yet led vicious lives, shall be consigned only to a long, but temporary, purgatory after death.[10] This doctrine he appears to have avowed for the rest of his life,[11] sometimes acknowledging, however, that those sinners who have been severely punished in this world, such as the antediluvians, the Sodomites and Pharaoh's host, will be pardoned, in the next.[12] After all, there is some reason to suspect that Jerome still remained, though in secret, a Universalist.[13]

[10.] Hieron. Comment. in Esaiam. Lib. xvi. (cap. lxvi. v. 24.) Written a. d. 409. Tom. iii. [11.] Hieron. Contra. Pelagian. Lib. i. cap. 9. Written about a. d. 415. [12.] Du Pin's Biblioth. Pat. Art. Jerome. [13.] See his Comment. in Esaiam. Lib. xvi. (cap. lxvi. v. 24.) Commenting upon these words of the prophet, *They shall go forth and look upon the carcasses of the men that have transgressed against me ; for their worm shall not die, neither shall their fire be quenched ; and they shall be an abhorring unto all flesh,* Jerome says, " this fire will burn as long as that matter " remains which feeds the voracious flame. If, therefore, any " one's conscience be infested with tares, which the enemy sowed " while the householder was asleep, the fire will burn and devour " them. And in the eyes of all the saints shall be manifested the " torments of those who, instead of laying gold, silver, precious " stones upon the foundation of the Lord, have built thereupon " hay, wood, stubble, the fuel of the eternal fire. Moreover, they " who would have these torments, though protracted through many " ages, come at length to an end, use the following texts ; *when* " *the fulness of the Gentiles shall have come in, then all Israel shall* " *be saved.* (Rom. xi. 25, 26.) Again : *God had concluded all* " *under sin, that he may have mercy upon all.* In another pas- " sage it is said, *I will sustain the wrath of the Lord, for I have* " *sinned against him, until he justify my cause, and bring forth* " *my judgement, and lead me into light.* (Micah vii. 9.) And " again : *I will bless thee O Lord, that thou wast angry with me.* " *Thou didst turn thy face from me ; but thou hast had compassion* " *upon me.* (Isa. xii. 1.) The Lord also says to the sinner, *when* " *the wrath of my fury shall have passed, I will heal thee again.* " Accordingly it is said, in another place, *how great is the multi-* " *tude of thy favors, O Lord, which thou hast laid up in secret, for* " *them that fear thee!* (Ps. xxi. 19.) All which texts they repeat, " in order to maintain that after punishments and torture, there " will be a refreshing, which must now be hidden from those to

III. Nor did he stand altogether alone in the church. The orthodox of this age may be divided into five classes, with respect to their views of future punishment and the final extent of salvation : 1, The most rigid among them believed that none would hereafter be saved, except those who died in the true faith, and in the exercise of godliness ; and most, if not all of these held, for the less deserving saints, a mild purgatory, by which they were to be thoroughly cleansed, before their admission into heaven. Such were the sentiments of the famous Augustine,[14] the oracle of the western church, who was, however, disposed, at times, to mitigate the severity of damnation.[15] 2, Another class held, in substance with the more ancient fathers Lactantius, Hilary, Basil and Ambrose, that all would finally be saved, who continued to the last in the catholic faith and discipline, whatever were their moral characters ; but that such

" whom fear is necessary, that while they fear the torments they " may desist from sin. We ought to leave it to the wisdom of " God alone, whose measure not only of mercy, but of torment is " just, and who knows whom to judge, and in what manner, and " how long to punish. We may only say, as becomes human " frailty, *Lord, contend not with me in thy fury, nor in thy wrath* " *take me away.* (Ps.) And as we believe in the eternal torments " of the devil and of all deniers and impious men who have said in " their heart *There is no God ;* so we may suppose that the sentence " of the Judge on those sinners and impious persons who never- " theless are Christians, and whose works are to be tried and purg- " ed in the fire, will be moderated and mixed with mercy." Considering Jerome's usual positiveness, and especially his violence in the late contention, I cannot satisfactorily account for the foregoing language, so moderate if not even equivocal, without supposing that he himself secretly agreed with those Restorationists of whom he speaks.

[14] Augustin. De Civitate Dei Lib. xx. cap. 1. and xxi. 24, and 26. See also Du Pin's Biblioth. Patrum, Art. Augustine.

[15] Augustin, Enchiridion ad Laurentium, cap. 112, 113. De Fide. et Op. cap. 23, 26.

of them as lived wickedly should suffer a long and excruciating trial by fire in the future world, before their reception to bliss. This, probably, was the common, the popular belief; and Jerome must be numbered among its *professed* advocates. 3, Others believed that all would eventually be saved, who had been baptized in the catholic church, and had partaken of the eucharist, into whatever crimes, errors and heresies they might afterwards have fallen; alleging in their support, the declarations of the Saviour, that *whoever eateth of this bread, shall live forever*, and the remark of the apostle, that the *church is the body of Christ.* 4, Many of the orthodox, though they held agreeably to the decision of the late councils against Origen, that the devil and his angels would suffer endless punishment, believed, nevertheless, that all mankind, without exception, would be saved; the wicked, after ages of torment in hell. 5, The last class of the orthodox, which was perhaps small, held that God had indeed threatened future misery on the impenitent, but that the saints, at the great judgement day, would so earnestly intercede with the Almighty in behalf of the world, that all mankind, even the impious and the infidels, would be saved, without any suffering at all; while the devil and his angels should be abandoned to endless torture. To prove the right of God to remit his threatenings, they adduced the judgement denounced, but not executed, upon Nineveh.[16] The two classes, last

[16.] Augustin. De Civit. Dei Lib. xxi. cap. 17—24.

named, seem to have formed, if we reckon them together, a large proportion of the orthodox.*

All this variety of opinion appears to have been tolerated in the church; and it is natural to suppose that there were some who still held in secret, with Origen, that all intelligent creatures, including the apostate angels, would ultimately be reconciled to God.

IV. This last opinion, heretical as it A. D. 410, had been adjudged, was certainly spread-to 415. ing, and openly taught, in the north-eastern province of Spain, that now bears the name of Catalonia. About fifty miles beyond the mouth of the Ebro, stands the modern city of Tarragona, on the venerable ruins of the ancient metropolis, Tarraco; which, from the summit of a gentle eminence, overlooked the Mediterranean to the south, and a fertile country inland.[17] Two of the citizens, by the name of Avitus, having spent some time in the East, returned not far from A. D. 410; and one of them brought from Jerome, in Palestine, the correct translation of Origen's books *Of Principles,* together with a long *Letter* pointing out their erroneous doctrines.[18] But the antidote proved only a partial preventive. While the two friends rejected some of Origen's speculations, they adopted others; and with the assistance of one Basil, a Gre-

---

* Augustin, Enchiridion, cap. 112. " *Quam plurimi*" is the phrase by which he denotes the number of those who did not believe that eternal punishment would be actually inflicted.

[17] Swinburne's Travels in Spain.   [18] Hieronymi Epist. xciv. ve 59, ad Avitum. See Sect. ii. of this chapter, Note 9.

cian, they proceeded to teach among the people the following peculiar tenets: 1, That all things had, from eternity, a real existence in the mind of Deity. 2, That angels, human souls and demons were of one uniform, equal substance, and originally of the same rank; and that their present diversity is the consequence of their former deserts. 3, That this world was made for the punishment and purification of the souls which had sinned in the pre-existent state. 4, That the flames of future torment are not material fire but only the remorse of conscience. 5, That they are not endless; for, although they are called *everlasting*, yet that word, in the original Greek, does not, according to its etymology and its frequent use, signify *endless*, but answers only to the duration of an age; so that every sinner, after the purification of his conscience, shall return into the unity of the body of Christ. 6, That the devil himself will, at length, be saved, when all his wickedness shall have been subdued. 7, That Christ had been employed, before his advent on earth, in preaching to the angels and exalted powers. 8, That the sun, moon and stars are to be reckoned among those intelligent rational creatures who, according to St. Paul, were made subject to vanity, and likewise to hope.[19]

These doctrines, together with the separate heresy of the Priscillianists which flourished in Spain, caused so much disturbance at Tarraco and its neighborhood, that two of the bishops at length sent a deputation on the subject to Augustine in Africa; and he imme-

[19.] Orosii Consultatio sive Commonitorium ad Augustin. inter Augustini Opp. Tom. vi. Edit. Basil. 1569.

diately wrote, in return, a small book
A. D. 415. *Against the Priscillianists and Origenists*, but chiefly against the latter. In opposition to their views of future punishment, he asserted the materiality of its fire, and laboriously defended
the eternity of its duration; attempting to maintain
that the original word, translated *everlasting*, always
signified *endless*. But, because there might be some
exceptions, as he at the same time inconsistently admitted, he then changed his ground, and resorted to
that declaration of Christ, *These shall go away into
everlasting punishment, but the righteous into life
eternal*, (Matt. xxv. 46,) where the same Greek
word was applied to the torments of the damned, and
to the bliss of the saints: so that if the Origenists
would, through compassion, limit the duration of the
former, they must also restrict that of the latter. But,
if this should not convince them, how could they
elude that declaration of the prophet Isaiah, *Their
worm shall not die, neither shall their fire be quenched?* (Isa. lxvi. 24.) [20]

Such is the order and substance of his arguments.
It is remarkable, that here we meet with the earliest
attempt at criticism on that original word which has
been the subject of so much cavilling in modern
times. But Augustine, a Latin writer, was too imper-
fectly acquainted with the Greek language to define
its terms; and, if we may judge from what we have
observed in our own day, his criticisms were accounted satisfactory, by the determined believers in endless

---

[20] Augustini Lib. Contra Priscillianistas et Origenistas, Tom. vi.

misery, but absurd, by the Universalists. A few years afterwards, in composing a general body of divinity, he repeated some of these arguments, with several additions, and combatted the notions of all the several classes just mentioned, who extended the happiness of heaven beyond the number who died in faith and holiness.[21] He has furnished the moderns with many of the trite but popular objections, which are now alleged from the Scriptures, against the salvation of all mankind.*

[21.] Augustin. De Civit. Dei Lib. xxi. cap. 23—24.

* As a specimen of his reasoning, or declamation, which with *him* was original, I subjoin an entire chapter from his great work, *The City of God.*

"And in the first place we should ascertain why the Church
"has refused to allow people to dispute in favor of a purification
"and release of the devil himself, after very great and lasting
"punishments: It was not that so many holy men, so well in-
"structed in the Old and New Testaments, grudged any of the
"angels a purification, and the bliss of heaven after so great tor-
"ments; but it was because they saw it impossible to annul or
"weaken that divine sentence which the Lord declared he would
"pronounce in the judgement, *Depart from me, ye cursed, into*
"*eternal fire, prepared for the devil and his angels.* (Matt. xxv.
"41.)   For thus it is shown that the devil and his angels are to
"burn in eternal fire.   As it is written in the Apocalypse: *The*
"*devil who deceived them was cast into the lake of fire and brim-*
"*stone, where are the beast and the false prophet; and they shall*
"*be tormented day and night forever and ever.* (Rev. xx. 10.)
"What is called in the other passage *eternal,* is here expressed
"by *forever and ever:* by which words the divine Scripture is
"wont to mean nothing but what is endless in duration.   And
"there is no other reason, nor can one more just and manifest be
"found, why we should hold it fixed and immutable in the sin-
"cerest piety, that the devil and his angels are never to return
"to righteousness and the life of the holy, than that the Scrip-
"ture, which deceives no one, says that God spared them not (2
"Pet. ii. 4,) but delivered them up to be kept in prisons of infer-
"nal darkness, in order to be punished at the last judgement, when
"they shall be sent into eternal fire, where they shall be tor-
"mented forever and ever.   This being the case, how can all, or
"any of mankind, after a certain period, be restored from the
"eternity of this punishment, and not immediately weaken that
"faith by which we believe the torments of the demons will be

V. But however inconclusive his arguments may have been deemed, the great authority of his opinin-

"endless? For if all or any of those to whom it shall be said, "*Depart from me, ye cursed, into eternal fire, prepared for the* "*devil and his angels*, shall not always remain there, what rea- "son have we to believe that the devil and his angels will always "remain there? Will the sentence of God which is pronounced "both against the evil angels and men, be true with respect to "the angels, and false with respect to men? Thus it will plainly "be, if not what God said, but what men suspect, avail the most. "But because that cannot be the case, they who would shun "eternal torments, ought, while there is time, to yield to the "divine precept, instead of arguing against God. And again: "how can we suppose eternal torment to be only a fire of long "duration, and yet eternal life to be without end, when in the "very same passage, and in one and the same sentence, Christ "said with reference to both, *These shall go away into eternal* "*punishment, but the righteous into eternal life?* (Matt. xxv. 46.) "As both are eternal, both certainly ought to be understood either "as of long duration but with an end, or else as perpetual, with "no end. For they are connected together: on the one hand, "eternal punishment; on the other eternal life. And it is very "absurd to say, in this one and the same sense, that eternal life "will be without end, and eternal punishment will have an end. "Whence, as the eternal life of the saints will be without end, "so also the eternal punishment of those who shall suffer it, will, "without any doubt, have no end." De Civitate Dei Lib. xxi. cap. 23. This remains, even to the present day, the most popu- lar, and perhaps the most plausible argument used against the doctrine of Universal Salvation; and yet it is founded on one of the most palpable blunders into which the church has fallen: that of applying to eternity what Christ declared should be ac- complished in his own generation. Compare Matt. xxv. 31—, with its immediate connexion, Matt. xxiv. 30—34; and also with Matt. x. 23—xvi. 27, 28.—Mark viii. 38, ix. 1.—Luke ix. 26, 27.

Another chapter of the same work, furnishes us with the orig- inal, I believe, whence has been derived one of the popular methods of justifying the infliction of endless torments: "But to "human notions eternal punishment seems hard and unjust, be- "cause that in the weakness of our mortal senses we are destitute "of that most exalted and pure wisdom by which we could real- "ize how great was the wickedness committed in the first trans- "gression. For in proportion as man enjoyed God, was the "magnitude of his impiety in forsaking God; and he was worthy "of eternal evil, who destroyed in himself that good which might "have been eternal. And the whole mass of the human race "was therefore condemned, because that he who first introduced "sin, was punished together with his posterity which had its root "in him; so that none could be released from this just and merions, especially in the western churches, must have checked the progress of any doctrine which he was known so decidedly to oppose. Already were his talents, his virtues, and his faithfulness regarded with a general homage, such as had been enjoyed by none of the Christian doctors, since the time of the more vigorous and enterprizing, but less amiable Anthanasius. In the West, his decisions were received with almost universal deference; and in the East, his name was regarded with great, though perhaps not equal, veneration. A long and intimate familiarity with the Scriptures, a competent share of learning, and a large fund of general information, which had been rather hastily collected, supplied his strong and capacious mind with subjects for reflection, and provided his argumentative genius with the weapons of controversy, which, however, he generally managed with moderation. In general, he treated his opponents with an indulgence to which they were unaccustomed, and which would appear with advantage in the theological warfare of a later and more refined age. That he sometimes dissembled for truth's sake, and that he

"ited penalty, but by mercy and unmerited grace. And thus
"mankind are so situated that in some of them the power of
"merciful grace may be exhibited; and in the rest, the power of
"vindictive justice. For both could not be manifested upon all;
"because if all should remain in the sufferings of their just dam-
"nation, in none would appear the merciful grace of redemption,
"and if all should be translated from darkness into light, in none
"would appear the severity of vengeance. Of the latter class
"there are many more than of the former; that thus might be
"shown what was due to all. And if it had been inflicted upon
"all, none could, with propriety, have called in question the
"justice of the vengeance; and the release of so many as are saved
"therefrom, should be an occasion of the greatest thanksgiving
"for the gift of redemption." De Civitate Dei Lib. xxi. cap. 12.
N. B. This was written about A. D. 420, or 426.

21*

countenanced the legal persecution of schismatics, when he could not persuade them to-reenter the catholic church, may in justice be imputed to the pernicious but approved maxims of his times. Augustine was a great and a good man. Yet he was the father of the present orthodox system of total depravity, irresistible grace, and sovereign, partial election.

VI. By introducing this system of doctrine into the church, he unknowingly laid upon the cause of Universalism a remote, but eventually, a more fatal check, than even the decisions of a council could have imposed. Hitherto, none of the catholic Christians had gone farther, in their very lowest descents into orthodoxy, than to represent, that from the fall of Adam, all his posterity inherited a mortal constitution, and such an unhappy weakness of soul, as combined with the depravity of the flesh, caused a propensity to sin ; and that the supernatural influences of God's spirit were necessary to aid, not strictly to create good resolutions, and to render them effectual. But this divine agency, they had ever held, was always received or rejected, cherished or suppressed, yielded to or resisted, by the free will of the creature ; and they had never disputed, that all had competent power, both natural and moral, to avail themselves of its assistance. It was proffered sincerely to all, for the single purpose of preserving in holiness such as were already pure, and of reclaiming the sinful ; for, it was unequivocally the will of God that all should be saved. There may, indeed, have been some who entertained a vague notion that the devil and his angels, when they apostatized, sunk below the reach of divine mercy, and that impenitent sinners, when they die, pass the irremeable line. But, that God had sought to prevent the fatal catastrophe, appears to have been doubted by none ; and, that his decrees were concerned in procuring it, was a thought from which every one would have shrunk with horror.

So long as it was the invariable opinion that God sincerely aimed at the repentance and salvation of all his erring creatures, it is easy to discover that a silent but strong influence was constantly bearing the more reflecting minds towards Universalism ; since it was unreasonable to suppose that the will of an immutable Deity could ever totally abandon its aim, or that Omnipotence would be forever frustrated in its objects by the impotence of man. Resulting from this view there was also a favorable, though often indefinite, persuasion of the general goodness of God, which tended to suggest doubts of the eternal infliction of a torment as fruitless as it was unmerciful. But when Christians became accustomed to consider it the arbitrary determination of the almighty Sovereign to save a part, and a part only, and at the same time to abandon the rest to certain and complete ruin, the doctrine of endless misery stood on its own proper and substantial foundation, — the divine counsel ; for, it was not likely that the neglected and helpless wretches would be saved, when their recovery was not actually desired by God.[22]

22. I do not forget, what may at first seem inconsistent with this reasoning, that the high Calvinism of Whitfield and his school, was the immediate occasion of the rise of the present sect of Universalists. But, then, the leading preachers of Whitfield's connexion did not usually dwell on the black side of the picture.

VII. This change of doctrine, one of
A. D. 412,   the most momentous which has ever oc-
to 418.   curred, seems to have taken place in the
church, like many others, by accident
rather than by design. Two British monks, Pelagius
and his disciple Celestius, residing at Rome early in
this century, imbibed some peculiar sentiments from
certain [23] Christians who had studied in the East.
Though these sentiments were silently spreading in
the city, little notice was taken of them ; and Pelagius continued to enjoy a high and deserved reputation for the purity of his character and for the warmth
of his devotion to the church. Going at length into
Africa, he formed some acquaintance with Augustine ;
and then pursued his course on a visit to John, in
Palestine, leaving Celestius at Carthage. Here, the
latter was soon involved in a charge of heresy ; and
he was condemned at the council of Carthage, in A.
D. 412, for teaching, what was certainly a considerable variation from the popular belief of the age, that
Adam was created mortal, and that his transgression
affected none of his posterity, but himself alone.   To

The favorite themes on which many of them used to expatiate,
with all the fervor of enthusiasm, were, the complete pardon
purchased by Christ, the free, unconditional gift of salvation, and
the omnipotent energy of God's spirit in converting sinners.
When these encouraging topics were so zealously urged, without
a corresponding regard for the decree of damnation, it was but
one step forward to the hope, the conclusion, that God would
have all men to be saved ; and to this step, the strong tide of
their new feelings, their view of the Messiah's increasing and
victorious kingdom, as well as the testimonies of Scripture, im-
pelled them, often before they were thoroughly aware.

[23]. It has been supposed that one Rufinus, a Syrian (a friend
and not the opponent of Jerome) brought this doctrine from Asia
Minor, and perhaps from Theodorus of Mopsuestia, to Rome,
and here taught it to Pelagius.

these particulars we may here add some others which were involved during the progress of the succeeding controversy, and which complete the doctrine of Pelagianism : that as mankind are now born pure, they are able, after transgression, to repent, reform, and arrive at length to the highest degrees of virtue and piety, even to perfection, by the exercise merely of their own natural powers ; that though the external excitements of divine grace are necessary to rouse their endeavors, yet they have no need of any internal agency of the Holy Ghost ; that infant baptism does not wash away sin, but is only a ceremony of admittance into the church of Christ ; and that good works are meritorious as the conditions of salvation. Such, it appears, were the real tenets of Pelagius and Celestius, though they were sometimes unjustly charged, with disowning the necessity of the grace of God, in every sense relative to human actions, and with denying the utility of infant baptism.

On the condemnation of Celestius, in the council of Carthage, Augustine began to preach and to write against the heresy, with his characteristic tenderness at first towards its authors, but always with a cool, invincible determination to destroy their doctrine, root and branch. But, in the long contest which followed, he himself went over, by degrees, to the opposite extreme ; and influenced, perhaps, by the early bias of his Manichean principles,[24] he maintained, what

[24.] See Appendix to Chapter v. Sect. 2. Note (2.) It is a curious circumstance that nearly all the fathers who had been converted from other religions, always retained some of the peculiarities of their former doctrines, notwithstanding they became the most strenuous opposers of those systems, taken as a

was new in the church, that Adam's transgression had so thoroughly corrupted all his posterity, that, by nature, they could do only evil, and that nothing but the irresistible spirit of the Almighty could incline their wills to good, and induce them, contrary to their nature, to accept of his grace. God alone was, from first to last, the immediate agent of their counternatural conversion; and on his arbitrary pleasure only did it depend, whether the impotent sinner should be renovated. From these premises he advanced to the necessary conclusion, that God had foreordained whom to convert, and finally to save, without reference to any thing which they should perform; while he had likewise predetermined to pass by all the remainder of the fallen race. Such was the first organization of the present orthodox system, so far as it regards total depravity, election and reprobation.[25]

whole. Witness the converts from the Greeks, who corrupted Christianity with their old philosophy; and those from the Magian religion, who introduced the monstrous fables of the Gnostics.

[25]. The difference between Augustine's doctrine and that of Calvin, on election and reprobation, though small, is such as to betray the crudeness of the master, and the finishing touches of his scholar. Augustine seems to have held that God did not ordain the fall of Adam, and that it was after that event occurred, and when it had become certain that the whole race would be born totally depraved and therefore under helpless bondage to sin, that the elect were chosen and the reprobate abandoned. The original plan of creation did not embrace such a result. But Calvin and other Reformers, with a better digested arrangement, carried back the separating decree to the past ages of eternity; so that mankind were originally created for their respective destinations. Augustine was by no means thoroughly systematic: He held that Christ died for all men; that even genuine conversion is no security of final happiness, as the subjects may afterwards fatally relapse and perish; and that the grace of perseverance alone is the pledge of personal election. No infants, who had not been baptized, could be saved; because, regeneration was effected only in the rite of water baptism.

With quite different views, the Pelagians were also attacked by other cotemporary writers, and among the rest by Jerome, with his accustomed violence.

VIII. During the first three or four A. D. 413, years of his troubles, Pelagius resided in to 420. Palestine, enjoying the patronage of John of Jerusalem ; and when, in A. D. 416, he was arraigned, on a charge of heresy, before a synod at Diospolis, near Joppa, that prelate earnestly defended him, and procured his entire acquittal.[26] But John did not live to witness the conclusion of the controversy. A peaceful death closed his career in the beginning of A. D. 417, at about the age of sixty. He was somewhat famous in his day, but chiefly for the part he bore in the contests which agitated the church. We discover nothing in his life, that evinces superior learning, talents, or piety ; and as he has been generally described, he betrays considerable petulance, timidity, and wary cunning. In justice to him, however, we must remember that his history is collected wholly from his opponents, and chiefly from his bitter enemies. His friends, it is certain, gave him the character of a worthy and pious man ; and even Pope Anastasius and Augustine addressed him in terms of respect and esteem. Indeed, such as he is actually described, it would be no disparagement to the generality of his cotemporaries to compare them with him. He was a zealous patron of the monastic life, and joined in the prevailing veneration of relics ; and his last days were honored, to adopt the language of those times, by the miraculous

[26.] Fleury's Eccl. Hist. Book xxiii. chap. 19, 20.

discovery of the bodies of Stephen the first martyr, of Nicodemus who came to our Saviour by night, and of Gamaliel the master of St. Paul. These remains, undoubtedly of some nameless persons, drew vast concourses on their exhibition, excited universal awe, and of course wrought numerous miracles, according to the invariable custom of relics, in that age.[27]

In taking our final leave of John of Jerusalem, we must also bid adieu to one who has borne a still more conspicuous part in the events of this history. Jerome died, very old, at Bethlehem, in the year 420 ; but the account we have already given of his life and conduct, sufficiently exhibits his character, without the tediousness of a formal analysis.

IX. Of all the ancient Universalists, A. D. 420, the more respectable for good sense and to 428. sober judgement, if we may rely on the opinion of modern critics,[28] than Theodorus bishop of Mopsuestia, a very eminent orthodox father, and a voluminous writer. Belonging to an illustrious Syrian family in Antioch, he was placed under the instruction of the renowned heathen sophist and critic, Libanius ; and then, in company with the celebrated Chrysostom, he studied divinity in the school of Diodorus, whom we have named as the Universalist bishop of Tarsus. At the close of his studies, he appears to have been ordained a presbyter in his native city. Here, also, we soon afterwards

---

[27] Fleury's Eccl. Hist. Book xxiii. chap. 22, 23.   [28] Beausobre, (Hist. de Manichee Lib. i. chap. 4. Tom. i. p. 288.) Lardner, (Credibility &c. Chap. Theodore of Mopsuestia) and Mosheim, (Eccl. Hist. Cent. v. Part ii. chap. 2, 3.) speak in the highest terms of his useful talents and apparent sound judgement.

find him engaged, with Chrysostom, instructing youths in a monastery, where he had the famous Nestorius for one of his pupils. In the year 392, a little before the death of his master Diodorus, he was appointed bishop of Mopsuestia, which stood nearly forty miles eastward of Tarsus, and occupied both banks of the river Pyramus. Here, he passed a long episcopate, of about thirty-six years, in composing numerous commentaries and polemical works ; maintaining, the mean while, the reputation of a distinguished preacher, at Antioch, at Constantinople, and over all the East.

Like his master Diodorus, he followed the natural and simple mode of interpretation ; and it would seem, from some fragments, which alone have descended to us, of his writings, that he cultivated this method with more judgement, than a large part even of our modern commentators. So much did he dislike the allegorical expositions of Origen, of whom he was no admirer, that he published a work against them.* Though he held the tenets for which Pelagius was condemned, and though he was, perhaps, the source whence they were indirectly transmitted to that unfortunate heretic, yet his orthodoxy seems never to have been impeached during his life-time. It appears, also, that he avowed, with impunity, the restoration of the wicked from hell, long after the contest with the Origenists had brought it into disrepute. " They, " says he, " who have chosen the good, shall, in the future " world, be blessed and honored. But the wicked, " who have committed evil the whole period of their

* Facundi Hermianensis de Tribus Capit. Lib. iii. cap. 6. inter Sirmondi Opp. Tom. ii. p. 362.

" lives, shall be punished till they learn, that, by con-
" tinuing in sin, they only continue in misery.   And
" when, by this means, they shall have been brought
" to fear God, and to regard him with a good-will,
" they shall obtain the enjoyment of his grace.   For,
" he never would have said, *Until thou hast paid the*
" *uttermost farthing*, (Matt. v. 26,) unless we could
" be released from punishment, after having suffered
" adequately for sin ; nor would he have said, *He*
" *shall be beaten with many stripes*, and again, *He*
" *shall be beaten with few stripes*, (Luke xii. 47, 48,)
" unless the punishments to be endured for sin, will
" have an end. "*   We learn, also, from Photius, of
the ninth century, who was one of the most trusty
ecclesiastical critics of antiquity, that he found, in
another work of Theodorus, " the notion of Origen
" concerning the termination of the punishments of the
" future state. "†

He maintained that the reason why God permitted
sin, was, that it would be ultimately made to subserve
the good of mankind.‡   According to Photius, he held
that Adam was created mortal, that mankind inherit
no moral corruption from him ; that infants are born
without sin ; and that mankind sin, not by nature, but
by their free-will ; or rather, he opposes the contrary
opinions, which, he says, were taught by some western Christians, alluding, probably, to Augustine and

---

* Assemani Biblioth. Orient. Tom. iii. Par. i. p. 323.   † Photii
Biblioth. Cod. 177.   The work of Theodorus, which Photius here
quotes, must have been written about as late as the year 420 ; since
it is evident, from its topics, that the Pelagian controversy had
already made considerable noise, even in the East.   ‡ See Du
Pin's Biblioth. Pat. 5th Cent. Art. Theodorus of Mopsuestia.

his party.[29] He was always a firm and steady opposer of Arianism ; but it is suspected that he was the father of Nestorianism, a doctrine which arrived, though in a blind and very circuitous way, to little else than the simple humanity of Jesus Christ. He died undisturbed, however, in the catholic communion, in A. D. 428, aged not far, probably, from seventy years.

But, after his death, he was often reproached for his Pelagianism, and for his connexion with his scholar Nestorius ; and, in the middle of the next century, he was anathematized, on the latter account, by the Fifth General council. Accordingly, his works, for the most part, have either perished, or been preserved only in the Syriac language, among the Nestorians of the East.[30]

X. Directing our attention, from Cilic
A. D. 430, ia, down the Mediterranean coast to the
to 450. Holy Land, we discover that here Universalism prevailed, about this time, to a considerable extent among the monks, especially around Cesarea in Palestine. But the glimpse we obtain of the matter, is casual and imperfect, and soon obstructed by surrounding darkness. We only know that Origenism had openly appeared in the country,

---

[29] Photii Bib. Cod. 177.   [30] Besides fragments of his writings among the acts of the Fifth General Council, in Facundus Hermianensis, and in Photius, it is supposed that the *Commentary on the Psalms*, under the name of Theodorus, in Catena Corderii, belongs to our author. It is said also that his *Commentaries on the Twelve Minor Prophets*, exist in manuscript in the Emperor's Library at Vienna, in the Library of St. Mark at Venice, and in the Library of the Vatican. These, however, form but a very small part of the ancient catalogue of his works.

with a numerous party of advocates ; and that the particulars, in their doctrine, which gave most offence, were the pre-existence of souls, and the universal restoration. Against both of these points, Euthymius, the chief abbot who then presided over the monasteries in the desert between Jerusalem and the Dead Sea, opposed his utmost zeal and indignation,[31] but with what effect we are not informed. It does not appear, however, that any of the party were arraigned, nor their tenets condemned. We naturally suspect that their faith had always lingered around the churches where Origen preached, and where Alexander, Theoctistus and John presided ; and there is some reason to suppose, that it continued to exist in the country, till it broke out, as we shall learn, sixty or seventy years afterwards, and spread through a large part of Palestine.

But, with a single exception that will A. D. 450, be noticed at the close, we seek in vain, to 500. in the remainder of the present century, for any traces of the doctrine. It had grown unpopular. For though it had not been judicially branded with the indelible mark of heresy, save when it embraced the salvation of the devil and his angels, yet even in its restricted form, as extending only to the restoration of all mankind, it had been pointed out as an obnoxious and kindred error ; and the repose of the public, as well as the quiet of the individual, must have suggested the prudence of con-

---

[31.] Vita Euthymii, per Cyrillum Scythopolitanum, inter Cotelerii Monumenta Græc. Ecclesiæ Tom. iv. p. 52. See also a Paraphrase on this work, by Symeon Metaphrastes, in Tom. ii.

cealment. Even the familiar name of Origenism
almost wholly disappears, during this period.[32] We
may, indeed, discover a favorable disposition in the
ecclesiastical historians, Socrates, Sozomen and Theodoret ; of whom, the two first defended the reputation
of its former advocates, and the last neglected to insert
it in his general Catalogue of heresies. But on the
other hand, it appears that Antipater, bishop of Bostra
in Arabia, undertook to refute the *Apology* of Pamphilus and Eusebius *for Origen* ; and that, about the
same time, a Council at Rome, in A. D. 496, either
gave or followed the example.[33]

A. D. 450, to 500.

XI. But other and more interesting
causes may be assigned for the silence
which pervades the ecclesiastical writings
of this period, with regard to Universa-

[32.] To this period, if not to a later, may perhaps be assigned the
anonymous *Apology for Origen, in five books*, which Photius describes (Biblioth. Cod. 117.) without fixing its date. According to
him, it was of little value. The author, it appears, mentioned
Clemens Alexandrinus, Dionysius the Great, and even Demetrius,
as witnesses in favor of Origen ; and he strove, particularly, to
defend Pamphilus and Eusebius, which shows that it was after
they had been reproached for their Apology, perhaps by Jerome,
perhaps by Antipater. He also acknowledged and maintained
Origen's doctrine of Pre-existence and some other heterodox notions ; but he denied that Origen had been guilty of the following
errors charged upon him ; 'That the Son is not to be invoked, is
not absolutely good, and knows not the Father as he knows himself ; That rational natures enter into brutes, that there is a transmigration into different kinds of bodies ; That the soul of Christ
was that of Adam ; That there is no eternal punishment for sinners, nor resurrection of the flesh ; That magic is not evil, and
that the influence of the stars governs our conduct ; That the only
begotten Son will, hereafter, possess no kingdom ; That the holy
angels came into the world as fallen creatures, not to assist others ;
That the Father cannot be seen by the Son ; that the Cherubim
are merely the thoughts of the Son ; That Christ, the image of
God, so far as he is the image, is not the true God.' [33.] Huet,
Origenian. Lib. ii. cap. 4. Sect. ii. § 24, 25.

lism. There is no wonder it should have been overlooked, or if known to exist, that it should have been
suffered to pass unnoticed, when subjects far different,
and of the most distracting nature, engrossed the attention of all christendom. The Roman Empire in the
West was going to wreck amidst the boisterous and
conflicting waves that rolled in upon it from the fierce
North ; and it finally sunk under the repeated assaults
of the barbarians, in the year 476. Odoacer, king of
the Heruli, enjoyed the spoils, and stretched his sceptre over all Italy. Other conquerors advanced from
the exhaustless regions of barbarism, and, in their turn,
wrested the power from the recent victors. From
Rome to Britain, from the Danube to Africa, all was
a scene of anxiety and distress. Amidst the general
commotion, the church beheld, with equal chagrin
and fear, the exiled Arians return along with the in-
vading hosts of their barbarian converts, and, under
the patronage of the Huns, Goths and Vandals, assume the pre-eminence in Italy, Gaul and the African
provinces. The catholics now dreaded, and they
sometimes felt, the scourge of retribution ; but they
still retained sufficient spirit to wage, at intervals, a
polemical contest with the Pelagians and Semi-Pela-
gians. The Roman pontiffs, however, had other subjects of interest, in the terrible and shameful contentions that raged, with unprecedented violence and
duration, in the eastern churches.

The Empire of the East, though little annoyed by
foreign enemies, was agitated by the desperate quarrels
of the clergy, who have left, on the records of this age,
one of the blackest stains that disgrace the pages of

ecclesiastical history. The great archbishopric of Egypt, which had hitherto maintained its superiority among the eastern dioceses, watched, with an envious eye, the growing influence of the new see of Constantinople, which was rapidly ascending to a rank next that of Rome ; and the two successive prelates of Alexandria, who inherited the vices and the jealousy of Theophilus, had already shaken Nestorius and, after him Flavian, from the episcopal throne of the rival city, by means of some intricate questions concerning the union of the divine and human natures of Christ. All the East, from the Nile and the Bosphorus to the Euphrates, took sides for a long contest, in which honor and freedom were staked, and deposition and banishment were the penalty of failure. The artifices, the outrageous injustice, and shameless effrontery, which prevail in the most degenerate courts in times of violent faction, disgraced three General Councils,[34] in quick succession, and procured for one of them, even in that age, an appellation which truly belonged to all, *The Assembly of Robbers.* The indignant spectator gladly turns from these deplorable scenes ;[35] and we may only remark, that before the close of this century, the Nestorian, Eutychian and Monophysite heresies were successively condemned, as they arose,

---

[34.] At Ephesus, in A. D. 431; at the same place, in A. D. 449 ; and at Chalcedon, in A. D. 451. That in A. D. 449 is not reckoned, by the Catholics, among the General Councils, because the legates of the Pope were excluded.

[35.] Of this contest Gibbon (Decline and Fall &c. chap. xlvii.) has given a description to the life, which though slightly marked with his infidel irony, seems well supported, and does not differ, materially, from the narrative of the Catholic Fleury, (Eccl. Hist. Book xxv. and onwards.)

and that amidst riots, intrigue, bribery, kicks and blows, was settled the present orthodox faith concerning the two natures of Christ : that his divinity and humanity are most intimately united in one person, while they are nevertheless distinct.

XII. Near the close of the century, About we find a single instance of Universalism, A. D. 500. in the remote country, however, of Mesopotamia, and beyond the bounds of the Roman Empire. At Edessa, about seventy miles east of the upper waters of the Euphrates, and twenty-six northwest of the ancient Haran,* the abbot Stephan Bar-Sudaili presided over a cloister of monks, and maintained a distinguished reputation among those Christians who held the simple unity of the divine and human nature of Christ. But deviating, at length, from the common faith of his brethren, he proceeded to teach that future punishments will finally come to an end ; that wicked men and devils, having been purified, will obtain mercy ; and that all things will be brought into unity with God, so that, as St. Paul expresses it, he shall become all in all.[36] Whether he succeeded, to any extent, in propagating this doctrine among the churches of Mesopotamia and Syria, we are not informed. We only know that it soon called forth the complaints of some of his brethren, who stigmatized it as heresy ;[37] and that he left

---

* See Buckingham's Travels in Mesopotamia &c. chap. iii.—v.
[36]. Assemani Biblioth. Orient. Tom. ii. pp. 30—33, 291. See, too, Neander's remarks, Allgemeine Geschichte der christlich. Religion u. s. w. 2n. Band 3te. Abtheil. § 793—795. [37]. Assemani Bib. Orient. Tom. i. p. 303. Tom. ii. pp. 30—33.

Edessa, and went into Palestine, — perhaps, to associate with the Origenists there.

XIII. Nothing remains but to close with a passing notice of the Manicheans. Under this appellation, which had now grown somewhat indefinite, may be comprehended about all the Gnostic Christians of this century; for the Priscillianists, who were numerous in Spain, and a few Marcionites, scattered in various parts, were often classed, and not very improperly, with the more genuine followers of Mani, who lurked in every quarter of christendom. All of them had been led, by their intercourse with the Roman world, to modify their general system, and to omit some of their fables ; but they always adhered to their fundamental doctrine of two original Principles, the distinct causes of good and evil. On one solitary point we may prefer their views to those entertained by a large part of the orthodox : they contemplaated Deity in the unchangeable character of universal and perfect benevolence. This important sentiment, together with their fanciful notion concerning the divine emanation of all souls, would naturally incline them to expect the eventual recovery of human nature ; but how far they approached towards this conclusion, does not distinctly appear. They still retained enough of their oriental peculiarities to render them intolerable to the Greek and Roman sects ; and, while the cruel laws of persecution compelled them to the most careful concealment, the sharp-sighted zeal of the bishops and governors often detected them through all their disguises.

CHAPTER IX.

I. The opening scene of our narrative lies in the barren solitude between Jerusalem and Bethlehem on the West, and the sunken coast of the Dead Sea, or lake Asphaltites, on the East. The wild and austere features of desolation, which pervade this mountainous desert, will readily occur to every one who has attentively studied the geography of Palestine. But it can scarcely be accounted a useless interruption, if we pause here to take a more careful and particular view of a region so full of interest, and which retains, to this day, nearly the same appearance it wore in the sixth century.

Beginning our survey at the north-eastern extremity, and standing on some elevated spot, if such there be, in the fields adjacent to the once flourishing Jericho, we should find ourselves in the midst of an uneven plain, of great length and considerable breadth. Its fertility departed, ages ago, with the banished tribes, and left little remains on the parched surface, except a kind of spiny grass, and a few detached groves and plantations. Two leagues to the East, the plain is divided by the reedy and shrub-covered banks of the Jordan, whose turbid waters hasten along through a narrow channel towards their entrance into the Dead

Sea. If we turn around, so as to face the north, we behold the level country lose itself in the distance. But close at hand appears the miserable village of Arab huts, which occupy a little space on the site of the ancient Jericho; and several spots of beautiful vegetation, here and there improved into gardens, mark the course which the streams from Elisha's Fountain, a little distant, still maintain through the surrounding barrenness. If we cast our eyes to the West, the huge, precipitous mountain of Quarantania, at the distance of only three miles, stands full before us, and lifts to heaven those naked cliffs, whence, tradition says, the tempter showed our Saviour all the kingdoms of this world. Looking past the southern side of the mountain, we discover, a little farther off, in the way to Jerusalem, the wild congregation of barren hills that form the boundary of the plain. Rising just behind the first range, are seen tops of rifted and shapeless mountains, among whose deep and tremendous ravines, lies, hidden from our view, the Desert of the Temptation. Far in the rear, beyond a succeeding tract of less elevation, and of less sterility, we might perhaps descry, through some fortunate opening, the low, triple summits of Mount Olivet, at the distance of eighteen miles to the southwest, shutting out the city of Jerusalem from the eastern prospect.

As we turn round to the left, from the quarter of Mount Olivet, with our backs upon Jericho, the eye still ranges along the broken mass of hills, a few miles southward, where the plain terminates at their bases, or is invaded by their more advanced and sep-

arate crags.   Beyond them, we catch the glimpse of
remoter eminences, appearing here and there above
the horizon, and by their dismal whiteness betraying
the solitude and decay which reign in the interior.
Traversing, with a sidelong glance, the successive
ridges down to the left, as they approach the Dead
Sea, we perceive their height gradually increasing to
the very brink, where they suddenly fall off, to make
room for the bed of the lake.   The lake itself may
be seen, still farther around to the eastward, coming
up into the limits of the plain ; and nothing but an
intervening promontory shuts out, from our eye, the
whole expanse of waters spreading southward to
undiscernible distance.

From our post of observation, it is but five or six
miles, over a sandy tract, to the nearest part of the
Dead Sea ; and if, quitting the fields of Jericho, we
now proceed thither, and follow the shore down to
the South, we come at length to the mountainous
border already surveyed.   Here we enter on a wide
beach, which runs the whole remaining length, perhaps, of the lake, between the margin of the waves
and the lofty battlement of cliffs on the West.   Advancing along this desolate valley, we traverse heaps
of sand, and patches of dry mud, covered thick with
salt ; and sometimes a solitary and stunted shrub
shakes the dust from its scanty foliage, in the wind.
On our right, we see the towering masses of rock still
bearing onward, but frequently broken by huge chasms
that wind in many intricacies through their heavy
range.   The dreary lake now spreads full before us,
to the South ; but its extremity is beyond the reach

of the eye. To the East, however, we see its contracted breadth, at the distance of ten or fifteen miles, bounded by the dark, and to appearance, perpendicular mountains of Arabia, which stand on the opposite shore like a stupendous wall. Not a solitary peak seems to break the uniformity of their continuous summit; we only perceive slight inflections, here and there, as though the hand of the painter, who drew this horizontal line across the sky, had sometimes trembled in the bold execution.

After following the wide strand or valley for six or eight miles, to the South, we may turn to the right, and seek our way up the precipices. Arrived at the summit of the range, the whole country, as far as Mount Olivet in the north-west, the hills of Bethlehem in the West, and those of Tekoa in the south-west, bursts at once in desolate majesty, upon our sight. Plains and narrow glens without verdure or inhabitant, hills whose aged rocks are themselves decaying into dust, sharp ridges and misshapen points in the distance, fill up the scene. Throughout a large part of this tract, the spirit of religious madness, of fanatical seclusion, might find accommodations in the profound labyrinths channelled out between solid cliffs, and in numerous caverns, some of them almost inaccessible. Even close around the summit on which we stand, we may look down into chasms that sink to the very base.

If we look to the North, the plain of Jericho appears; if to the South, the concourse of mountains stretches off beyond the outlet of the Cedron, and finally fades in the prospect amidst the vast Desert of

23

Ruba. Below us, to the West, extends a considerably wide plain, through which, in ancient times, lay the road from Jericho to Hebron. Descending from the heights, and crossing this open space westwardly, our course runs among little hillocks of chalk and sand, and some scattered patches of herbage; till, at the end of three miles, we come to the boundary. Here we begin to climb through the narrow gorges of another chain of mountains, white, arid, and dusty; and not a solitary shade, not a plant, not even the last effort of vegetation, a single tuft of moss, meets the eye as we proceed. Four or five miles, in the same direction, brings us to the edge of the long, tremendous chasm, through which, in the rainy season, gushes the torrent Cedron, on its south-eastward course from Jerusalem to the Dead Sea. Through a sudden opening, that city itself may be descried, looking like a confused heap of rocks, nearly a dozen miles to the north-west; and the naked summits that rise on every quarter above us, command a prospect of the eastern lake. Proceeding, now, a small distance up the channel of the Cedron, we discover, in its very bed, and two or three hundred feet below us, the ancient monastery of St. Sabas, surrounded with numerous cells in the precipices, and still occupied as a convent.[1]

[1] For the account of this region, see Relandi Palæstina Illustrata; Pococke's Description of the East, Vol. ii. Part 1. pp. 30—45; Sandys's Travels, Book iii. Maundrell's Journey to Jerusalem; Dr. E. D. Clark's Travels through Greece, Egypt and the Holy Land, Chap. 17, 18; and Chateaubriand's Travels, Part iii. Several striking hints may be gathered from Cyrilli Scythopolitani Vita S. Sabæ, inter Coteleri Mon. Eccl. Græcæ Tom. iii. See, also, as the best work on Palestine, Robinson's Biblical Researches, &c.

II. At the beginning of the sixth cen-
A. D. 500.   tury, this great solitude had long been
peopled with monks.   Many lauras, or
collections of recluse cells and caverns, were prepared
in different quarters ; and monasteries, or regular con-
vents, were erected in other parts.   Of the former,
the most famous, at this period, was the laura of St.
Sabas, the remains of which we have just surveyed.
It was founded, less than twenty years before, by the
distinguished abbot of that name ; and five or six
thousand monks had already gathered in the deep
channel of the Cedron, under the protection of his
reputed miracles and sanctity.   A very successful
struggle, of more than fifty years, against every natural mode of human existence, had conferred on Sabas
a venerable preeminence over the whole desert ; and
a mild and patient temper gave his authority a sort of
fatherly character.   With these qualifications, it is no
wonder that the scrupulous exactness of his faith, the
wretchedness of his appearance, and the supposed
gifts of commanding rain from heaven, and of shutting
the mouths of wild beasts, should make him known
abroad, in that age, as " the light and ornament of all
Palestine."

Between the years 501 and 506, an
A. D. 501,   old [2] difficulty broke out anew in the
— 506.   midst of his own laura.   Forty of his
monks became greatly dissatisfied ; and
he, who seldom contended with opposition, left the
place and retired to a cave near Scythopolis.   After

[2]. Vit. Sabæ cap, 19,

awhile he returned; but finding the malecontents increased now to the number of sixty, and grown utterly irreconcileable, he again departed. This sudden and unexpected absence gave his enemies occasion to flatter themselves, at least to report, that he was devoured by wild beasts; and, going to Jerusalem, they entreated Elias, the bishop of that city, to appoint them another abbot. Their report, however, did not gain credit; and Elias was by no means disappointed, when, some time afterwards, he beheld Sabas himself, with several disciples from his new retirement, enter the Holy City, on the anniversary festival of the Dedication of the Temple. The bishop solemnly adjured him to return to his laura, and wrote a letter to the monks there, commanding them to receive him with honors, and submit to his authority. But when Sabas arrived and produced the letter in public, the disaffected rose in rebellion, assailed one of the buildings in their wrath, and overthrew it into the torrent. The rioters, to the number of sixty, then took their course over the hills, south-westwardly, to the laura of Succa, probably about eight or ten miles distant.[3] Applying there in vain for admittance, they proceeded onwards, till they entered the deep valley under the southern side of the hill on which stood the ruined village of Tekoa. Here, finding a little water, and some old

---

[3] The laura of Succa was not far from Tekoa, either to the North or to the South; (compare Vit. Sabæ cap. 36, with Vit. Cyriaci, inter Cotelerii Mon. Eccl. Græcæ Tom. iv. pp. 117, 118.) but in which of these directions, cannot be determined. The form of the expression, however, in Vit. Sabæ, seems to intimate that it was towards the laura of Sabas from Tekoa.

forsaken cells, they took up their abode, and called the place Nova Laura, or the new laura.* Having no church, they were obliged, for awhile, to hold their public exercises in an old one at Tekoa, dedicated to the ancient prophet Amos, once an inhabitant of this village.[4] Sabas, having obtained information of the place of their retreat, visited them with necessary supplies; and procuring afterwards, from Elias at Jerusalem, a sum of gold for the purpose,

A. D. 507. he built them a church, and dedicated it in A. D. 507. His beneficence seemed to reconcile them; and they allowed him to place over their laura a superior, who governed it in quiet for seven years.[5]

A. D. 514. III. On the death of this overseer, his successor admitted, through ignorance it is said, four Origenists; of whom the chief were Nonnus, whose earlier history is entirely unknown, and one Leontius of Byzantium, or Constantinople. Their distinguishing tenet appears to have been the pre-existence of human souls; but to this, it seems, we must add that of universal restoration.[6] Both these opinions, however, remained undis-

---

* I think Nova Laura must have been in what is now called Wady Jehar. (See Robinson's Bib. Researches, vol. ii. p. 185.) It was in a deep valley, not far to the South of Tekoa.

[4.] Amos i. 1.   [5.] Vit. Sabæ cap. 33—36.   [6.] That Nonnus and Leontius were Universalists is not absolutely certain, though very probable. I here subjoin the best evidence I have found of the fact: 1. Symeon Metaphrastes, a Greek writer of the tenth century, who recomposed the lives of the saints from the original documents, but who is by no means indisputable authority, adduces, in his Life of Cyriacus, (Cotelerii Mon. Eccl. Græcæ Tom. iv. pp. 117, 118.) the testimony of Cyrill of Scythopolis, a credible witness, that Nonnus and Leontius avowed the doctrines of pre-existence and Universal Restoration. 2. Cyrill himself, who

covered, at least unreproved, for about six months ;
when a new superior, the third in succession, being
appointed at Nova Laura, soon detected the alarming
doctrine, and, by the authority of Elias of Jerusalem,
expelled the believers.   They retired to other parts of
the country, and propagated their senti-
A. D. 517. ments in silence.   Two or three years
afterwards, Elias himself was deposed
amid some of the ecclesiastical revolutions which, in
the East, yet followed the Nestorian controversy of the
preceding century ; and when John succeeded to the
bishopric of Jerusalem, the Origenists came and asked
to be restored to their laura.   But he, being informed
by Sabas of their heresy, denied their request.   Leontius, indeed, was received, at length, into the great
laura of Sabas himself ; but the moment he became
known, the aged father drove him away.

Better fortune, however, awaited the outcasts : Not
many years afterwards, one Mamas, on succeeding
to the care of Nova Laura, admitted, it seems without

by the way, was a monk of Sabas's Laura, and a cotemporary of
Nonnus and Leontius, invariably represents them as teaching
Pre-existence ; and he also says (Vit. Sabæ cap. 36,) that they
derived it from Origen, Evagrius and Didymus.   Now, in the
doctrine of these fathers the two notions of Pre-existence and
Restoration were so inseparably connected, as the beginning and
end of their system, that whoever followed them in one, could
hardly avoid adopting the other.   3. Domitian, archbishop of
Galatia, a convert and patron of Nonnus and Leontius, was certainly an advocate of both these notions ; (Facundi Hermianensis
Defens. Trium Capit. inter Sirmondi Opp. Tom. ii. pp. 384, 385,)
and Facundus, a cotemporary, observes that it was particularly
on account of these tenets that his party was accused.   Several
other circumstances might be mentioned in favor of their Universalism ; and nothing, so far as I know, can be found to the con
trary.

hesitation,[7] Nonnus, Leontius, and their party to the cordial fellowship of the brotherhood. There followed such an increase of Origenism in the country, as to produce considerable uneasiness ; and an opportunity soon offered of introducing the affair to the attention of the ambitiously orthodox emperor Justinian : Some public grievances rendering it necessary to send an agent to the court of Constantinople, the bishops of Palestine unanimously deputed Sabas, whose sanctity had long been venerated in the imperial palace, and known throughout all the East. He accordingly visited the capital ; and, having accomplished his business, was about to

A. D. 531. take his leave, when the doting emperor humbly asked what revenues he should bestow on the monasteries and lauras of the desert, in order to secure their prayers for himself and his government. ' Grant the petitions that I have ' brought,' replied the abbot, ' and in recompense ' God will add to your dominions, Africa, Rome, ' and the whole of the western empire ; upon one ' condition, however, — that you deliver the churches ' from the three heresies of Arius, Nestorius, and ' Origen.' The obedient emperor loaded him with gifts, promised whatever he desired, and anathematized those heresies ; but whether he then issued any special decree against them, does not appear.[8]

---

7. Cyrill says (Vita Sabæ,) that Mamas did not know their sentiments; but how could he be ignorant, after the previous disturbances?

8. Vit. Sabæ cap. 36; and 70—74. Fleury's Eccl. History, Book xxxiii. chap. 3.

IV. Sabas died at his laura, in the end
A. D. 532. of the year 531, soon after his return from
Constantinople ; and the Origenists of
Nova Laura, feeling themselves relieved from the op-
pression of his great authority, began to propagate
their doctrine, with less reserve. Their success was,
if possible, more than proportioned to their zeal. In
a short time they converted all the most learned in
their own cells, placed their partizans over some of
the neighboring monasteries, spread their opinions
through several large communities of monks in the
desert, and established them even in the great laura of
Sabas.

Among their adherents, perhaps among the new
converts, were two persons, introduced now for the
first time to our notice, who afterwards rose to considerable eminence, and bore a distinguished part in
the ecclesiastical history of the period. Domitian was
abbot of a monastery in a desert ; and Theodorus
Ascidas was deacon, or one of the principal officers,
of Nova Laura. Both were Origenists ; both, probably Universalists, — such, at least, did Domitian avow
himself.[9] Going, about this time, to Constantinople,

---

9. Facundus, a cotemporary author, says (Defens. Trium Capitul.
Lib. iv. cap. 4, inter Sirmondi Opp. Tom. ii. pp. 384, 385,) "Do-
"mitian, formerly bishop of Ancyra in Galatia, writing a book to
"Pope Vigilius, complained of those who contradicted the doc-
"trine of Origen, that human souls existed before the body in a
"certain happy state, and that all who are consigned to everlast-
"ing torments shall be restored, together with the devil and his
"angels, to their primeval blessedness. Domitian also asserts
"that '*they have even anathematized the most holy and renowned
"doctors, on account of those things which were agitated in favor
"of Pre-existence, and Universal Restoration. This they have
"done under pretence of condemning Origen ; but in reality, con-
"demning all the saints who were before him, and who have been*

they were accompanied by Nonnus and Leontius ; and, through the recommendation of the latter, who seems to have had some influence in his native city, our two adventurers obtained the patronage of Eusebius, a favorite bishop at court. By his means, they were then introduced to the emperor himself ; and, concealing their sentiments and peculiar attachments, they so far won the partiality of Justinian, that he placed them over the two extensive bishoprics in Asia Minor. Domitian was elevated to that of Galatia, and immediately ordained at its metropolitan city, Ancyra ; Theodorus Ascidas, at Cesarea, in the large and influential see of Cappadocia, was seated on the same episcopal throne which had been honored by the ancient, and perhaps more worthy fathers, Firmilian and Basil the Great. Neither of the new prelates, it would seem, spent much of their time in their respective diocesses ; but, following the fashion of that age, resorted, among a crowd of other bishops, to the court of Constantinople, and there engaged in the intrigues of the palace and of the church. Theodorus long maintained a considerable ascendancy over the measures, though not over the faith, of the royal polemic himself, and frequently perverted the imperial authority to purposes, which, if discovered, would have been instantly condemned. Amidst the honors to which he had been advanced, and the splendor with which he was surrounded, he did not forget his old associates in the solitude of Palestine, but continued to exert, in their behalf, all the influence he dared to employ in

"*after him.*" This book of Domitian was written, probably, about the year 546, or a little after.

such a cause. Nor were they, on their part, unconscious of the increased advantages they might derive from the countenance, however cautiously granted, of two powerful friends at court. Emboldened by the patronage, and encouraged by their good fortune, the Origenists labored with redoubled energy, and in a short time succeeded in diffusing their doctrine through the whole of Palestine; an undertaking which was the more readily accomplished on account of the former prevalence of Origenism in the country.[10]

V. About five years after the death of Sabas, his second successor, Gelasius, on being elected over the great laura, determined to check the prevailing heresy among his own flock; and, to this end, he consulted a few of his yet orthodox brethren, and appointed the *Treatise* of Antipater of Bostra *against Origen*, to be read publicly in the church. But this indignity only provoked a disturbance; and Gelasius soon found it necessary, in prosecuting his scheme, to expel some of the leaders of the opposition, among whom was one of his deacons. It was too late, however, for violent measures; the expulsion of their leaders roused the spirit of the rest, and forty others were soon afterwards driven away. The outcasts repaired immediately to Nova Laura, where they enjoyed the protection of Nonnus, Leontius, and their brethren, and assisted in propagating their faith among the various monasteries in the neighborhood.[11] The next year, Eusebius, the

A. D. 537.

10. Vit. Sabæ cap. 77—83. 11. Cyrill's story (Vit. Sabæ cap. 84,) of their hostile expedition for the purpose of destroying the great laura, of the supernatural darkness which blinded and misled them so that they could not find the well-known place, &c. is incredible, unless

episcopal courtier who had introduced Domitian and Theodorus to Justinian, happened at Jerusalem; and Leontius, in company with the outcasts from the great laura, embraced the opportunity to carry before him a complaint against the abbot, for their expulsion. The haughty bishop assumed the seat of judgement; and sending for Gelasius, ordered him either to receive the Origenists, or else to expel their accusers. The timid, or perhaps politic, abbot returned, upon this, to the laura of Sabas, and choosing the latter alternative, dismissed six of his orthodox monks, probably with their own consent. These, however, went directly to Antioch, related to Ephraim, the powerful archbishop of that city, the affair of Origenism in Palestine, and showed him the books of Antipater of Bostra against the doctrine. Ephraim immediately called a provincial synod at Antioch, and procured, for the first time since the days of Theophilus and Jerome, an anathema against the heresy; but on what particular points, is unknown.

When the news of this procedure reached Palestine, the Origenists were, of course, alarmed. Leontius had sailed for Constantinople; but Nonnus went to Peter, the present bishop of Jerusalem, and importuned him to erase the name of Ephraim from the sacred diptychs, or official registers of bishops in fellowship and communion. Leontius at Constantinople also exerted his influence to procure the excommunication of the archbishop of Antioch; and Domitian and Theodorus

we admit, with him, the miraculous interference of the deceased Sabas.

strove to compel the patriarch of Jerusalem to execute
the proposed measure.   Already was there a strong
disaffection against Peter, among the monks of the
desert ; and, to screen himself from the indignation
which, it was easy to foretell, the course he had
adopted would arouse, he contrived to procure some
of the orthodox abbots to write a tract against Origenism, and in favor of Ephraim of Antioch.   This
was, accordingly, composed, and presented to him ;
and Peter immediately directed it, together with some
writings of his own, pointing out the heresies and the
disorders of the Origenists, to the emperor Justinian at
Constantinople.   The monks, entrusted with these
documents, arrived at the imperial city, attached
themselves to the deacon Pelagius, legate from the
Pope of Rome, and an enemy to Theodorus ; and,
by their united exertions, soon succeeded in laying
the matter in form before the emperor.[12]

VI. Justinian, who had now sat about a dozen
years on the throne of the eastern empire, was one
of the few sovereigns whose ruling ambition has been
to shine in theological disputes, and to acquire, by
superior orthodoxy and austere mortifications, the
proud epithet of *The Pious*.   Nothing could be
more gratifying, than this reference of the affair of
Origenism to his judgement and decision.   He lost
no time, therefore, in ordering a long *Edict* to be
drawn up, addressed *to Mennas*, arch-
A. D. 539, bishop of Constantinople, and published
—540. as early as the year 540.   " We are
told, " says he, " of some who, not hav-

[12.] Vit. Sabæ cap. 85. And Fleury's Eccl. Hist. Book **xxxiii**.
Chap. 3, 4.

"ing the fear of God before their eyes, have forsaken
"the truth, without which there is no salvation, and
"departed from the doctrine of the Scriptures and of
"the catholic fathers, by adhering to Origen, and
"maintaining his impious notions, which are like
"those of the Arians, Manicheans, and other here-
"tics." He then proceeds to recount, in a formal
catalogue, and under six heads, the errors attributed
to Origen: "1. That the Father is greater than the
"Son, and the Son greater than the Holy Ghost, as
"the Holy Ghost is superior to other spirits; and that
"the Son cannot behold the Father, nor the Holy
"Ghost see the Son. 2. That the power of God is
"limited, because he can create and govern only a
"certain number of souls, and a certain quantity of
"matter; that every species of being was coeternal
"with the Deity; that there have already been, and
"that there will hereafter be, several worlds in suc-
"cession, so that the Creator has never been without
"creatures. 3. That rational spirits were clothed
"with bodies, only for their punishment; and that
"the souls of men, in particular, were at first pure
"and holy intelligences, who, becoming weary of
"divine contemplation, and inclining to evil, were
"confined in earthly bodies, as a retribution and chas-
"tisement for their former follies. 4. That the sun,
"the moon, the stars, and the waters above the heav-
"ens, are animated and rational creatures. 5. That, in
"the resurrection, human bodies will be changed into
"a spherical shape. 6. That wicked men and devils
"will at length be discharged from their torments, and
"re-established in their original state." Each of

24

these six errors, Justinian attempts to refute by authorities from the Scriptures and fathers; but he directs his labors more particularly against the *third*, concerning pre-existence, and against the *sixth*, concerning the Restoration. Then, addressing Mennas, he adds, " we therefore exhort you to assemble all the " bishops and abbots of Constantinople, and oblige " them to anathematize in writing the impious Origen " Adamantius, together with his abominable doctrines, " and especially the articles we have pointed out. " Send copies of what shall be transacted, to all other " bishops and to all superiors of monasteries, that they " may follow the example ; and, for the future, let " there be no bishops nor abbots ordained, who do not " first condemn Origen and all other heretics, accord- " to custom. We have already written thus to Pope " Vigilius, and to the rest of the patriarchs. " After a collection of heretical extracts from the books of Origen, the emperor subjoins nine anathemas ; six, against the forementioned errors ; and three against the following on the incarnation. " 1. That the human soul of " Jesus Christ existed long before it was united to the " Word ; 2. That his body was formed, in the virgin " before its union either with the Word, or with his " own soul ; and 3. That he will, hereafter, be cruci- " fied for the salvation of the devils. " To conclude, there is a tenth anathema against the person of Origen and against those of his followers.[13]

13. See Du Pin's Biblioth. Pat. Vol. v. Art. Hist. of Fifth General Council. And Fleury's Eccl. Hist. Book xxxiii. chap. 4. I know not where to look for an entire copy of this very important document, Justinian's Edict to Mennas, except in Harduin's Concilia, Tom. iii. p. 243 ; and this valuable collection is out of my reach.

This sweeping decree, which aimed full against Universalism, went forth, of course, as a law of the realm; and Justinian's ambition to shine in the church conspired with his natural jealousy as a sovereign, to ensure the rigid enforcement of his orders. Accordingly, the bishops then residing at Constantinople were immediately assembled in council, by the patriarch Mennas, to subscribe the Edict; and soon afterwards, Pope Vigilius at Rome, Zoilus on the archiepiscopal throne of Alexandria, Ephraim at Antioch, and Peter at Jerusalem, obeyed the mandate and followed the example. Even Domitian of Ancyra and Theodorus of Cappadocia, though favorites, were obliged to yield to the imperial command; and, rather than suffer expulsion, they affixed their names to the anathemas which condemned some of their own sentiments.[14]

VII. In Palestine, however, there were A. D. 540, some bold and determined enough to withto 546. stand the emperor's authority. Alexander, bishop of Abyla,[15] who is known only by the part he bore in this affair, refused to subscribe the decree; and Nonnus, together with his party in general, remained faithful to their cause, at the expense of exclusion from the catholic communion, and of banishment from Nova Laura. But their powerful patron, Theodorus of Cappadocia, soon heard of their treatment; and, sending for certain agents of the

[14.] Fleury's Eccl. Hist. Book xxxiii. ch. 4. And Du Pin's Biblioth. Patrum Vol. v. Art. Hist. of Fifth Gen. Council. [15.] There were several cities or villages, by the name of Abyla, or Abila, in the northern part of Palestine (See Relandi Palæst Illust.) and this was probably one of them.

church of Jerusalem who resided at Constantinople, he angrily threatened to deprive their bishop, Peter, of his see, unless he should give satisfaction to the outcasts, and restore them to their former standing. At the same time, he sent to Nonnus and his adherents, advising them to propose to their bishop a sort of compromise, in which he should only pronounce some indefinite form of words, annulling, in general terms, all anathemas which were not agreeable to the will of God. As the real and manifest intent, however, of this equivocal formality, was to imply a censure of the emperor's late Edict, Peter at first refused; but, fearing the dangerous influence of Theodorus at court, he at length privately pronounced the sentence, re-admitted the Origenists into their laura, and finally appointed two of their leading members his suffragans, or bishops in immediate attendance on his person. Emboldened by the success of this attempt, the partizans of Nonnus did not hesitate openly to preach their doctrine from house to house. It would have been honorable to them, had they proceeded no farther. But, remembering with resentment the indignities they had suffered from the orthodox, they unhappily turned back upon them the tide of contempt and abuse. Disputes and violent altercations were quickly succeeded by blows, which fell, of course, on the catholic or weaker party; for whom it soon became unsafe to appear abroad, especially in the city of Jerusalem. Finding their numbers unequal to the quarrel, they procured a reinforcement of a savage race of monks from the banks of the Jordan. When these arrived at the Holy City, and

joined the orthodox host, an engagement ensued ; but
the Origenists succeeded at last in putting them all to
flight, and in driving them as far as the great laura of
Sabas. Here, the vanquished retreated into a fortified
place, and their pursuers were, in their turn, obliged
to fly, after one of the most valorous of their enemies
had fallen, the only victim of the combat.

The public had long been too familiar with scenes
of this shameful character, to regard them with the
abhorrence they merited ; and it was probably the
urgent motive of self-preservation, alone, which induced the remnant of the orthodox, in the present
exigency, to seek the prevention of these disorders.
Accordingly, Gelasius, the abbot of the great laura,
set out on a journey to Constantinople, in order to
lay the affair before Justinian. But Theodorus of
Cappadocia, having notice of his arrival, contrived
to prevent all access to the emperor, so that, after
several ineffectual attempts, Gelasius was obliged to
depart without accomplishing his purpose. Returning towards Palestine, he died at a small city in
Phrygia ; and with him expired, for a season, the
hopes of the orthodox party in the desert of Judea.
For, when the monks of the great laura went to
Jerusalem to ask the appointment of a new abbot,
the suffragans of Peter, imitating the cunning of Theodorus, drove them away ; and immediately all the
monastic communities in that region, yielding to the
strong, popular current, were carried over, by flattery
or by fear, to the side of Origenism. Even the great
laura itself submitted, soon afterwards, to an abbot
appointed by the dominant party ; and the few ortho-

24*

dox leaders in the place forsook their long-venerated cells, and sought other retreats. But the very day, on which the triumphant Origenists saw the feeble remnant of their opposers retire, called them also to mourn the sudden and unexpected death
A. D. 546. of Nonnus at Nova Laura. This loss was the more severely felt, as Leontius, the other chief of the party, had died, a year or two before, at Constantinople. What was the real character of these two persons, and what their abilities, we have no satisfactory means to ascertain. That they had considerable influence among the monks, is evident ; and that they were feared and hated by their opposers, is certain. Should we judge of them, however, by their cotemporaries, we could boast neither of their intelligence, nor of their peaceable and Christian temper. Nonnus had the satisfaction of leaving their cause, though proscribed by the government, in a very prosperous condition throughout Palestine. At the great laura of Sabas, however, the orthodox regained an ascendancy, seven months after his death, and appointed a new abbot ; who was succeeded, in less than a year, by Conon, another of their most enterprizing leaders. The loss of this important place seemed, soon afterwards, more than made up to the Origenists, by a fortunate acquisition on their part : Peter, who had always
A. D. 547. opposed them, died about this time ; and, by their influence, their friend, Macarius, was chosen his successor in the bishopric of Jerusalem. But their affairs remained, for five or six years, unstable and fluctuating. A sedition followed the

election of the new prelate ; and Justinian command-
ed him to be expelled from his see. What was still
more injurious to their interests, the Origenists themselves had abused their success, and suffered prosperity to cherish a factious spirit, which divided them,
on some trivial question, into hostile parties.[16]

      VIII. Meanwhile, an artful plot was
A. D. 546, contrived and put in execution, at Con-
to 553. stantinople ; the particulars of which it is
necessary to relate, although they have
no other bearing on the doctrine of Universal Salvation, than as they led, eventually, to the assembling.
of the Fifth General council. Theodorus of Cappadocia had not forgotten the malicious interference of
Pelagius, in procuring the late imperial Edict against
Origen and his doctrines ; and he resolved to retaliate
upon his enemy, by taking advantage of some unsettled affairs in the old Nestorian controversy. He
happened to belong to a party that hated the memory
of the General council of Chalcedon, held in the middle of the last century ; while the Roman legate, on
the contrary, zealously supported its authority and
cherished its reputation. To impair its credit, and to
vex its advocates, Theodorus contrived to procure the
condemnation of some of the fathers whom it had approved. Among those of this class, he found the
name of Theodorus of Mopsuestia ; and ignorant,
probably, that he had been, in his day, a Universalist,
and knowing only that he was celebrated as an opposer of Origen, he thought that, by anathematizing

    [16.] Vit. Sabæ cap. 86—90. Fleury's Eccl. Hist. Book xxxiii. ch.
20, 40.

him, he should accomplish, at once, two important objects, — that of avenging, in some degree, the late indignities inflicted on the memory of his own favorite author ; and that also of bringing disgrace on the obnoxious council.

Accordingly, he cautiously suggested to his patron, the emperor, that he might easily effect a work in which he was laboriously engaged, the reconciliation of a certain party in the church, merely by condemning Theodorus of Mopsuestia, Theodoret of Cyrus, and Ibas of Edessa, together with the writings they had left in favor of Nestorianism. Justinian had not sufficient penetration to discover the subtlety of his adviser; and, with his characteristic officiousness, assumed the authority of pronouncing, for the whole church, upon one of the most hazardous topics he could have selected. But it was foreseen that, when he had once promulgated his decision, his theological vanity would be security against all retraction, and his pride of power a guarantee of his perseverance and final victory. Accordingly, Theodorus felt already assured of success, when he received a command to draw up an Edict in the Emperor's name, condemning the fathers in question, together with their obnoxious writings; which have since been known by the title of the *Three Chapters*. This Edict was published A. D. 546, in the form of a Letter addressed to the whole catholic church; and all bishops were required to subscribe its anathemas. Most of them, apparently against their conscience, complied, after some hesitation, and were liberally rewarded; but such as maintained their integrity and refused, were of course banished. A violent and general contention followed, for several years. Books were written on both sides. The Roman pontiff himself continually shuffled between fear of the sovereign's vengeance, and regard for the consistency of the church. The passions of men grew inflamed, till all christendom was so agitated that the usual expedient became necessary in order to allay, or rather to give vent to, the fermentation.[17]

IX. On the fourth of May, A. D. 553, the Fifth General council was therefore opened at Constantinople, under the eye of Justinian, by one hundred and fifty-one bishops from the Greek and African churches; and it was continued, with the accession of fourteen other bishops, till the second day of the following month. Every thing appears to have been managed, as was expected, according to the emperor's pleasure. The Three Chapters were condemned with extravagant expressions of zeal; and the person of Theodorus of Mopsuestia was anathematized, not for his Universalism, but for his alleged Nestorianism. Thus far, the artful bishop of Cappadocia saw his plan go into complete effect. But he could not stop the ponderous machinery which he had put in motion; and he was destined to feel, before the close of its operations, that his cunning had overreached itself. While he was, in reality, the prime but covert manager, steadily controling the results, by first suggesting

A. D. 553.

---

17. Fleury's Eccl. Hist. Book xxxiii. ch. 21—43.

to Justinian the course to be pursued, and then dictating, in his name, to the council, the subject of Origenism, entirely foreign from the business of the session, is said to have been suddenly brought before the obsequious conclave,[18] in spite of all his efforts to the contrary.   The emperor's attention had lately been directed to it by some incidents in Palestine; certain deputies from Jerusalem, with Conon, the Abbot of St. Sabas, at their head, urged its immediate consideration; and Justinian was by no means backward to show his zeal and faithfulness in the affair.   He despatched, it is thought, a message to the assembled bishops, exhorting them to examine the doctrine of " the impious Origen," and to condemn him and his followers, together with their tenets.   As a form which they might use in framing their decrees, he sent them the long Edict which he had published, thirteen or fourteen years before, with its catalogue of heresies and of anathemas.

On the receipt of these papers, the fathers of the council, it seems, hastened to pay obedience to the request; and the following decree served at once to commend them to their master, and to betray, to the eye of the historian, their servility to the imperial

[18] Here I follow Huet (Origenian. Lib. ii. cap. 4, Sect. iii. § 14—16,) Fleury (Eccl. Hist. Book xxxiii. ch. 40, 51,) and the testimony of antiquity, in preference to the authority of the modern historians, who contend that the affair of Origen, Didymus and Evagrius, was not examined in this Council, but only in that which was called together, at Constantinople, by Mennas, on receiving Justinian's Edict, in A. D. 540.   Without incurring the charge of pretending to decide this question, I may say, that the condemnation of Origen, Didymus and Evagrius, having been almost invariably attributed to the Fifth General council, has been received in the catholic church with the deference which is paid to the decisions of such a body.

dictation. " Whoever says, or thinks, that the souls
" of mankind pre-existed as intellectual, holy natures,
" but that growing weary of. divine contemplation
" they degenerated to their present character, and
" were sent into these bodies for the purpose of pun-
" ishment, let him be anathema. Whoever says, or
" thinks, that the human soul of Christ pre-existed,
" and became united to the Word before its incarna-
" tion and nativity of the blessed Virgin, let him be
" anathema. Whoever says, or thinks, that the body
" of Christ was first formed in the womb of the holy
" virgin, and that the Word and his pre-existent hu-
" man soul were afterwards united with it, let him be
" anathema. Whoever says, or thinks, that the divine
" Word is to become like the angelic and celestial
" powers, and thus be reduced to an equality with
" them, let him be anathema. Whoever says, or
" thinks, that in the resurrection human bodies are to
" be of a round, globular form, or whoever will not
" acknowledge that mankind are to rise in an erect
" posture, let him be anathema. Whoever says that
" the sun, the moon, the stars, and the waters above
" the heavens, are certain animated or intelligent
" powers, let him be anathema. Whoever says, or
" thinks, that Christ is to be crucified in the future
" world for the demons, as he was, in this, for men,
" let him be anathema. Whoever says, or thinks,
" that the power of God is limited, and that it has
" created all that it was able to embrace, let him be
" anathema. Whoever says, or thinks, that the tor-
" ments of the demons and of impious men are tem-
" poral, so that they will, at length, come to an end, or

"whoever holds a restoration either of the demons or
"of the impious, let him be anathema.   Anathema to
"Origen Adamantius, who taught these things among
"his detestable and accursed dogmas; and to every
"one who believes these things, or asserts them, or
"who shall ever dare to defend them in any part, let
"there be anathema: In Christ Jesus our Lord, to
"whom be glory forever.   Amen." [19]

In addition to these fulminating sentences, an act of
condemnation is said to have been passed, also, upon
those writings of Didymus of Alexandria and of Evagrius Ponticus, which advocated pre-existence and
universal restoration.[20]

X. The decree of a General council
was unalterable, and fixed the faith, at
least the creed, of the catholic church,
forever.   It only remains, that we men-
tion the effects of this decision, on the Origenists of
Palestine.   When the condemnatory acts were sent
to that province, they were subscribed by all the prelates, except Alexander of Abyla, who was accordingly expelled from his bishopric.   The monks of
Nova Laura also refused obedience, and withdrew
from the general communion.   The new patriarch of
Jerusalem, who had been appointed to that see during
the late council, endeavored to reclaim the dissenters;
but, at the end of eight months, finding all persuasion
vain, he availed himself of the emperor's authority,
and by force drove the Origenists out of the country.[21]

A. D. 553 and 554.

[19.] Summa Conciliorum, Auctore M. L. Bail. Tom. 1. p. 285,
286. Edit. Paris. 1672.   [20.] Vit. Sabæ cap. 90.   [21.] Ditto.

APPENDIX

TO THE ANCIENT HISTORY OF UNIVERSALISM.

[From A. D. 554, to A. D. 1500.]

I. Having brought the history of Universalism down to its complete and authoritative condemnation, we may, with all propriety, close the regular and connected narrative ; especially as we have followed it into the dim twilight preceding the long age of darkness. But as curiosity naturally looks onwards, with an enquiring eye, through the gloomy succession of centuries from the fifth General council to the era of the Reformation, I shall here annex such notices of the doctrine, during that period, as have occurred to me.

In the first Lateran council, convened
A. D. 649. at Rome, by Pope Martin I, in the year 649, against those who asserted but one will in Jesus Christ, the fathers repeated the anathema against Origen, and his followers, Didymus and Evagrius ; who, it will be recollected, had been, condemned only for Universalism.

The sixth General council, held at
A. D. 680. Constantinople in A. D. 680, recognized for some reason, the condemnation of Origen, Didymus and Evagrius : either from a suspicion that the heresy was still cherished ; or else from a casualty in the form of expression. The

25

principal business of this council, convened like the Lateran against the Monothelites, a sect so called from some distinguishing notions concerning the two natures of Christ, had not the least connexion with the subject of Origenism. Yet one of the declarations reads thus: "We agree with the holy and "universal, or general, councils in all things; espe-"cially with the last of them, the fifth, which was "assembled in this city against Theodorus of Mop-"suestia, Origen, Didymus and Evagrius."

A. D. 787.
The seventh General council also, which met, A. D. 787, at Nice in Bithynia, for the purpose of defending and establishing the use of images, relics, &c. in churches, has left on its records a sentence that may induce a suspicion that Universalism was not quite extinct: "we anathematize the fables of Origen, Did-"ymus and Evagrius."

A. D. 869.
And the eighth General council, at Constantinople in A. D. 869, likewise digressed from its proper objects, in order to pronounce an "anathema against Origen, who "advanced many errors; and against Evagrius and "Didymus, who are caught in the same abyss of per-"dition.[1]" This council was called together on the memorable quarrel which resulted in the separation of the Greek from the Latin church; and therefore it had no natural concern with the fathers here condemned.

The introduction of this foreign topic, in these successive Synods, is at least a circumstantial evidence that it was not altogether accidental; and that the obnoxious sentiments were thought to have some abettors, probably in the eastern church.

[1] For the sentences extracted from the Sixth, Seventh and Eighth Councils, see Hist. de l'Origenisme, par Louis Doucin, pp. 321, 322. For the notice of the Lateran Council, see Huetii Origenian. Lib. ii. cap. 4. Sect. iii. 17.

This indication is confirmed by a cir-
A. D. 713, cumstance that happens to have come
to 730. to our knowledge. Germanus, archbishop of Constantinople in the former
part of the eighth century, published a book, we
are told, to confute "the heretical doctrine that
"the demons shall be restored to their pristine state,
"and that those who die in their sins, shall, after
"certain punishments, be gathered into the num-
"ber of the blest. This impiety, so full of fables,
"he disproved, first, by the words of the Lord,
"then by the apostolic decrees; to which he
"adds also the testimonies of the prophets, which show
"clearly that as the enjoyment of the blest is eter-
"nal and ineffable, so also the punishment of sinners
"will be endless and infinite. And not only by these
"testimonies did he confound the profane and poison-
"ous error, but also by those of the holy fathers; and
"particularly by the very writings of him [Gregory
"Nyssen] whom this heresy perfidiously claimed as its
"patron. By means of all these authorities, he freed
"the whole ecclesiastical body from that scheme of
"fables so pernicious to the soul." In part of his
book, Germanus undertook the impracticable task of
showing that the ancient father, Gregory Nyssen, was
not an advocate of Universalism. The occasion of
this bold attempt is said to have been "because that
"they who favored the notion that the demons and
"the damned might be delivered, endeavored to mix
"the dark and pernicious poison of Origen's dreams
"with Gregory's luminous and salutary writings, and
"strove secretly to add an heretical madness to the
"virtue and renowned orthodoxy of him whom they
"knew to be distinguished for doctrine and eloquence,
"and the bright reputation of whose sanctity they
"knew was talked of by all." We are likewise told
that "those books of Gregory which the heretics
"craftily endeavored to bring to their aid, but which

" Germanus, the advocate of the truth, had preserved
" uninjured from their attempts, were *The Dialogue*
" *concerning the soul: The Catechetical Oration;*
" and the Book *concerning a Perfect Life.*" *

This account, taken from a writer of the ninth century, who was one of the most renowned ecclesiastical critics of all antiquity, shows that, about the time of Germanus, the heresy of universal restoration made some noise in the East.

II. In the western church there appeared, among several other sectaries, a preacher who claims our notice. Clement, a native of Ireland, seems to have been regularly ordained a presbyter, or minister, in the Romish communion. But he at length discarded its superstitions, renounced its authority, and rejected the whole mass of ecclesiastical canons, the decrees of the councils, and all the treatises and expositions of the fathers ; reserving to himself, probably, as the guide of his faith, the Bible alone, which was now forbidden the people. He taught that Christ, when he descended to hell, restored all the damned, even infidels and idolators ; and he differed, on what particulars we know not, from the catholic doctrine concerning predestination. Several independent congregations were gathered, under his ministry, in part of France and Germany ; and such was his progress as to awaken the attention of both the civil and ecclesiastical powers. In a council of twenty-three bishops, assembled A. D. 744, at Soissons in A. D. 744. France, by king Pepin, Clement was deposed from the priesthood, condemned among other heretics, and imprisoned. Boniface, archbishop of Mentz, and legate of the Holy See, presided, probably, in this council ; and he immediately sent to the pope an account of the affair. It was soon discovered

* Photii Bibliothec. Cod. 233. See note (62) to Sect. xviii. of the vi. Chap. of this History.

that Clement had left disciples even among the lower orders of the clergy ; and, in a council of seven bishops held, the following year, by pope Zachary, at Rome, he was again deposed, and anathematized, together with his followers, in case they should not renounce their error. Two years afterwards, the pope advised Boniface to call a council in his neighborhood, and ascertain whether Clement and certain other heretics would submit to the church ; and, in case of their obstinacy, to send them to Rome. It does not appear, however, that any thing further was done ; and it is probable that Clement died in prison. Boniface reported that he was guilty of adultery ;[2] but, as some such accusation was the customary expedient of the catholics on similar occasions, the story is unworthy of notice. Mosheim says, that " by the best and " most authentic accounts, Clement was much better " acquainted with the true principles and doctrines of " Christianity, than Boniface himself; and hence he " is considered by many as a confessor and sufferer for " the truth, in this barbarous age." [3] Priestly also thinks " it is probable that, if his sentiments and con- " duct were fully known, he would be ranked with the " most early reformers." [4]

III. The greatest scholar, and perhaps
A. D. 850,   the most philosophical genius, of the ninth
— 870.   century, was John Scotus Erigena, a na-
tive of Ireland, or of Scotland. At an early age, he visited Greece, especially Athens, and studied the Oriental as well as classic literature. On his return, he was invited, by Charles the Bald, to the court of France ; where he probably continued till

[2] Fleury's Eccl. Hist. xlii. ch. 39, 50, 52, 53, 54, 58. The orthodox enthusiast, Milner, applauds the soul-saving zeal of Boniface on this occasion ; and commends the *discipline* inflicted upon Clement and his associates. See his Hist. of the Church, Cent. viii. ch. 4.

[3] Mosheim's Eccl. Hist. Cent. viii. Pt. ii. ch. 5. § 2

[4] Priestley's Hist. of the Church. Period xv. Sect. v. p. 181.

his death, notwithstanding the accounts of his removal to England, on the request of Alfred the Great, to take charge of the college which that prince had founded at Oxford. His favorite study, it appears, was philosophy, in which he followed the doctrines of the New Platonism: that all things proceeded from God, and will eventually return to him. He distinguished himself, however, as an ecclesiastical writer. In this character, his influence was so hostile to the corrupt doctrines of that day, and especially to the papal hierarchy, that the court of Rome threatened to arraign him. He wrote against Transubstantiation, and the Augustinian scheme of Predestination; and it is said that he taught the opinion of Origen concerning the end of the punishment of the damned, and the final restoration of all fallen creatures.* He is classed among the mystic philosophers and theologians.

IV. From about the year 850, for two centuries onwards, both the Greek and the Roman or Latin churches enjoyed, within their respective communions, the golden age of profound ignorance and undisturbed orthodoxy. One of the most learned and impartial of the catholic historians says, " in this age of the church, " there were no controversies concerning articles of " faith, or doctrinal points of divinity, because there " were no heretics, nor other inquisitive persons, who " refined upon matters of religion, or undertook to " dive to the bottom of its mysteries. The sober part " contented themselves with yielding implicit faith to " whatever the churchmen thought fit to deliver from " the pulpit; and as for the profligate wretches, they " abandoned themselves to gross sensualities for the " gratification of their brutal appetites, rather than to

---

* As authorities for his Universalism, the Rev. T. J Sawyer has kindly furnished me with the following references: Doederlein, Institut. Theol. Christ. Vol. ii. p. 202. D. J. Otto Thiess ueber d. bibl. u. kirch. Lehrmeinung von Ewigkeit d. Hoellenstrafen, s. 24.

" the vices of the mind, to which none but ingenious
" persons are liable. Therefore, in this age of dark-
" ness and ignorance, the church, not being disturbed
" upon account of its doctrines, had nothing to do but
" to suppress the enormities which abounded with
" regard to discipline and manners." [5] A protestant
historian shall describe to us the real character of this
church, so unmolested by error, at this period : " Both
" in the eastern and western provinces, the clergy
" were, for the most part, composed of a most worth-
" less set of men, shamefully illiterate and stupid, igno-
" rant more especially in religious matters, equally
" enslaved to sensuality and superstition, and capable
" of the most abominable and flagitious deeds. This
" dismal degeneracy of the sacred order was, accord-
" ing to the most credible accounts, principally owing
" to the pretended chiefs and rulers of the universal
" church, who indulged themselves in the commission
" of the most odious crimes, and abandoned them-
" selves to the lawless impulse of the most licentious
" passions, without reluctance or remorse ; who con-
" founded, in short, all difference between just and
" unjust, to satisfy their impious ambition ; and whose
" spiritual empire was such a diversified scene of
" iniquity and violence, as never was exhibited under
" any of those temporal tyrants, who have been the
" scourges of mankind." [6] " Both Greeks and Latins
" placed the essence and life of religion, in the wor-
" ship of images and departed saints; in searching
" after, with zeal, and preserving, with a devout care
" and veneration, the sacred relics of holy men and
" women ; and in accumulating riches upon the priests
" and monks, whose opulence increased with the pro-
" gress of superstition. Scarcely did any Christian
" dare to approach the throne of God, without first
" rendering the saints and images propitious by a

5. Du Pin's Eccl. Hist. Vol. viii. ch. 6.   6. Mosheim's Eccl.
Hist. Cent. x. Pt. 2. ch. ii. 1.

"solemn round of expiatory rites and lustrations.
"The ardor, also, with which relics were sought, sur-
"passes almost all credibility : it had seized all ranks
"and orders among the people, and was grown into a
"sort of fanaticism and phrenzy ; and, if the monks
"are to be believed, the supreme Being interposed, in
"an especial and extraordinary manner, to discover to
"doating old wives, and bareheaded friars, the places
"where the bones or carcasses of the saints lay dis-
"persed or interred." [7] Such was the age of midnight
darkness.

V. But, though no new heresies, so called, arose at
this period within the two vast communities which arrogated to themselves the appellation of *The Church*,
yet one earlier and very powerful sect, that of the
Paulicians, still existed in the East, and, under several names, was spread in the West. It is in this he-
terogenous body that modern historians[8] have sought,
with some appearance of success, for the embryo
germ of the Reformation ; and it is among the same
people that we may discover some vague elements of
Universalism, confused and doubtful indeed at first,
but afterwards assuming a more distinct character,
and coming out into more decided results. The Paulicians were, at once, descendants and dissenters, from
the Manicheans ; with whose Gnosticism they were
considerably tainted, while they rejected the name
with the utmost abhorrence. " Extraordinary as it

[7.] Ditto. ch. iii. 1.

[8.] Mosheim (Eccl. Hist. Cent. x. Part 2. ch. v. 2. and Cent. xi.
Part 2. ch. v. compared with Cent. xii. Part 2. ch. v. &c.) has traced
the Paulicians down into the Albanenses, Albigenses, Cathari &c.
&c. Gibbon (Decline and Fall &c. ch. liv.) has followed the same
line of descent, and connected them with the Reformation; and so
has Priestly (Hist. of the church, Period xviii. Sect. vii. pp. 102—
104, &c.) Milner doubts their relation to the forerunners of the
Reformation, because he is not convinced of their dispersion
through Europe (Hist. of the Church, Cent. ix. ch. 2;) but he is
confident that they were very good saints. Catholic historians
agree fully with Gibbon, as it regards their connexion with the
Reformers.

" may appear, the same general principles, from
" which were derived, in the very age of the apostles,
" the earliest corruptions of the Christian doctrine,
" were the means of bringing about the reformation of
" Christianity ; and having effected this purpose, they
" are now become extinct. "[9]

Of the rise, doctrine, and progress of this sect,
many particulars are very uncertain ; but we may
venture to follow, with some confidence, one of the
most clear sighted masters of history,[10] whose account
has, in the present affair, been commended both by
the liberal and the bigoted, by the Protestant and the
Catholic, notwithstanding his general hostility to revealed religion. About the year 660, we
A. D. 660. first discover this people, in considerable
numbers, spreading quietly from the
neighborhood of Samosata, in the upper region of
the Euphrates, northeastwardly through Armenia,
and northwardly through Cappadocia and Pontus.
Descended from the Gnostics, who had never been
affected with the gradual corruptions of the Catholics,
they abhorred the use of images, of relics, pompous
ceremonies, and ecclesiastical domination ; and they
even dispensed with the rites of water baptism and
the Lord's supper. Their preachers were distinguished from their brethren by no title ; and no superiority
was allowed, except what arose from the austerity of
their lives, their zeal or their knowledge. - The Manichean books they rejected, and likewise the Jewish,
as they called the Old Testament ; but the New Testament, which in the orthodox church had almost disappeared from the laity, they received as the only

[9.] Priestly's Hist. of the Church, Period xviii. Sect. vii. pp. 103,
104.   [10.] Gibbon's Decline and Fall &c. ch. liv. Milner says
" the candor of Gibbon is remarkable in this part of his history.
" O, si sic omnia ! " and the learned Charles Butler (Book of the
Roman Catholic Church, Note at the end of Letter xii.) thinks
this the most interesting chapter of his work.

volume of sacred Scripture, and enjoined its diligent perusal on all the people. It is probable, however, that they disowned the two Epistles of St. Peter, and the Revelation of St. John ; and it is certain that their favorite books were the writings of St. Paul, from whom they, perhaps, took their name of Paulicians. Still, they held the Manichean notion of two original Principles, the Good and the Bad ; and they looked forward to the triumph of the former over his rival, either by the entire abolition,[11] or partial conquest, of death, sin and misery. The body with which Christ was seen upon earth, together with his crucifixion, they supposed to have been apparent only ; and of course it is probable that they denied his real resurrection, and that of mankind.

VI. Their Oriental notions might, A. D. 670, with propriety, be disliked by the church. to 845. But the downright simplicity of their institutions, their total disrespect of images and relics, their contempt of all those artifices by which the craft got their living, kindled against them the most implacable hatred ; and the orthodox emperors of the East resolved on their complete extermination. For an hundred and fifty years, they sustained a bloody persecution, with a patience and inoffensive meekness that converted even some of their executioners. But all human endurance may at length be overcome ; and when that sanguinary zealot, the empress Theodora, succeeded to the regency of the East, during her son's minority, she drove them beyond the bounds of forbearance. In those parts of Asia Minor where they abounded, and in Armenia, she confiscated their goods, and put to death by the sword, the gibbet and

11. I have ventured, without any express authority, to attribute to them a difference of opinion among themselves, on this point ; because such seems to have been the case with their predecessors, the Manicheans and other Gnostics, and also with their descendants, the Albigenses &c.

the flames, more than a hundred thousand of their number, making them expire slowly by a variety of the most excruciating torments. Those who escaped the horrible massacre, fled immediately for refuge to the Saracens, accepted with gratitude permission to build a city on the frontiers of Armenia, and entered into an alliance with their Mahometan protectors. They soon gathered an army, and marched back to avenge, on the Greeks, the sufferings of their martyred brethren. The war was carried on with alternate advantage, about forty years ; but, towards the close of the century, the power of the Paulicians was effectually broken, and they were obliged to seek security in the fastnesses of the Armenian mountains.

But they had already obtained a permanent footing in Europe. About the middle of the preceding century, in the midst of those persecutions they so patiently endured, a colony of them was transported, by one of the Greek emperors, from Asia to Thrace, westward of Constantinople. With a zeal which no sufferings could repress, they labored successfully to diffuse their doctrine among their northern neighbors, the Bulgarians, in the lower region of the Danube. After sustaining many hardships and cruelties for more than two hundred years, they were, at length, reinforced by another and very numerous colony from Armenia ; and they were also privileged with a full toleration of their faith. In course of time, they occupied a line of villages and castles from Thrace westwardly through Macedonia and Epirus ; and by the various chances of trade, of emigration and persecution, they became scattered in small numbers, over all Europe. Their Manichean or oriental principles would have been, perhaps, a fatal preventive to the reception of their faith among the people of the West, had it not been counteracted by the simplicity

A. D. 845, to 880.

A. D. 970, to 1100.

of their religious institutions.   A strong though secret discontent had been generally provoked by the avarice, the despotism, the mummery and the dissoluteness of the church of Rome ; and when the oppressed and neglected populace beheld a sect of professed Christians blameless in their lives, humble in their demeanor, and disclaiming all tyranny over the consciences of men, the spectacle was so attractive to many that they became partial converts to the new system, and adopted even its doctrines, though with various modifications.   From this amalgamation arose all those sects of the eleventh, twelfth, thirteenth, and fourteenth centuries, which the Catholic writers denominate Manicheans, but which are known to Protestants under the name of Albanenses, Albigenses, and Cathari.   This mongrel race, it is well known, spread through Italy, France and Germany ; and, for a long period, suffered from the church all the cruelty that cunning could devise and power inflict.   " It was " about the year 1150, that several parts of the conti- " nent had become pervaded by men, chiefly of the " poorer and laborious classes of life, who were form- " ing themselves into religious communities, distinct " from the established Catholic church, and who had " the Scriptures with them in their vernacular langua- " ges, and were intently and critically comparing the " tenets, system, and conduct of the papal clergy, " with the precepts and instructions of the evangelists " and apostles.   They were universally diffused.   In " France they were called Weavers, Poor of Lyons, " Waldenses, and Albigenses ; in Flanders, Piphles ; " and in Germany, Cathari.   They were at Bonn, " and in the diocese of Cologne ; they abounded near " the Alps and Pyrenees ; they were greatly diffused " through Provence and in Tholouse ; they existed in " Spain ; and had spread through Lombardy to Padua " and Florence, and some had even entered Naples.

" They were distinguished for their missionary spirit,
" and the caution with which they pursued it. "*

With various opinions as to the Manichean doctrine
of two original Principles, they were nevertheless united in denouncing, as antichristian, the authority, the
ceremonies, and the whole hierarchy, of the Romish
communion. It is probable that many of them held,
in some form, the doctrine of the salvation of all
souls ; for, of this they are accused by the Catholic
writers, who also assert that they denied a future
judgement and future punishment.[12]

VII. We find a solitary trace of Uni-
A. D. 1190. versalism, at this time, among the monks
of France. At the city of Nevers, which
stands on the river Loire, about a hundred and forty
miles south of Paris, one Raynold, who presided as
abbot over the monastery of St. Martin, was accused
in a council, held this year, at Sens, of maintaining
two errors, which were doubtless derived from the
Paulicians : 1, That the bread of the sacrament was
corruptible, and that it was digested, like other bread ;
and 2, that all men will eventually be saved, as Origen had taught.[13] What was the result of the complaint I know not.

VIII. It is, perhaps, impossible to
A. D. 1200, determine whether we ought to rank
to 1210. Amalric, or Amauri, an eminent professor of logic and theology at Paris,
among the Universalists. Like the celebrated Wick-

---

* History of England, by Sharon Turner, Vol. ii. pp. 381, 382.
Lond. 1815. N. B. This learned and philosophical historian follows Gibbon, in deducing the above named sects from the Paulicians.

[12] See Gabrielis Prateoli Marcossii Vita Hæreticorum, Art. Albanenses, Albigenses, &c. And Berti Breviarium Hist. Eccl.
Cent. viii.—xii. cap. 3. And Notitiæ Eccl. Pars Tertia, per So-
dalet. Academ Bambergensem, &c.

[13] Priestley's Hist. of the Christian Church, Period xviii. Sect.
ix. pp. 136, 137.

liffe,[14] he was charged with holding the pantheistical tenet that the Universe is God ; but it is certain that the whole tenor of the doctrine attributed to him, opposes that proposition, at least in its exceptionable sense. "According to Fleury, he held that, in order " to be saved, every person must believe that he is a ", member of Jesus Christ ; but, the pope condemn- " ing this opinion, he retracted it before his death. " Fleury also ascribes to the followers of Amauri an " opinion which is said to have taken its rise from a " book by Joachim, entitled *The Everlasting Gospel*, " viz. That Jesus Christ abolished the old law, and " that in his time commenced the dispensation of the " holy spirit, in which confession, baptism, the eucha- " rist, and other sacraments, would have no place ; " but that persons might be saved by the interior " grace of the Holy Spirit, without any external acts. " He moreover says that Amauri denied the resurrec- " tion, said that heaven and hell were in men's own " breasts, that the pope was Antichrist, and Rome " Babylon."[15] I shall now set down, in their own words, the catalogue which other Catholic writers have made of his errors : " 1, Amalric said that the " body of Christ was not otherwise present in the " bread of the sacrament, than as it is in other bread, " and in every thing else ; so that he denied transub- " stantiation. 2, He said that God had spoken by Ovid, " as much as by Augustine. 3, He denied the resurrec- " tion of the body, and likewise heaven and hell; saying " that whoever enjoyed the knowledge of God in himself, " enjoyed also heaven in himself, and that on the contra- " ry whoever committed deadly sin, experienced hell in " himself. 4, He asserted that to dedicate altars to the " saints, to burn incense to images, and to invoke the " saints, was Idolatry. 5, He affirmed, not only with the

14. Lenfant's Hist. of the Council of Constance, Book iii. ch. 42, Art. 28, vol. i. p. 419. 15. Priestley's Hist. of the Christ. Church, Period xix. Sect. xi. pp. 296—299.

" Armeni, that Adam and Eve would never have co-
" habited, had they continued in their first state, but
" also that there would have been no difference of
" sex, and that the multiplication of mankind would
" have been like that of the angels ; thus contradict-
" ing what is written in Genesis ; *God created man
" in his own image ; in his image created he him,
" male and female.* 6, He asserted that God is not
" to be seen in himself, but in his creatures, as the
" light is seen in the air. 7, He said that what would
" otherwise be mortal sin, would, if done in charity,
" be no sin : thus promising impunity to sinners. 8,
" He affirmed that those ideas which are in the divine
" mind, are both capable of being created, and actu-
" ally are created ; when Augustine on the contrary
" has declared, that there is nothing in the divine
" mind, but what is eternal and incommunicable. 9,
" He fancied that the soul of the contemplative, or
" happy saint would lose itself, as to its own nature,
" and return into that ideal existence which it had in
" the divine mind. 10, He taught that all creatures,
" in the end, would return into God, and be converted
" into him ; so that they will be one, individually,
" with him. "[16] As this account is given by his enemies, we must make an allowance in his favor ; and
it is not an unreasonable conclusion that he only opposed the corruptions and errors of the Church, that
he adopted some mystic notions which then prevailed
concerning spiritual union with Deity, and that he believed that God would finally become " all in all. "
With regard to the resurrection, he may have made, like
the celebrated Locke, some distinctions which gave
his adversaries occasion to charge him with denying it.
Some of the opinions of Amalric, or Amauri, as he
is generally called, were condemned by the University
of Paris, and likewise by Pope Innocent III. and, just

[16.] Summa Conciliorum, per M. L. Bail, Tom. i. p. 432.

before his death, the author was compelled to retract them.   But he left disciples ; and, in A. D. 1209, a council was called at Paris, in which ten priests or students of divinity were condemned to the flames, and four to perpetual imprisonment.   At the same time, the name of Amauri, who had died in peace, was anathematized, and his bones were dug up and thrown upon a dunghill.

IX. Salomon, metropolitan bishop of
A. D. 1222. Bassorah, on the Euphrates, about sev-
enty miles from its mouth, was a writer of considerable renown among the Nestorians of the East.   Some of his works, in the Syriac language, yet remain, though only in manuscript.   In one of them, he discusses the question, "Whether the demons and "sinners, who are now in hell, shall at length obtain "mercy, after having suffered their appointed punish-"ment, and been purified?"   In answer, he quotes the affirmative opinion of Theodorus of Mopsuestia, and of Diodorus of Tarsus, and subscribes to it himself.   He also endeavors to show, but it is said inconclusively, that other Nestorian writers taught the same doctrine.*

X. I present to the reader the follow-
A. D. 1230, ing account entire, as it stands in a cath-
to 1234. olic historian.   I add no remarks, because
every reflecting person will discover much incongruity between the different parts of the statement ; and every one, who is at all acquainted either with the habitual language of the old Romish authors concerning heretics, or with the odious representations that are even now given, in our own country, concerning Universalists, will readily understand the present case : "Among all the sects which started up, during the "thirteenth century, there was none more detestable "than that of the Stadings, which showed itself by

* Assemani Biblioth. Orientalis Tom. iii. Par. i. pp. 323, 324.

" the outrages and cruelties which it exercised, in
" Germany, A. D. 1230, against the catholics, and
" especially against the church-men. Those impious
" persons honored Lucifer, and inveighed against God
" himself, believing that he had unjustly comdemned
" that angel to darkness, that one day he would be
" re-established, and that they should be saved with
" him. Whereupon they taught, that, until that time,
" it was not requisite to do any thing which was pleas-
" ing to God, but quite the contrary. They were per-
" suaded that the devil appeared in their assemblies.
" They therein committed infamous things, and utter-
" ed strange blasphemies. It is said, that after they
" had received the eucharist, at Easter, from the hands
" of the [catholic] priest, they kept it in their mouths
" without swallowing it, in order to throw it away.
" Those heretics spread themselves in the bishopric of
" Breme, and in the frontiers of Friezland and Sax-
" ony ; and getting to a head, they massacred the
" ecclesiastics and monks, pillaged the churches and
" committed a world of disorders. Pope Gregory IX.
" excited the bishops and lords of those countries to
" make war against them, in order to extirpate that
" wicked race. The archbishop of Breme, the duke
" of Brabant, and the count of Holland, having raised
" forces, marched, in the year 1234, to engage them.
" They made a vigorous defence, but were at last de-
" feated and cut to pieces. Six thousand were killed
" upon the spot ; the rest perished in several ways,
" and they were all routed ; so that there were but
" few left, who were converted and returned to their
" obedience the next year. "[17]

XI. " The sect of the Lollards spread
A. D. 1315, " through Germany, and had for their
&c. — " leader, Walter Lollard, who began to
" disperse his errors about the year 1315.

[17] Du Pin's Eccl. Hist. Vol. xi. ch. ix. p. 153.

"They despised the sacraments of the [catholic]
"church, and derided her ceremonies and her consti-
"tutions, observed not the fasts of the church, nor its
"abstinences, acknowledged not the intercession of
"the [deceased] saints, and believed that the damned
"in hell, and the evil angels, should one day be saved.
"Trithemius, who recites the errors of these sectaries,
"says that Bohemia and Austria were infected with
"them; that there were above twenty-four thousand
"persons in Germany who held these errors; and that
"the greater part defended them with obstinacy, even
"unto death." [18]

XII. In England, Langham, archbish-
A. .D 1368. op of Canterbury, convened a council, in
A. D. 1368, and, with the advice of his
divines, gave judgement against thirty propositions
which were taught in his province. Among them,
"the following opinions were condemned: 1. Every
"man ought to have the free choice of turning to
"God, or from him; and according to this choice he
"will be saved or damned. 2. Baptism is not neces-
"sary to the salvation of infants. 3. No person will
"be damned for original sin only. 4. Grace, as it is
"commonly explained, is an illusion; and eternal life
"may be acquired by the force of nature. 5. Noth-
"ing can be bad merely because it is forbidden. 6.
"The fruit that Adam was forbidden to eat, was for-
"bidden because it was in itself bad. 7. Man is
"necessarily mortal, Jesus Christ included, as well as
"other animals. 8. All the damned, even the de-
"mons, may be restored and become happy. 9. God
"cannot make a reasonable creature impeccable, or
"free from a liability to sin. It was an honor to the
"age and to the country," says Priestley, "to produce
"such sentiments as these; but it was but a sudden

[18]. Du Pin's Eccl. Hist. Vol. xii. ch. viii. p. 113.

"blaze in the midst of much thick darkness, and, as
"far as appears, was soon extinguished." [19]

XIII. "In the year 1411, a sect was
A. D. 1400, "discovered in Flanders, and more espe-
to 1412. "cially at Brussels, which owed its origin
"to an illiterate man, whose name was
"Ægidius Cantor, and to William of Hildenissen, a
"Carmelite monk, and whose members were distin-
"guished by the title of *Men of Understanding*.
"There were many things" says Mosheim, "repre-
"hensible in the doctrine of this sect, which seemed
"to be chiefly derived from the theology of the Mys-
"tics. For they pretended to be honored with celestial
"visions, denied that any could arrive at a perfect
"knowledge of the holy Scriptures, without the extra-
"ordinary succors of a divine illumination; declared
"the approach of a new revelation from heaven, more
"complete and perfect than the gospel of Christ;
"maintained that the resurrection was already accom-
"plished in the person of Jesus, and that no other
"resurrection was to be expected; affirmed that the
"inward man was not defiled by the outward actions,
"whatever they were; that the pains of hell were to
"have an end, and that, not only all mankind, but
"even the devils themselves, were to return to God,
"and be made partakers of eternal felicity. This sect
"seems to have been a branch of that of *The Breth-*
"*ren and Sisters of the Free Spirit;* since they
"declared that a new dispensation of grace and spir-
"itual liberty was to be promulgated to mortals by the
"Holy Ghost. It must, however, be acknowledged,
"on the other hand, that their absurdities were min-
"gled with several opinions which showed that they
"were not totally void of *understanding;* for they
"maintained, among other things, 1. that Christ alone

[19]. Priestley's Hist. of the Christian Church, Period xx. Sect.
xii. pp. 498, 499. See also Du Pin's Eccl. Hist. Vol. xii. ch. viii.
p. 115.

"had merited eternal life and felicity for the human
"race, and that, therefore, men could not acquire this
"inestimable privilege by their own actions alone;
"2. that the priests, to whom the people confessed
"their transgressions, had not the power of absolving
"them, but that it was Christ alone in whom this
"authority was vested; and 3. that voluntary pen-
"ance and mortification were not necessary to salva-
"tion. These propositions however, and some others,
"were declared heretical by Peter D'Ailly, bishop of
"Cambray, who obliged William of Hildenissen to
"abjure them, and who opposed with the greatest
"vehemence and success the progress of this sect." [20]
Such is Mosheim's account, which is the most particular I have seen.

XIV. John Picus, earl of Mirandola
A. D. 1480, and Concordia, a distinguished scholar in
to 1494. Italy, alarmed the church, about this period, by advancing some opinions which
properly come under our notice. From infancy he
had evinced a remarkable quickness of mind and a
prodigious memory. At the age of fourteen, he studied
law at Bologne; and, afterwards, spent seven years in
visiting the most famous universities of France and
Italy, and in conversing with the learned of those
countries. He then went to Rome; and in A. D.
1486, when he was only twenty-one years old, he
published, in this city, nine hundred propositions upon
various subjects in the several branches of theology,
magic, the cabalistic art, and philosophy, and engaged
to maintain them in public disputation, according to a
custom of those times. These propositions were, for
the most part, either of a metaphysical kind, or of a
character merely verbal; but among them were the
following, of a more important nature: "Jesus Christ
"did not descend into hell in person, but only in

---

[20]. Mosheim's Eccl. Hist. Cent. xv. Part ii. ch. v. 4.

" effect ; Infinite pain is not due even to mortal sin ; " because sin is finite, and therefore merits but finite " punishment ; Neither crosses nor images ought to be " adored ; There is more reason to believe that Origen " was saved, than that he was damned &c." But, instead of a controversy which he had challenged, he found that other means were likely to be employed in refuting him. His enemies sounded the alarm of heresy ; the pope appointed commissioners to examine his publications ; and, to his dismay, they at length brought in a judgement censuring the foregoing propositions, together with nine others, some of which seemed to disagree with the doctrine of transubstantiation. Upon this, Picus wrote an Apology, and by means of metaphysical subtleties, explained away the heretical character of the obnoxious propositions, and humbly submitted himself to the Holy See. As to his former statement concerning the demerit of sin, he now endeavored to reconcile it with the doctrine of endless misery. After all, the pope forbade the reading of his books ; and, sometime afterwards, when Picus had retired from Rome, he was cited to appear before the tribunal of the church. But while this was yet pending, he obtained an absolution from the pontiff, in the year 1493. After this, he devoted himself wholly to the study of the Scriptures, and to controversial writings, resigning his earldom, and distributing all his goods among the poor. He died at Florence, A. D. 1494, aged only twenty-nine years.[21]

XV. In the year 1498, a Spanish A. D. 1490, prelate, by the name of Peter D'Aranda, to 1498. was degraded and condemned to perpetual imprisonment in the castle of St. Angelo at Rome, on being convicted, it is said, of Judaism. He was bishop of Calahorra in Old Castile, near the river Ebro ; and he held the office of Master of the

---

[21] Du Pin's Eccl. Hist. vol. xiii. ch. 4. pp. 95, 96.

sacred palace. He is said to have taught that the Jewish religion acknowledged but one Principle, while the Christian recognized three, — alluding probably to the doctrine of the trinity. "In his prayers he said, "*Glory to the Father*, without adding, *to the Son*, or, "*to the Holy Ghost*. He said that indulgences were "of no avail, but were invented for the profit that "was drawn from them; that there was neither pur-"gatory nor hell, but only paradise. He observed no "fasts, and said mass after dinner. From his saying "mass, or receiving the Lord's supper, it is evident "he was not a Jew, but probably a Unitarian Chris-"tian." [22]

[22.] Priestley's Hist. of the Christian Church, Period xxi. Sect. vii.

NOTE. A few errors have escaped in the spelling of proper names. The most of them, however, are such as will be easily detected by the reader. The author was unable to examine many of the proof-sheets, as he lived at a distance from the place of publication.

Printed in the United States
54961LVS00003B/47